THE VISAGES OF ADAM

Philosophical Readings on the Nature of Man

The Visages of Adam

Philosophical Readings on the Nature of Man

edited by

H. A. NIELSEN

UNIVERSITY OF NOTRE DAME PRESS
NOTRE DAME — LONDON

Acknowledgments

Grateful acknowledgment herewith is made to the following for permission to reprint the material listed below.

Nicomachean Ethics: from *The Oxford Translation of Aristotle,* translated by W. D. Ross. By permission of the Clarendon Press, Oxford.

"What Then Must I Do?": from S. Kierkegaard, *Purity of Heart Is to Will One Thing.* Harper & Row, Publishers, Incorporated, copyright 1938, 1948.

"Characterisation of the Will to Live": from Arthur Schopenhauer, *The Will to Live,* edited by Richard Taylor. Doubleday & Company, copyright 1962.

"The Vanity of Existence": from Arthur Schopenhauer, *The Will to Live,* edited by Richard Taylor. Doubleday & Company, copyright 1962.

"The Ego and Its Relation to Others": from Gabriel Marcel, *Homo Viator. Introduction to a Metaphysics of Hope,* translated by Emma Craufurd. Harper & Row, Publishers, Incorporated.

The Politics of Aristotle: translated by B. Jowett. By permission of the Clarendon Press, Oxford.

The City of God: from *Basic Writings of Saint Augustine,* edited by Whitney J. Oates, vol. II. Random House, Inc. Alfred A. Knopf, Inc., New York.

"On Man in the Cosmos": from *Paracelsus: Selected Writings,* edited by Jolande Jacobi, translated by Norbert Guter-

v

Preface

Between the period of the ancient Greeks and the present day, thousands of philosophical works have been written on the subject of man's nature and what it means to come up for a turn at existing as a human being. In this collection of readings the editor's intent was to quarry from that massive literature some patient discussions, and some angry ones, bearing upon the personal, interpersonal, and religious dimensions of human life. The readings taken together are addressed to the question of how the individual ought to regard his own existence. Part One considers man as a subject in himself, i.e., as the kind of being that can strike up a dialogue with himself and by means of it clarify for himself what he really thinks of his existence. Part Two considers man in relation to the visible setting in which he makes his way, a setting that opens up possibilities for him and at the same time imposes physical and moral limits. Part Three concerns itself again with the isolated individual, this time in relation to the claim that he is no mere offspring of natural process but a creature.

The abundance and variety of philosophical studies in this area raise problems for the anthologist. Justice is invariably on the side of those who complain that a collection of less than twenty readings must leave out some obviously worthy authors. As regards variety, the readings were picked to include only those whose basic points of view are strongly in evidence today. Even where a particular selection dates back to antiquity, the student is sure to encounter its main theme in variant forms, and the primary purpose of this collection is to acquaint him with the matter of such encounters.

Note to the Teacher

These readings are designed for a one-semester freshman or sophomore introduction to the philosophical literature that deals with human nature. They are selected from works all philosophical in spirit, though not all of a piece as regards either the value their authors place on human existence or the styles in which they express their competing views. Each of the three groups of readings opens with an introduction that discusses the main theme of that group, and closes with a brief list of related readings that the teacher can supplement according to his own emphases. Trial classroom use of these readings over two years showed that they contain more material than some teachers would care to cover in one semester. Rather than reduce the number of readings, it seemed preferable to leave the teacher a little room to choose among them. The individual selections are meant to be ample enough to display their authors' wares, yet of a length adapted to a single reading assignment.

During the evolution of these readings the editor received extensive help from Reverend James Doig, C.S.C., and Professors A. Edward Manier and Robert Turley, all of Notre Dame's department of philosophy. My thanks go also to the president of the University, Reverend Theodore M. Hesburgh, C.S.C., who some years ago gave me the idea for a set of readings in this general area, and to other officials of the

University for cooperating at every point with the editor, who is, however, alone accountable for any and all faults in this work.

H. A. N.

Contents

PART ONE
Three Ways of Looking at a Human

Introduction

The first part of these readings will exhibit three more or less distinct and competing views of what man is and how the individual ought to regard his existence. The reader, bearing in mind that these philosophers are talking about humankind and hence about himself, should be prepared at any point to question the correctness and canniness of their judgments.

Each of the three basic ways of looking at human nature is broad enough to accommodate a variety of thinkers, early and modern. The first, represented by Socrates in Plato's *Apology,* and less poignantly by Aristotle in his *Nicomachean Ethics,* accents the personal condition of the individual, his unknowings about himself, and his capacity for finding out about himself and about the things which are ultimately hurtful or good for him. A second way looks at man's nature, not directly or from within but indirectly, through some ancient or modern cosmic picture, as instanced below by the universal atomism of Lucretius and by Schopenhauer's doctrine of the Will to Live. A third way, Christian in its fundamental conceptions, is continuous with the Socratic way in its emphasis on the individual person, but goes further by submitting that God has dissolved the Socratic unknowings and revealed man's true condition along with the means of his rescue from it. This third way is represented by Kierkegaard and Marcel in part one. Although many philosophers of human nature resist being fitted conveniently into one of these three slots, it is often possible to get a philosopher's thought into some kind of preliminary focus by noticing how nearly he fits.

The first reading in part one is Plato's *Apology*. In the person of its main character, Socrates, we meet a man whose questions all point in one direction: How ought a man to live? The objective sciences concern him almost not at all. An individual's primary task, as he represents it, is to penetrate the darkness that surrounds his own existence, not to crack the mysteries of the physical world. It might just happen, Socrates suspects, that each human must go on being himself forever: How should he live this life in the face of that possibility? Even an encyclopedic knowledge of "the skies above and the earth below" is no substitute for the answer to that question.

In the *Nicomachean Ethics* Aristotle's discussions of man's chief good seeks to stabilize the quaking domain of moral decision by specifying principles and goals of human conduct. The result expresses in very general terms an essentially Socratic yearning for a well-defined life-task. Aristotle no more than his predecessor can speak from Mount Sinai and command that man follow his orders, but he can and does remind his readers—in common terms such as "good," "happiness," and "virtue"—that of all creatures only man can conceive, however dimly, of such a thing as an exemplary life. Though he is more diffident and naturalistic than Socrates on the subject of death and would hardly claim to be personally guided by a god, Aristotle's conviction of the seriousness of life is of a piece with that of Socrates.

Lucretius (Titus Lucretius Carus), Roman poet-philosopher of the first century B.C., echoer and praiser of the Greek

Introduction

thinker Epicurus, speaks of human nature by way of deductions from a system of cosmological principles. First among
these is a kind of super-law: "Nothing can proceed from
nothing, and nothing can return to nothing." Tiny solid
corpuscles, the elements of all things, exist from eternity in
infinite numbers. These plus empty space exhaust the cata-
logue of reality. For details readers may consult Books I and
II of his metaphysical poem *On the Nature of Things*. In
Book III, from which our selection is taken, Lucretius moves
from this sweeping survey of the universe to a discussion
of mind and body, life and death, and the nature of humankind. The principle that guides his reasoning appeared on
the scene centuries before Lucretius and is still toughly
surviving despite the arguments of Socrates and others against
it. It is this: cosmological theory (or natural science, or both)
can give the individual a fixed star by which he can know
where he is going and can set his compass for life. Socrates,
the *Apology* relates, put away scientific matters as useless for
guiding one's life. Aristotle, himself the founder of some
respectable sciences, would think it foolishness to boast that
man, by thinking very hard, can set final limits to the real
or fathom his own being by means of a physical theory. Lucretius, on the other hand, takes his reader aside and in effect
asks him to set aside as old-fashioned those Greek doubts
and scruples. Here the reader must search his own mind.

Turning to the Danish philosopher and religious writer
Søren Kierkegaard, we come back to a Socratic concern with
personal existence and selfhood, now in a Christian rather
than a pagan setting. The selection from *Purity of Heart*
points up the task involved in existing consciously as an
individual and the forces one must overcome to carry it
through.

INTRODUCTION

Arthur Schopenhauer, in the next readings, develops a grim, no-nonsense picture of human life, a picture which advertises itself as liberated from all softness and illusion. A human being, even a full-time thinker, can of course be mistaken in supposing himself so liberated. In any event, Schopenhauer's conclusions claim to be based upon a sweeping view of the whole panorama of life and death on this planet, a somewhat narrower field of vision than Lucretius commanded but essentially the same kind.

Coming around once more to the anatomy of the human self, Christianly understood, we find in Gabriel Marcel's war-years essay an informal psychological analysis. Once again the emphasis is Socratic. "The Ego and Its Relation to Others" asks how one can tell whether he is rising or sinking as a person, and suggests a way of telling.

Plato (427?-347 B.C.)

The Apology of Socrates

How you have felt, O men of Athens, at hearing the speeches of my accusers, I cannot tell; but I know that their persuasive words almost made me forget who I was, such was the effect of them; and yet they have hardly spoken a word of truth. But many as their falsehoods were, there was one of them which quite amazed me: I mean when they told you to be upon your guard, and not to let yourself be deceived by the force of my eloquence. They ought to have been ashamed of saying this, because they were sure to be detected as soon as I opened my lips and displayed my deficiency; they certainly did appear to be most shameless in saying this, unless by the force of eloquence they mean the force of truth: for then I do indeed admit that I am eloquent. But in how different a way from theirs! Well, as I was saying, they have hardly uttered a word, or not more than a word, of truth; but you shall hear from me the whole truth: not, however, delivered after their manner, in a set oration duly ornamented with words and phrases. No, indeed! but I shall use the words and arguments which occur to me at the moment; for I am certain that this is right, and that at my time of life I ought not to be appearing before you, O men of Athens, in the character of a juvenile orator: let no one expect this of me. And I must beg of you to grant me one favor, which is this—if you hear me using the same words in my defence which I have been in the habit of using, and which most of you may have heard in the *agora*, and at

the tables of the money-changers, or anywhere else, I would
ask you not to be surprised at this, and not to interrupt me.
For I am more than seventy years of age, and this is the first
time that I have ever appeared in a court of law, and I am
quite a stranger to the ways of the place; and therefore I
would have you regard me as if I were really a stranger,
whom you would excuse if he spoke in his native tongue,
and after the fashion of his country: that I think is not an
unfair request. Never mind the manner, which may or may
not be good; but think only of the justice of my cause, and
give heed to that: let the judge decide justly and the speaker
speak truly.

And first, I have to reply to the older charges and to my
first accusers, and then I will go to the later ones. For I have
had many accusers, who accused me of old, and their false
charges have continued during many years; and I am more
afraid of them than of Anytus and his associates, who are
dangerous, too, in their own way. But far more dangerous are
these, who began when you were children, and took possession of your minds with their falsehoods, telling of one Socrates, a wise man, who speculated about the heaven above,
and searched into the earth beneath, and made the worse
appear the better cause. These are the accusers whom I
dread; for they are the circulators of this rumor, and their
hearers are too apt to fancy that speculators of this sort do
not believe in the gods. And they are many, and their charges
against me are of ancient date, and they made them in days
when you were impressible—in childhood, or perhaps in
youth—and the cause when heard went by default, for there
was none to answer. And, hardest of all, their names I do
not know and cannot tell; unless in the chance of a comic
poet. But the main body of these slanderers who from envy
and malice have wrought upon you—and there are some of
them who are convinced themselves, and impart their convictions to others—all these, I say, are most difficult to deal

with; for I cannot have them up here, and examine them, and therefore I must simply fight with shadows in my own defence, and examine when there is no one who answers. I will ask you then to assume with me, as I was saying, that my opponents are of two kinds—one recent, the other ancient; and I hope that you will see the propriety of my answering the latter first, for these accusations you heard long before the others, and much oftener.

Well, then, I will make my defence, and I will endeavor in the short time which is allowed to do away with this evil opinion of me which you have held for such a long time; and I hope I may succeed, if this be well for you and me, and that my words may find favor with you. But I know that to accomplish this is not easy—I quite see the nature of the task. Let the event be as God wills: in obedience to the law I make my defence.

I will begin at the beginning, and ask what the accusation is which has given rise to this slander of me, and which has encouraged Meletus to proceed against me. What do the slanderers say? They shall be my prosecutors, and I will sum up their words in an affidavit: "Socrates is an evildoer, and a curious person, who searches into things under the earth and in heaven, and he makes the worse appear the better cause; and he teaches the aforesaid doctrines to others." That is the nature of the accusation, and that is what you have seen yourselves in the comedy of Aristophanes; who has introduced a man whom he calls Socrates, going about and saying that he can walk in the air, and talking a deal of nonsense concerning matters of which I do not pretend to know either much or little—not that I mean to say anything disparaging of anyone who is a student of natural philosophy. I should be very sorry if Meletus could lay that to my charge. But the simple truth is, O Athenians, that I have nothing to do with these studies. Very many of those here present are witnesses to the truth of this, and to them I appeal. Speak then, you who have heard me, and tell your neighbors whether any of you have ever known me hold forth in few words or in many upon matters of this sort. . . . You hear their answer. And from what they say of this you will be able to judge of the truth of the rest.

As little foundation is there for the report that I am a teacher, and take money; that is no more true than the other. Although, if a man is able to teach, I honor him for being paid. There is Gorgias of Leontium, and Prodicus of Ceos, and Hippias of Elis, who go the round of the cities, and are able to persuade the young men to leave their own citizens, by whom they might be taught for nothing, and come to them, whom they not only pay, but are thankful if they may be allowed to pay them. There is actually a Parian philosopher residing in Athens, of whom I have heard; and I came to hear of him in this way: I met a man who has spent a world of money on the Sophists, Callias the son of Hipponicus, and knowing that he had sons, I asked him: "Callias," I said, "if your two sons were foals or calves, there would be no difficulty in finding someone to put over them; we should hire a trainer of horses or a farmer probably who would improve and perfect them in their own proper virtue and excellence; but as they are human beings, whom are you thinking of placing over them? Is there anyone who understands human and political virtue? You must have thought about this as you have sons; is there anyone?" "There is," he said. "Who is he?" said I, "and of what country? and what does he charge?" "Evenus the Parian," he replied; "he is the man, and his charge is five minæ." Happy is Evenus, I said to myself, if he really has this wisdom, and teaches at such a modest charge. Had I the same, I should have been very proud and conceited; but the truth is that I have no knowledge of the kind, O Athenians.

I dare say that someone will ask the question, "Why is this, Socrates, and what is the origin of these accusations of

10

you: for there must have been something strange which you have been doing? All this great fame and talk about you would never have arisen if you had been like other men: tell us, then, why this is, as we should be sorry to judge hastily of you." Now I regard this as a fair challenge, and I will endeavor to explain to you the origin of this name of "wise," and of this evil fame. Please to attend them. And although some of you may think I am joking, I declare that I will tell you the entire truth. Men of Athens, this reputation of mine has come of a certain sort of wisdom which I possess. If you ask me what kind of wisdom, I reply, such wisdom as is attainable by man, for to that extent I am inclined to believe that I am wise; whereas the persons of whom I was speaking have a superhuman wisdom, which I may fail to describe, because I have it not myself; and he who says that I have, speaks falsely, and is taking away my character. And here, O men of Athens, I must beg you not to interrupt me, even if I seem to say something extravagant. For the word which I will speak is not mine. I will refer you to a witness who is worthy of credit, and will tell you about my wisdom— whether I have any, and of what sort—and that witness shall be the god of Delphi. You must have known Chærephon; he was early a friend of mine, and also a friend of yours, for he shared in the exile of the people, and returned with you. Well, Chærephon, as you know, was very impetuous in all his doings, and he went to Delphi and boldly asked the oracle to tell him whether—as I was saying, I must beg you not to interrupt—he asked the oracle to tell him whether there was anyone wiser than I was, and the Pythian prophetess answered that there was no man wiser. Chærephon is dead himself, but his brother, who is in court, will confirm the truth of this story.

Why do I mention this? Because I am going to explain to you why I have such an evil name. When I heard the answer, I said to myself, What can the god mean? and what is the interpretation of this riddle? for I know that I have no wisdom, small or great. What can he mean when he says that I am the wisest of men? And yet he is a god and cannot lie; that would be against his nature. After a long consideration, I at last thought of a method of trying the question. I reflected that if I could only find a man wiser than myself, then I might go to the god with a refutation in my hand. I should say to him, "Here is a man who is wiser than I am; but you said that I was the wisest." Accordingly I went to one who had the reputation of wisdom, and observed to him —his name I need not mention; he was a politician whom I selected for examination—and the result was as follows: When I began to talk with him, I could not help thinking that he was not really wise, although he was thought wise by many, and wiser still by himself; and I went and tried to explain to him that he thought himself wise, but was not really wise; and the consequence was that he hated me, and his enmity was shared by several who were present and heard me. So I left him, saying to myself, as I went away: Well, although I do not suppose that either of us knows anything really beautiful and good, I am better off than he is—for he knows nothing, and thinks that he knows. I neither know nor think that I know. In this latter particular, then, I seem to have slightly the advantage of him. Then I went to another, who had still higher philosophical pretensions, and my conclusion was exactly the same. I made another enemy of him, and of many others besides him.

After this I went to one man after another, being not unconscious of the enmity which I provoked, and I lamented and feared this: but necessity was laid upon me—the word of God, I thought, ought to be considered first. And I said to myself, Go I must to all who appear to know, and find out the meaning of the oracle. And I swear to you, Athenians, by the dog I swear!—for I must tell you the truth—the result of my mission was just this: I found that the men most in repute were all but the most foolish; and that some inferior men were really wiser and better. I will tell you the tale of my wanderings and of the "Herculean" labors, as I may call them, which I endured only to find at last the oracle irrefutable. When I left the politicians, I went to the poets; tragic, dithyrambic, and all sorts. And there, I said to myself, you will be detected; now you will find out that you are more ignorant than they are. Accordingly, I took them some of the most elaborate passages in their own writings, and asked what was the meaning of them—thinking that they would teach me something. Will you believe me? I am almost ashamed to speak of this, but still I must say that there is hardly a person present who would not have talked better about their poetry than they did themselves. That showed me in an instant that not by wisdom do poets write poetry, but by a sort of genius and inspiration; they are like diviners or soothsayers who also say many fine things, but do not understand the meaning of them. And the poets appeared to me to be much in the same case; and I further observed that upon the strength of their poetry they believed themselves to be the wisest of men in other things in which they were not wise. So I departed, conceiving myself to be superior to them for the same reason that I was superior to the politicians.

At last I went to the artisans, for I was conscious that I knew nothing at all, as I may say, and I was sure that they knew many fine things; and in this I was not mistaken, for they did know many things of which I was ignorant, and in this they certainly were wiser than I was. But I observed that even the good artisans fell into the same error as the poets; because they were good workmen they thought that they also knew all sorts of high matters, and this defect in them overshadowed their wisdom—therefore I asked myself on behalf of the oracle, whether I would like to be as I was, neither having their knowledge nor their ignorance, or like them in both; and I made answer to myself and the oracle that I was better off as I was.

This investigation has led to my having many enemies of the worst and most dangerous kind, and has given occasion also to many calumnies, and I am called wise, for my hearers always imagine that I myself possess the wisdom which I find wanting in others: but the truth is, O men of Athens, that God only is wise; and in this oracle he means to say that the wisdom of men is little or nothing; he is not speaking of Socrates, he is only using my name as an illustration, as if he said, He, O men, is the wisest, who, like Socrates, knows that his wisdom is in truth worth nothing. And so I go my way, obedient to the god, and make inquisition into the wisdom of anyone, whether citizen or stranger, who appears to be wise; and if he is not wise, then in vindication of the oracle I show him that he is not wise; and this occupation quite absorbs me, and I have no time to give either to any public matter of interest or to any concern of my own, but I am in utter poverty by reason of my devotion to the god.

There is another thing—young men of the richer classes, who have not much to do, come about me of their own accord; they like to hear the pretenders examined, and they often imitate me, and examine others themselves; there are plenty of persons, as they soon enough discover, who think that they know something, but really know little or nothing: and then those who are examined by them instead of being angry with themselves are angry with me: This confounded Socrates, they say; this villainous misleader of youth!—and then if somebody asks them, Why, what evil does he practice or teach? they do not know, and cannot tell; but in order that they may not appear to be at a loss, they repeat the ready-made charges which are used against all philosophers about teaching things up in the clouds and under the earth, and having no gods, and making the worse appear the better cause; for they do not like to confess that their pretence of knowledge has been detected—which is the truth: and as they are numerous and ambitious and energetic, and are all in battle array and have persuasive tongues, they have filled your ears with their loud and inveterate calumnies. And this is the reason why my three accusers. Meletus and Anytus and Lycon, have set upon me; Meletus, who has a quarrel with me on behalf of the poets; Anytus, on behalf of the craftsmen; Lycon, on behalf of the rhetoricians: and as I said at the beginning, I cannot expect to get rid of this mass of calumny all in a moment. And this, O men of Athens, is the truth and the whole truth; I have concealed nothing, I have dissembled nothing. And yet I know that this plainness of speech makes them hate me, and what is their hatred but a proof that I am speaking the truth?—this is the occasion and reason of their slander of me, as you will find out either in this or in any future inquiry.

I have said enough in my defence against the first class of my accusers; I turn to the second class, who are headed by Meletus, that good and patriotic man, as he calls himself. And now I will try to defend myself against them: these new accusers must also have their affidavit read. What do they say? Something of this sort: That Socrates is a doer of evil, and corrupter of the youth, and he does not believe in the gods of the State, and has other new divinities of his own. That is the sort of charge; and now let us examine the particular counts. He says that I am a doer of evil, who corrupts the youth; but I say, O men of Athens, that Meletus is a doer of evil, and the evil is that he makes a joke of a serious matter, and is too ready at bringing other men to trial from a pretended zeal and interest about matters in which he really never had the smallest interest. And the truth of this I will endeavor to prove.

Come hither, Meletus, and let me ask a question of you. You think a great deal about the improvement of youth?

15

Yes, I do.

Tell the judges, then, who is their improver; for you must know, as you have taken the pains to discover their corrupter, and are citing and accusing me before them. Speak, then, and tell the judges who their improver is. Observe, Meletus, that you are silent, and have nothing to say. But is not this rather disgraceful, and a very considerable proof of what I was saying, that you have no interest in the matter? Speak up, friend, and tell us who their improver is.

The laws.

But that, my good sir, is not my meaning. I want to know who the person is, who, in the first place, knows the laws.

The judges, Socrates, who are present in court.

What do you mean to say, Meletus, that they are able to instruct and improve youth?

Certainly they are.

What, all of them, or some only and not others?

All of them.

By the goddess Here, that is good news! There are plenty of improvers, then. And what do you say of the audience— do they improve them?

Yes, they do.

And the Senators?

Yes, the Senators improve them.

But perhaps the ecclesiasts corrupt them?—or do they too improve them?

They improve them.

Then every Athenian improves and elevates them; all with the exception of myself; and I alone am their corrupter? Is that what you affirm?

That is what I stoutly affirm.

I am very unfortunate if that is true. But suppose I ask you a question: Would you say that this also holds true in the case of horses? Does one man do them harm and all the world good? Is not the exact opposite of this true? One man

16

is able to do them good, or at least not many; the trainer of
horses, that is to say, does them good, and others who have to
do with them rather injure them? Is not that true, Meletus,
of horses, or any other animals? Yes, certainly. Whether you
and Anytus say yes or no, that is no matter. Happy indeed
would be the condition of youth if they had one corrupter
only, and all the rest of the world were their improvers. And
you, Meletus, have sufficiently shown that you never had a
thought about the young: your carelessness is seen in your
not caring about matters spoken of in this very indictment.

And now, Meletus, I must ask you another question:
Which is better, to live among bad citizens, or among good
ones? Answer, friend, I say; for that is a question which may
be easily answered. Do not the good do their neighbors good,
and the bad do them evil?

Certainly.

And is there anyone who would rather be injured than
benefited by those who live with him? Answer, my good
friend; the law requires you to answer—does anyone like to
be injured?

Certainly not.

And when you accuse me of corrupting and deteriorating
the youth, do you allege that I corrupt them intentionally or
unintentionally?

Intentionally, I say.

But you have just admitted that the good do their neighbors good, and the evil do them evil. Now is that a truth
which your superior wisdom has recognized thus early in life,
and am I, at my age, in such darkness and ignorance as not
to know that if a man with whom I have to live is corrupted
by me, I am very likely to be harmed by him, and yet I corrupt him, and intentionally, too? that is what you are saying,
and of that you will never persuade me or any other human
being. But either I do not corrupt them, or I corrupt them
unintentionally, so that on either view of the case you lie.

17

If my offence is unintentional, the law has no cognizance of unintentional offences: you ought to have taken me privately, and warned and admonished me; for if I had been better advised, I should have left off doing what I only did unintentionally—no doubt I should; whereas you hated to converse with me or teach me, but you indicted me in this court, which is a place not of instruction, but of punishment.

I have shown, Athenians, as I was saying, that Meletus has no care at all, great or small, about the matter. But still I should like to know, Meletus, in what I am affirmed to corrupt the young. I suppose you mean, as I infer from your indictment, that I teach them not to acknowledge the gods which the State acknowledges, but some other new divinities or spiritual agencies in their stead. These are the lessons which corrupt the youth, as you say.

Yes, that I say emphatically.

Then, by the gods, Meletus, of whom we are speaking, tell me and the court, in somewhat plainer terms, what you mean! for I do not as yet understand whether you affirm that I teach others to acknowledge some gods, and therefore do believe in gods and am not an entire atheist—this you do not lay to my charge; but only that they are not the same gods which the city recognizes—the charge is that they are different gods. Or, do you mean to say that I am an atheist simply, and a teacher of atheism?

I mean the latter—that you are a complete atheist.

That is an extraordinary statement, Meletus. Why do you say that? Do you mean that I do not believe in the god-head of the sun or moon, which is the common creed of all men?

I assure you, judges, that he does not believe in them; for he says that the sun is stone, and the moon earth.

Friend Meletus, you think that you are accusing Anaxagoras; and you have but a bad opinion of the judges, if you fancy them ignorant to such a degree as not to know that those doctrines are found in the books of Anaxagoras the

Clazomenian, who is full of them. And these are the doctrines which the youth are said to learn of Socrates, when
there are not unfrequently exhibitions of them at the theatre
(price of admission one drachma at the most); and they
might cheaply purchase them, and laugh at Socrates if he
pretends to father such eccentricities. And so, Meletus, you
really think that I do not believe in any god?

I swear by Zeus that you believe absolutely in none at all.

You are a liar, Meletus, not believed even by yourself.
For I cannot help thinking, O men of Athens, that Meletus
is reckless and impudent, and that he has written this indictment in a spirit of mere wantonness and youthful bravado.
Has he not compounded a riddle, thinking to try me? He
said to himself: I shall see whether this wise Socrates will
discover my ingenious contradiction, or whether I shall be
able to deceive him and the rest of them. For he certainly
does appear to me to contradict himself in the indictment as
much as if he said that Socrates is guilty of not believing
in the gods, and yet of believing in them—but this surely
is a piece of fun.

I should like you, O men of Athens, to join me in examining what I conceive to be his inconsistency; and do you,
Meletus, answer. And I must remind you that you are not
to interrupt me if I speak in my accustomed manner.

Did ever man, Meletus, believe in the existence of human
things, and not of human beings? . . . I wish, men of Athens,
that he would answer, and not be always trying to get up
an interruption. Did ever any man believe in horsemanship, and not in horses? or in flute-playing and not in flute-
players? No, my friend; I will answer to you and to the court,
as you refuse to answer for yourself. There is no man who
ever did. But now please to answer the next question: Can
a man believe in spiritual and divine agencies, and not in
spirits or demigods?

He cannot.

19

I am glad that I have extracted that answer, by the assistance of the court; nevertheless you swear in the indictment that I teach and believe in divine or spiritual agencies (new or old, no matter for that); at any rate, I believe in spiritual agencies, as you say and swear in the affidavit; but if I believe in divine beings, I must believe in spirits or demigods; is not that true? Yes, that is true, for I may assume that your silence gives assent to that. Now what are spirits or demigods? are they not either gods or the sons of gods? Is that true?

Yes, that is true.

But this is just the ingenious riddle of which I was speaking: the demigods or spirits are gods, and you say first that I don't believe in gods, and then again that I do believe in gods; that is, if I believe in demigods. For if the demigods are the illegitimate sons of gods, whether by the Nymphs or by any other mothers, as is thought, that, as all men will allow, necessarily implies the existence of their parents. You might as well affirm the existence of mules, and deny that of horses and asses. Such nonsense, Meletus, could only have been intended by you as a trial of me. You have put this into the indictment because you had nothing real of which to accuse me. But no one who has a particle of understanding will ever be convinced by you that the same man can believe in divine and superhuman things, and yet not believe that there are gods and demigods and heroes.

I have said enough in answer to the charge of Meletus: any elaborate defence is unnecessary; but as I was saying before, I certainly have many enemies, and this is what will be my destruction if I am destroyed; of that I am certain; not Meletus, nor yet Anytus, but the envy and detraction of the world, which has been the death of many good men, and will probably be the death of many more; there is no danger of my being the last of them.

Someone will say: And are you not ashamed, Socrates, of

a course of life which is likely to bring you to an untimely end? To him I may fairly answer: There you are mistaken: a man who is good for anything ought not to calculate the chance of living or dying; he ought only to consider whether in doing anything he is doing right or wrong—acting the part of a good man or of a bad. Whereas, according to your view, the heroes who fell at Troy were not good for much, and the son of Thetis above all, who altogether despised danger in comparsion with disgrace; and when his goddess mother said to him, in his eagerness to slay Hector, that if he avenged his companion Patroclus, and slew Hector, he would die himself—"Fate," as she said, "waits upon you next after Hector"; he, hearing this, utterly despised danger and death, and instead of fearing them, feared rather to live in dishonor, and not to avenge his friend. "Let me die next," he replies, "and be avenged of my enemy, rather than abide here by the beaked ships, a scorn and a burden of the earth." Had Achilles any thought of death and danger? For wherever a man's place is, whether the place which he has chosen or that in which he has been placed by a commander, there he ought to remain in the hour of danger; he should not think of death or of anything, but of disgrace. And this, O men of Athens, is a true saying.

Strange, indeed, would be my conduct, O men of Athens, if I who, when I was ordered by the generals whom you chose to command me at Potidæa and Amphipolis and Delium, remained where they placed me, like any other man, facing death—if, I say, now, when, as I conceive and imagine, God orders me to fulfil the philosopher's mission of searching into myself and other men, I were to desert my post through fear of death, or any other fear; that would indeed be strange, and I might justly be arraigned in court for denying the existence of the gods, if I disobeyed the oracle because I was afraid of death: then I should be fancying that I was wise when I was not wise. For this fear of death is indeed the pretence of wisdom, and not real wisdom, being the appearance of knowing the unknown; since no one knows whether death, which they in their fear apprehend to be the greatest evil, may not be the greatest good. Is there not here conceit of knowledge, which is a disgraceful sort of ignorance? And this is the point in which, as I think, I am superior to men in general, and in which I might perhaps fancy myself wiser than other men—that whereas I know but little of the world below, I do not suppose that I know: but I do know that injustice and disobedience to a better, whether God or man, is evil and dishonorable, and I will never fear or avoid a possible good rather than a certain evil. And therefore if you let me go now, and reject the counsels of Anytus, who said that if I were not put to death I ought not to have been prosecuted, and that if I escape now, your sons will all be utterly ruined by listening to my words—if you say to me, Socrates, this time we will not mind Anytus, and will let you off, but upon one condition, that you are not to inquire and speculate in this way any more, and that if you are caught doing this again you shall die—if this was the condition on which you let me go, I should reply: Men of Athens, I honor and love you; but I shall obey God rather than you, and while I have life and strength I shall never cease from the practice and teaching of philosophy, exhorting anyone whom I meet after my manner, and convincing him, saying: O my friend, why do you who are a citizen of the great and mighty and wise city of Athens, care so much about laying up the greatest amount of money and honor and reputation, and so little about wisdom and truth and the greatest improvement of the soul, which you never regard or heed at all? Are you not ashamed of this? And if the person with whom I am arguing says: Yes, but I do care; I do not depart or let him go at once; I interrogate and examine and cross-examine him, and if I think that he has no virtue, but only says that he has, I reproach him with undervaluing the greater, and overvaluing the less. And this I should say to everyone whom I meet, young and old, citizen and alien, but especially to the citizens, inasmuch as they are my brethren. For this is the command of God, as I would have you know; and I believe that to this day no greater good has ever happened in the State than my service to the God. For I do nothing but go about persuading you all, old and young alike, not to take thought for your persons and your properties, but first and chiefly to care about the greatest improvement of the soul. I tell you that virtue is not given by money, but that from virtue come money and every other good of man, public as well as private. This is my teaching, and if this is the doctrine which corrupts the youth, my influence is ruinous indeed. But if anyone says that this is not my teaching, he is speaking an untruth. Wherefore, O men of Athens, I say to you, do as Anytus bids or not as Anytus bids, and either acquit me or not; but whatever you do, know that I shall never alter my ways, not even if I have to die many times.

Men of Athens, do not interrupt, but hear me; there was an agreement between us that you should hear me out. And I think that what I am going to say will do you good: for I have something more to say, at which you may be inclined to cry out; but I beg that you will not do this. I would have you know that, if you kill such a one as I am, you will injure yourselves more than you will injure me. Meletus and Anytus will not injure me: they cannot; for it is not in the nature of things that a bad man should injure a better than himself. I do not deny that he may, perhaps, kill him, or drive him into exile, or deprive him of civil rights; and he may imagine, and others may imagine, that he is doing him a great injury: but in that I do not agree with him; for the evil of doing as Anytus is doing—of unjustly taking away another man's life—is greater far. And now, Athenians, I am not going to argue for my own sake, as you may think, but for yours, that you may not sin against the God, or lightly reject his boon by condemning me. For if you kill me you will not easily find another like me, who, if I may use such a ludicrous figure of speech, am a sort of gadfly, given to the State by the God; and the State is like a great and noble steed who is tardy in his motions owing to his very size, and requires to be stirred into life. I am that gadfly which God has given the State and all day long and in all places am always fastening upon you, arousing and persuading and reproaching you. And as you will not easily find another like me, I would advise you to spare me. I dare say that you may feel irritated at being suddenly awakened when you are caught napping; and you may think that if you were to strike me dead, as Anytus advises, which you easily might, then you would sleep on for the remainder of your lives, unless God in his care of you gives you another gadfly. And that I am given to you by God is proved by this: that if I had been like other men, I should not have neglected all my own concerns, or patiently seen the neglect of them during all these years, and have been doing yours, coming to you individually, like a father or elder brother, exhorting you to regard virtue; this, I say, would not be like human nature. And had I gained anything, or if my exhortations had been paid, there would have been some sense in that: but now, as you will perceive, not even the impudence of my accusers dares to say that I have ever exacted or sought pay of anyone; they have no witness of that. And I have a witness of the truth of what I say; my poverty is a sufficient witness.

Someone may wonder why I go about in private, giving advice and busying myself with the concerns of others, but do not venture to come forward in public and advise the State. I will tell you the reason of this. You have often heard me speak of an oracle or sign which comes to me, and is the divinity which Meletus ridicules in the indictment. This sign I have had ever since I was a child. The sign is a voice which comes to me and always forbids me to do something which I am going to do, but never commands me to do anything, and this is what stands in the way of my being a politician. And rightly, as I think. For I am certain, O men of Athens, that if I had engaged in politics, I should have perished long ago and done no good either to you or to myself. And don't be offended at my telling you the truth: for the truth is that no man who goes to war with you or any other multitude, honestly struggling against the commisssion of unrighteousness and wrong in the State, will save his life; he who will really fight for the right, if he would live even for a little while, must have a private station and not a public one.

I can give you as proofs of this, not words only, but deeds, which you value more than words. Let me tell you a passage of my own life, which will prove to you that I should never have yielded to injustice from any fear of death, and that if I had not yielded I should have died at once. I will tell you a story—tasteless, perhaps, and commonplace, but nevertheless true. The only office of State which I ever held, O men of Athens, was that of Senator; the tribe Antiochis, which is my tribe, had the presidency at the trial of the generals who had not taken up the bodies of the slain after the battle of Arginusæ; and you proposed to try them all together, which was illegal, as you all thought afterwards; but at the time I was the only one of the Prytanes who was opposed to the illegality, and I gave my vote against you; and when the orators threatened to impeach and arrest me, and have me taken away, and you called and shouted, I made up my mind that I would run the risk, having law and justice with me, rather than take part in your injustice because I feared imprisonment and death. This happened in the days of the democracy. But when the oligarchy of the Thirty was in power, they sent for me and four others into the rotunda, and bade us bring Leon the Salaminian from

Salamis, as they wanted to execute him. This was a speci-men of the sort of commands which they were always giving with the view of implicating as many as possible in their crimes; and then I showed, not in words only, but in deed, that, if I may be allowed to use such an expression, I cared not a straw for death, and that my only fear was the fear of doing an unrighteous or unholy thing. For the strong arm of that oppressive power did not frighten me into doing wrong; and when we came out of the rotunda the other four went to Salamis and fetched Leon, but I went quietly home. For which I might have lost my life, had not the power of the Thirty shortly afterwards come to an end. And to this many will witness.

Now do you really imagine that I could have survived all these years, if I had led a public life, supposing that like a good man I had always supported the right and had made justice, as I ought, the first thing? No, indeed, men of Athens, neither I nor any other. But I have been always the same in all my actions, public as well as private, and never have I yielded any base compliance to those who are slanderously termed my disciples or to any other. For the truth is that I have no regular disciples: but if anyone likes to come and hear me while I am pursuing my mission, whether he be young or old, he may freely come. Nor do I converse with those who pay only, and not with those who do not pay; but any one, whether he be rich or poor, may ask and answer me and listen to my words; and whether he turns out to be a bad man or a good one; that cannot be justly laid to my charge, as I never taught him anything. And if anyone says that he has ever learned or heard anything from me in private which all the world has not heard, I should like you to know that he is speaking an untruth.

But I shall be asked, Why do people delight in continually conversing with you? I have told you already, Athenians; the whole truth about this: they like to hear the cross examination of the pretenders to wisdom; there is amusement in this. And this is a duty which the God has imposed upon me, as I am assured by oracles, visions, and in every sort of way in which the will of divine power was ever signified to anyone. This is true, O Athenians; or, if not true, would be soon refuted. For if I am really corrupting the youth, and have corrupted some of them already, those of them who have grown up and have become sensible that I gave them bad advice in the days of their youth should come forward as accusers and take their revenge; and if they do not like to come themselves, some of their relatives, fathers, brothers, or other kinsmen, should say what evil their families suffered at my hands. Now is their time. Many of them I see in the court. There is Crito, who is of the same age and of the same *deme* with myself; and there is Critobulus his son, whom I also see. Then again there is Lysanias of Sphettus, who is the father of Æschines—he is present; and also there is Antiphon of Cephisus, who is the father of Epignes; and here are the brothers of several who have associated with me. There is Nicostratus the son of Theosdotides, and the brother of Theodotus (now Theodotus himself is dead, and therefore he, at any rate, will not seek to stop him); and there is Paralus the son of Demodocus, who had a brother Theages, and Adeimantus the son of Ariston, whose brother Plato is present; and Æantodorus, who is the brother of Apollodorus, whom I also see. I might mention a great many others, any of whom Meletus should have produced as witnesses in the course of his speech; and let him still produce them, if he has forgotten; I will make way for him. And let him say, if he has any testimony of the sort which he can produce. Nay, Athenians, the very opposite is the truth. For all these are ready to witness on behalf of the corrupter, of the destroyer of their kindred, as Meletus and Anytus call me; not the corrupted youth only—there might have been a motive for that—but their uncorrupted elder relatives. Why

27

should they too support me with their testimony? Why, indeed, except for the sake of truth and justice, and because they know that I am speaking the truth, and that Meletus is lying.

Well, Athenians, this and the like of this is nearly all the defence which I have to offer. Yet a word more. Perhaps there may be someone who is offended at me, when he calls to mind how he himself, on a similar or even a less serious occasion, had recourse to prayers and supplications with many tears, and how he produced his children in court, which was a moving spectacle, together with a posse of his relations and friends; whereas I, who am probably in danger of my life, will do none of these things. Perhaps this may come into his mind, and he may be set against me, and vote in anger because he is displeased at this. Now if there be such a person among you, which I am far from affirming, I may fairly reply to him: My friend, I am a man, and like other men, a creature of flesh and blood, and not of wood or stone, as Homer says; and I have a family, yes, and sons, O Athenians, three in number, one of whom is growing up, and the two others are still young; and yet I will not bring any one of them hither in order to petition you for an acquittal. And why not? Not from any self-will or disregard of you. Whether I am or am not afraid of death is another question, of which I will not now speak. But my reason simply is that I feel such conduct to be discreditable to myself, and you, and the whole State. One who has reached my years, and who has a name for wisdom, whether deserved or not, ought not to debase himself. At any rate, the world has decided that Socrates is in some way superior to other men. And if those among you who are said to be superior in wisdom and courage, and any other virtue, demean themselves in this way, how shameful is their conduct! I have seen men of reputation, when they have been condemned, behaving in the strangest manner: they seemed to fancy that they were going

28

The Apology of Socrates

to suffer something dreadful if they died, and that they could
be immortal if you only allowed them to live; and I think
that they were a dishonor to the State, and that any stranger
coming in would say of them that the most eminent men of
Athens, to whom the Athenians themselves give honor and
command, are no better than women. And I say that these
things ought not to be done by those of us who are of reputation; and if they are done, you ought not to permit them;
you ought rather to show that you are more inclined to condemn, not the man who is quiet, but the man who gets up
a doleful scene, and makes the city ridiculous.

But, setting aside the question of dishonor, there seems to
be something wrong in petitioning a judge, and thus procur-
ing an acquittal instead of informing and convincing him.
For his duty is, not to make a present of justice, but to give
judgment; and he has sworn that he will judge according to
the laws, and not according to his own good pleasure; and
neither he nor we should get into the habit of perjuring ourselves—there can be no piety in that. Do not then require
me to do what I consider dishonorable and impious and
wrong, especially now, when I am being tried for impiety on
the indictment of Meletus. For if, O men of Athens, by
force of persuasion and entreaty, I could overpower your
oaths, then I should be teaching you to believe that there
are no gods, and convict myself, in my own defence, of not
believing in them. But that is not the case; for I do believe
that there are gods, and in a far higher sense than that in
which any of my accusers believe in them. And to you and
to God I commit my cause, to be determined by you as is
best for you and me.

There are many reasons why I am not grieved, O men of
Athens, at the vote of condemnation. I expected this, and
am only surprised that the votes are so nearly equal; for I
had thought that the majority against me would have been

29

far larger; but now, had thirty votes gone over to the other side, I should have been acquitted. And I may say that I have escaped Meletus. And I may say more; for without the assistance of Anytus and Lycon, he would not have had a fifth part of the votes, as the law requires, in which case he would have incurred a fine of a thousand drachmæ, as is evident.

And so he proposes death as the penalty. And what shall I propose on my part, O men of Athens? Clearly that which is my due. And what is that which I ought to pay or to receive? What shall be done to the man who has never had the wit to be idle during his whole life; but has been careless of what the many care about—wealth and family interests, and military offices, and speaking in the assembly, and magistracies, and plots, and parties. Reflecting that I was really too honest a man to follow in this way and live, I did not go where I could do no good to you or to myself; but where I could do the greatest good privately to everyone of you, thither I went, and sought to persuade every man among you that he must look to himself, and seek virtue and wisdom before he looks to his private interests, and look to the State before he looks to the interests of the State; and that this should be the order which he observes in all his actions. What shall be done to such a one? Doubtless some good thing, O men of Athens, if he has his reward; and the good should be of a kind suitable to him. What would be a reward suitable to a poor man who is your benefactor, who desires leisure that he may instruct you? There can be no more fitting reward than maintenance in the Prytaneum, O men of Athens, a reward which he deserves far more than the citizen who has won the prize at Olympia in the horse or chariot race, whether the chariots were drawn by two horses or by many. For I am in want, and he has enough; and he only gives you the appearance of happiness, and I give you the reality. And if I am to estimate the penalty justly, I say that maintenance in the Prytaneum is the just return.

The Apology of Socrates

Perhaps you may think that I am braving you in saying this, as in what I said before about the tears and prayers. But that is not the case. I speak rather because I am convinced that I never intentionally wronged anyone, although I cannot convince you of that—for we have had a short conversation only; but if there were a law at Athens, such as there is in other cities, that a capital cause should not be decided in one day, then I believe that I should have convinced you; but now the time is too short. I cannot in a moment refute great slanders; and, as I am convinced that I never wronged another, I will assuredly not wrong myself. I will not say of myself that I deserve any evil, or propose any penalty. Why should I? Because I am afraid of the penalty of death which Meletus proposes? When I do not know whether death is a good or an evil, why should I propose a penalty which would certainly be an evil? Shall I say imprisonment? And why should I live in prison, and be the slave of the magistrates of the year—of the Eleven? Or shall the penalty be a fine, and imprisonment until the fine is paid? There is the same objection. I should have to lie in prison, for money I have none, and I cannot pay. And if I say exile (and this may possibly be the penalty which you will affix), I must indeed be blinded by the love of life if I were to consider that when you, who are my own citizens, cannot endure my discourses and words, and have found them so grievous and odious that you would fain have done with them, others are likely to endure me. No, indeed, men of Athens, that is not very likely. And what a life should I lead, at my age, wandering from city to city, living in ever-changing exile, and always being driven out! For I am quite sure that into whatever place I go, as here so also there, the young men will come to me; and if I drive them away, their elders will drive me out at their desire: and if I let them come, their fathers and friends will drive me out for their sakes.

Someone will say: Yes, Socrates, but cannot you hold your

tongue, and then you may go into a foreign city, and no one will interfere with you? Now I have great difficulty in making you understand my answer to this. For if I tell you that this would be a disobedience to a divine command, and therefore that I cannot hold my tongue, you will not believe that I am serious; and if I say again that the greatest good of man is daily to converse about virtue, and all that concerning which you hear me examining myself and others, and that the life which is unexamined is not worth living—that you are still less likely to believe. And yet what I say is true, although a thing of which it is hard for me to persuade you. Moreover, I am not accustomed to think that I deserve any punishment. Had I money I might have proposed to give you what I had, and have been none the worse. But you see that I have none, and can only ask you to proportion the fine to my means. However, I think that I could afford a mina, and therefore, I propose that penalty: Plato, Crito, Critobulus, and Apollodorus, my friends here, bid me say thirty minæ, and they will be the sureties. Well then, say thirty minæ, let that be the penalty; for that they will be ample security to you.

Not much time will be gained, O Athenians, in return for the evil name which you will get from the detractors of the city, who will say that you killed Socrates, a wise man; for they will call me wise even although I am not wise when they want to reproach you. If you had waited a little while, your desire would have been fulfilled in the course of nature. For I am far advanced in years, as you may perceive and not far from death. I am speaking now only to those of you who have condemned me to death. And I have another thing to say to them: You think that I was convicted through deficiency of words—I mean, that if I had thought fit to leave nothing undone, nothing unsaid, I might have gained an acquittal. Not so; the deficiency which led to my conviction was not of words—certainly not. But I had not the boldness

or impudence or inclination to address you as you would
have liked me to address you, weeping and wailing and
lamenting, and saying and doing many things which you
have been accustomed to hear from others, and which, as I
say, are unworthy of me. But I thought that I ought not to
do anything common or mean in the hour of danger: nor do
I now repent of the manner of my defence, and I would
rather die having spoken after my manner, than speak in
your manner and live. For neither in war nor yet at law
ought any man to use every way of escaping death. For often
in battle there is no doubt that if a man will throw away
his arms, and fall on his knees before his pursuers, he may
escape death; and in other dangers there are other ways of
escaping death, if a man is willing to say and do anything.
The difficulty, my friends, is not in avoiding death, but in
avoiding unrighteousness; for that runs faster than death. I
am old and move slowly, and the slower runner has overtaken me, and my accusers are keen and quick, and the faster
runner, who is unrighteousness, has overtaken them. And
now I depart hence condemned by you to suffer the penalty of death, and they, too, go their ways condemned by the
truth to suffer the penalty of villainy and wrong; and I must
abide by my award—let them abide by theirs. I suppose that
these things may be regarded as fated—and I think that they
are well.

And now, O men who have condemned me, I would fain
prophesy to you; for I am about to die, and that is the hour
in which men are gifted with prophetic power. And I
prophesy to you who are my murderers, that immediately
after my death punishment far heavier than you have inflicted on me will surely await you. Me you have killed
because you wanted to escape the accuser, and not to give
an account of your lives. But that will not be as you suppose: far otherwise. For I say that there will be more accusers
of you than there are now; accusers whom hitherto I have

restrained: and as they are younger they will be more severe with you, and you will be more offended at them. For if you think that by killing men you can avoid the accuser censuring your lives, you are mistaken; that is not a way of escape which is either possible or honorable; the easiest and noblest way is not to be crushing others, but to be improving yourselves. This is the prophecy which I utter before my departure, to the judges who have condemned me.

Friends, who would have acquitted me, I would like also to talk with you about this thing which has happened, while the magistrates are busy, and before I go to the place at which I must die. Stay then awhile, for we may as well talk with one another while there is time. You are my friends, and I should like to show you the meaning of this event which has happened to me. O my judges—for you I may truly call judges—I should like to tell you of a wonderful circumstance. Hitherto the familiar oracle within me has constantly been in the habit of opposing me even about trifles, if I was going to make a slip or error about anything; and now as you see there has come upon me that which may be thought, and is generally believed to be, the last and worst evil. But the oracle made no sign of opposition, either as I was leaving my house and going out in the morning, or when I was going up into this court, or while I was speaking, at anything which I was going to say; and yet I have often been stopped in the middle of a speech; but now in nothing I either said or did touching this matter has the oracle opposed me. What do I take to be the explanation of this? I will tell you. I regard this as a proof that what has happened to me is a good, and that those of us who think that death is an evil are in error. This is a great proof to me of what I am saying, for the customary sign would surely have opposed me had I been going to evil and not to good.

Let us reflect in another way, and we shall see that there is great reason to hope that death is a good, for one of two

things: either death is a state of nothingness and utter uncon-
sciousness, or, as men say, there is a change and migration of
the soul from this world to another. Now if you suppose
that there is no consciousness, but a sleep like the sleep of
him who is undisturbed even by the sight of dreams, death
will be an unspeakable gain. For if a person were to select
the night in which his sleep was undisturbed even by dreams,
and were to compare with this the other days and nights of
his life, and then were to tell us how many days and nights
he had passed in the course of his life better and more pleasantly than this one, I think that any man, I will not say a
private man, but even the great king, will not find many such
days or nights, when compared with the others. Now if death
is like this, I say that to die, is gain; for eternity is then
only a single night. But if death is the journey to another
place, and there, as men say, all the dead are, what good, O
my friends and judges, can be greater than this? If indeed
when the pilgrim arrives in the world below, he is delivered
from the professors of justice in this world, and finds the
true judges who are said to give judgment there, Minos and
Rhadamanthus and Æacus and Triptolemus, and other
sons of God who were righteous in their own life, that pil-
grimage will be worth making. What would not a man give
if he might converse with Orpheus and Musæus and Hesiod
and Homer? Nay, if this be true, let me die again and again.
I, too, shall have a wonderful interest in a place where I can
converse with Palamedes, and Ajax the son of Telamon, and
other heroes of old, who have suffered death through an
unjust judgment; and there will be no small pleasure, as I
think, in comparing my own sufferings with theirs. Above
all, I shall be able to continue my search into true and false
knowledge; as in this world, so also in that; I shall find out
who is wise, and who pretends to be wise, and is not. What
would not a man give, O judges, to be able to examine the
leader of the great Trojan expedition; or Odysseus or Sisy

PLATO

phus, or numberless others, men and women too! What infinite delight would there be in conversing with them and
asking them questions! For in that world they do not put a
man to death for this; certainly not. For besides being happier in that world than in this, they will be immortal, if
what is said is true.

Wherefore, O judges, be of good cheer about death, and
know this of a truth—that no evil can happen to a good man,
either in life or after death. He and his are not neglected by
the gods; nor has my own approaching end happened by
mere chance. But I see clearly that to die and be released
was better for me; and therefore the oracle gave no sign. For
which reason also, I am not angry with my accusers, or my
condemners; they have done me no harm, although neither
of them meant to do me any good; and for this I may gently
blame them.

Still I have a favor to ask of them. When my sons are
grown up, I would ask you, O my friends, to punish them;
and I would have you trouble them, as I have troubled you,
if they seem to care about riches, or anything, more than
about virtue; or if they pretend to be something when they
are really nothing—then reprove them, as I have reproved
you, for not caring about that for which they ought to care,
and thinking that they are something when they are really
nothing. And if you do this, I and my sons will have received
justice at your hands.

The hour of departure has arrived, and we go our ways—
I to die, and you to live. Which is better, God only knows.

36

Aristotle (384-322 B.C.)

Nicomachean Ethics

BOOK I, CHAPTERS 7–13

7. Let us again return to the good we are seeking, and ask what it can be. It seems different in different actions and arts; it is different in medicine, in strategy, and in the other arts likewise. What then is the good of each? Surely that for whose sake everything else is done. In medicine this is health, in strategy victory, in architecture a house, in any other sphere something else, and in every action and pursuit the end; for it is for the sake of this that all men do whatever else they do. Therefore, if there is an end for all that we do, this will be the good achievable by action, and if there are more than one, these will be the goods achievable by action.

So the argument has by a different course reached the same point; but we must try to state this even more clearly. Since there are evidently more than one end, and we choose some of these (e.g. wealth, flutes,[1] and in general instruments) for the sake of something else, clearly not all ends are final ends; but the chief good is evidently something final. Therefore, if there is only one final end, this will be what we are seeking, and if there are more than one, the most final of these will be what we are seeking. Now we call that which is in itself worthy of pursuit more final than that which is worthy of pursuit for the sake of something else and that

[1] Cf. Pl. *Euthyd.* 289 C.

which is never desirable for the sake of something else more final than the things that are desirable both in themselves and for the sake of that other thing, and therefore we call final without qualification that which is always desirable in itself and never for the sake of something else.

Now such a thing happiness, above all else, is held to be; for this we choose always for itself and never for the sake of something else, but honour, pleasure, reason, and every virtue we choose indeed for themselves (for if nothing resulted from them we should still choose each of them), but we choose them also for the sake of happiness, judging that by means of them we shall be happy. Happiness, on the other hand, no one chooses for the sake of these, nor, in general, for anything other than itself.

From the point of view of self-sufficiency the same result seems to follow; for the final good is thought to be self-sufficient. Now by self-sufficient we do not mean that which is sufficient for a man by himself, for one who lives a solitary life, but also for parents, children, wife, and in general for his friends and fellow citizens, since man is born for citizenship. But some limit must be set to this; for if we extend our requirement to ancestors and descendants and friends' friends we are in for an infinite series. Let us examine this question, however, on another occasion;[2] the self-sufficient we now define as that which when isolated makes life desirable and lacking in nothing; and such we think happiness to be; and further we think it most desirable of all things, without being counted as one good thing among others—if it were so counted it would clearly be made more desirable by the addition of even the least of goods; for that which is added becomes an excess of goods, and of goods the greater is always more desirable. Happiness, then, is something final and self-sufficient, and is the end of action.

[2] i. 10, 11, ix. 10.

Presumably, however, to say that happiness is the chief good seems a platitude, and a clearer account of what it is is still desired. This might perhaps be given, if we could first ascertain the function of man. For just as for a flute-player, a sculptor, or any artist, and, in general, for all things that have a function or activity, the good and the 'well' is thought to reside in the function, so would it seem to be for man, if he has a function. Have the carpenter, then, and the tanner certain functions or activities, and has man none? Is he born without a function? Or as eye, hand, foot, and in general each of the parts evidently has a function, may one lay it down that man similarly has a function apart from all these? What then can this be? Life seems to be common even to plants, but we are seeking what is peculiar to man. Let us exclude, therefore, the life of nutrition and growth. Next there would be a life of perception, but *it* also seems to be common even to the horse, the ox, and every animal. There remains, then, an active life of the element that has a rational principle; of this, one part has such a principle in the sense of being obedient to one, the other in the sense of possessing one and exercising thought. And, as "life of the rational element" also has two meanings, we must state that life in the sense of activity is what we mean; for this seems to be the more proper sense of the term. Now if the function of man is an activity of soul which follows or implies a rational principle, and if we say "a so-and-so" and "a good so-and-so" have a function which is the same in kind, e.g. a lyre-player and a good lyre-player, and so without qualification in all cases, eminence in respect of goodness being added to the name of the function (for the function of a lyre-player is to play the lyre, and that of a good lyre-player is to do so well): if this is the case [and we state the function of man to be a certain kind of life, and this to be an activity or actions of the soul implying a rational principle, and the function of a good man to be the good and noble performance of these,

39

and if any action is well performed when it is performed in accordance with the appropriate excellence: if this is the case] human good turns out to be activity of soul in accordance with virtue, and if there are more than one virtue, in accordance with the best and most complete.

But we must add "in a complete life." For one swallow does not make a summer, nor does one day; and so too one day, or a short time, does not make a man blessed and happy.

Let this serve as an outline of the good; for we must presumably first sketch it roughly, and then later fill in the details. But it would seem that any one is capable of carrying on and articulating what has once been well outlined, and that time is a good discoverer or partner in such a work; to which facts the advances of the arts are due; for any one can add what is lacking. And we must also remember what has been said before,[3] and not look for precision in all things alike, but in each class of things such precision as accords with the subject-matter, and so much as is appropriate to the inquiry. For a carpenter and a geometer investigate the right angle in different ways; the former does so in so far as the right angle is useful for his work, while the latter inquires what it is or what sort of thing it is; for he is a spectator of the truth. We must act in the same way, then, in all other matters as well, that our main task may not be subordinated to minor questions. Nor must we demand the cause in all matters alike; it is enough in some cases that the *fact* be well established, as in the case of the first principles; the fact is the primary thing or first principle. Now of first principles we see some by induction, some by perception, some by a certain habituation, and others too in other ways. But each set of principles we must try to investigate in the natural way, and we must take pains to state them definitely since they have a great influence on what follows. For the begin-

[3] 1094b 11–27.

ning is thought to be more than half of the whole, and many of the questions we ask are cleared up by it.

8. We must consider it, however, in the light not only of our conclusion and our premisses, but also of what is commonly said about it; for with a true view all the data harmonize, but with a false one the facts soon clash. Now goods have been divided into three classes,[4] and some are described as external, others as relating to soul or to body; we call those that relate to soul most properly and truly goods, and psychical actions and activities we class as relating to soul. Therefore our account must be sound, at least according to this view, which is an old one and agreed on by philosophers. It is correct also in that we identify the end with certain actions and activities; for thus it falls among goods of the soul and not among external goods. Another belief which harmonizes with our account is that the happy man lives well and does well; for we have practically defined happiness as a sort of good life and good action. The characteristics that are looked for in happiness seem also, all of them, to belong to what we have defined happiness as being. For some identify happiness with virtue, some with practical wisdom, others with a kind of philosophic wisdom, others with these, or one of these, accompanied by pleasure or not without pleasure; while others include also external prosperity. Now some of these views have been held by many men and men of old, others by a few eminent persons; and it is not probable that either of these should be entirely mistaken, but rather that they should be right in at least some one respect or even in most respects.

With those who identify happiness with virtue or some one virtue our account is in harmony; for to virtue belongs virtuous activity. But it makes, perhaps, no small difference whether we place the chief good in possession or in use, in

---

[4] Pl. *Euthyd.* 279 AB, *Phil.* 48 E, *Laws,* 743 E.

state of mind or in activity. For the state of mind may exist without producing any good result, as in a man who is asleep or in some other way quite inactive, but the activity cannot; for one who has the activity will of necessity be acting, and acting well. And as in the Olympic Games it is not the most beautiful and the strongest that are crowned but those who compete (for it is some of these that are victorious), so those who act win, and rightly win, the noble and good things in life.

Their life is also in itself pleasant. For pleasure is a state of *soul,* and to each man that which he is said to be a lover of is pleasant; e.g. not only is a horse pleasant to the lover of horses, and a spectacle to the lover of sights, but also in the same way just acts are pleasant to the lover of justice and in general virtuous acts to the lover of virtue. Now for most men their pleasures are in conflict with one another because these are not by nature pleasant, but the lovers of what is noble find pleasant the things that are by nature pleasant; and virtuous actions are such, so that these are pleasant for such men as well as in their own nature. Their life, therefore, has no further need of pleasure as a sort of adventitious charm, but has its pleasure in itself. For, besides what we have said, the man who does not rejoice in noble actions is not even good, since no one would call a man just who did not enjoy acting justly, nor any man liberal who did not enjoy liberal actions; and similarly in all other cases. If this is so, virtuous actions must be in themselves pleasant. But they are also *good* and *noble,* and have each of these attributes in the highest degree, since the good man judges well about these attributes; his judgement is such as we have described.[5] Happiness then is the best, noblest,

[5] I.e., he judges that virtuous actions are good and noble in the highest degree.

and most pleasant thing in the world, and these attributes are not severed as in the inscription at Delos—

> Most noble is that which is justest, and best is health;
> But pleasantest it is to win what we love.

For all these properties belong to the best activities; and these, or one—the best—of these, we identify with happiness.

Yet evidently, as we said,[6] it needs the external goods as well; for it is impossible, or not easy, to do noble acts without the proper equipment. In many actions we use friends and riches and political power as instruments; and there are some things the lack of which takes the lustre from happiness, as good birth, goodly children, beauty; for the man who is very ugly in appearance or ill-born or solitary and childless is not very likely to be happy, and perhaps a man would be still less likely if he had thoroughly bad children or friends or had lost good children or friends by death. As we said,[6] then, happiness seems to need this sort of prosperity in addition, for which reason some identify happiness with good fortune, though others identify it with virtue.

9. For this reason also the question is asked, whether happiness is to be acquired by learning or by habituation or some other sort of training, or comes in virtue of some divine providence or again by change. Now if there is any gift of the gods to men, it is reasonable that happiness should be god-given, and most surely god-given of all human things inasmuch as it is the best. But this question would perhaps be more appropriate to another inquiry; happiness seems, however, even if it is not god-sent but comes as a result of virtue or some process of learning or training, to be among the most god-like things; for that which is the prize and end of virtue seems to be the best thing in the world, and something god-like and blessed.

[6] 1098b 26–9.

43

It will also on this view be very generally shared; for all who are not maimed as regards their potentiality for virtue may win it by a certain kind of study and care. But if it is better to be happy thus than by chance, it is reasonable that the facts should be so, since everything that depends on the action of nature is by nature as good as it can be, and similarly everything that depends on art or any rational cause, and especially if it depends on the best of all causes. To entrust to chance what is greatest and most noble would be a very defective arrangement.

The answer to the question we are asking is plain also from the definition of happiness; for it has been said[7] to be a virtuous activity of soul, of a certain kind. Of the remaining goods, some must necessarily pre-exist as conditions of happiness, and others are naturally co-operative and useful as instruments. And this will be found to agree with what we said at the outset;[8] for we stated the end of political science to be the best end, and political science spends most of its pains on making the citizens to be of a certain character, viz. good and capable of noble acts.

It is natural, then, that we call neither ox nor horse nor any other of the animals happy; for none of them is capable of sharing in such activity. For this reason also a boy is not happy; for he is not yet capable of such acts, owing to his age: and boys who are called happy are being congratulated by reason of the hopes we have for them. For there is required, as we said,[9] not only complete virtue but also a complete life, since many changes occur in life, and all manner of chances, and the most prosperous may fall into great misfortunes in old age, as is told of Priam in the Trojan Cycle; and one who has experienced such changes and has ended wretchedly no one calls happy.

[7] 1098ᵃ 16.
[8] 1094ᵃ 27.
[9] 1098ᵃ 16–18.

Nicomachean Ethics

10. Must no one at all, then, be called happy while he lives; must we, as Solon says,[10] see the end? Even if we are to lay down this doctrine, is it also the case that a man *is* happy when he is *dead*? Or is not this quite absurd, especially for us who say that happiness is an activity? But if we do not call the dead man happy, and if Solon does not mean this, but that one can then safely *call* a man blessed as being at last beyond evils and misfortunes, this also affords matter for discussion; for both evil and good are thought to exist for a dead man, as much as for one who is alive but not aware of them, e.g. honours and dishonours and the good or bad fortunes of children and in general of descendants. And this also presents a problem; for though a man has lived happily up to old age and has had a death worthy of his life, many reverses may befall his descendants—some of them may be good and attain the life they deserve, while with others the opposite may be the case; and clearly too the degrees of relationship between them and their ancestors may vary indefinitely. It would be odd, then, if the dead man were to share in these changes and become at one time happy, at another wretched; while it would also be odd if the fortunes of the descendants did not for *some* time have *some* effect on the happiness of their ancestors.

But we must return to our first difficulty;[11] for perhaps by a consideration of it our present problem might be solved. Now if we must see the end and only then call a man happy, not as being happy but as having been so before, surely this is a paradox, that when he is happy the attribute that belongs to him is not to be truly predicated of him because we do not wish to call living men happy, on account of the changes that may befall them, and because we have assumed happiness to be something permanent and by no means easily

[10] Hdt. i. 32.
[11] Cf. 1. 10.

45

changed, while a single man may suffer many turns of fortune's wheel. For clearly if we were to keep pace with his fortunes, we should often call the same man happy and again wretched, making the happy man out to be a "chameleon and insecurely based."[12] Or is this keeping pace with his fortunes quite wrong? Success or failure in life does not depend on these, but human life, as we said,[13] needs these as mere additions, while virtuous activities or their opposites are what constitute happiness or the reverse.

The question we have now discussed confirms our definition. For no function of man has so much permanence as virtuous activities (these are thought to be more durable even than knowledge of the sciences), and of these themselves the most valuable are more durable because those who are happy spend their life most readily and most continuously in these; for this seems to be the reason why we do not forget them. The attribute in question,[14] then, will belong to the happy man, and he will be happy throughout his life; for always, or by preference to everything else, he will be engaged in virtuous action and contemplation, and he will bear the chances of life most nobly and altogether decorously, if he is "truly good" and "four square beyond reproach."[15]

Now many events happen by chance, and events differing in importance; small pieces of good fortune or of its opposite clearly do not weigh down the scales of life one way or the other, but a multitude of great events if they turn out well will make life happier (for not only are they themselves such as to add beauty to life, but the way a man deals with them may be noble and good), while if they turn out ill

[12] Source unknown.
[13] 1099a 31-b 7.
[14] Durability.
[15] Simonides, fr. 4 Diehl.

they crush and maim happiness; for they both bring pain with them and hinder many activities. Yet even in these nobility shines through, when a man bears with resignation many great misfortunes, not through insensibility to pain but through nobility and greatness of soul.

If activities are, as we said,[16] what gives life its character, no happy man can become miserable; for he will never do the acts that are hateful and mean. For the man who is truly good and wise, we think, bears all the chances of life becomingly and always makes the best of circumstances, as a good general makes the best military use of the army at his command and a good shoemaker makes the best shoes out of the hides that are given him; and so with all other craftsmen. And if this is the case, the happy man can never become miserable—though he will not reach blessedness, if he meet with fortunes like those of Priam.

Nor, again, is he many-coloured and changeable; for neither will he be moved from his happy state easily or by any ordinary misadventures, but only by many great ones, nor, if he has had many great misadventures, will he recover his happiness in a short time, but if at all, only in a long and complete one in which he has attained many splendid successes.

Why then should we not say that he is happy who is active in accordance with complete virtue and is sufficiently equipped with external goods, not for some chance period but throughout a complete life? Or must we add "and who is destined to live thus and die as befits his life"? Certainly the future is obscure to us, while happiness, we claim, is an end and something in every way final. If so, we shall call happy those among living men in whom these conditions are, and are to be, fulfilled—but happy *men*. So much for these questions.

[16] I. 9.

11.* That the fortunes of descendants and of all a man's friends should not affect his happiness at all seems a very unfriendly doctrine, and one opposed to the opinions men hold; but since the events that happen are numerous and admit of all sorts of difference, and some come more near to us and others less so, it seems a long—nay, an infinite—task to discuss each in detail; a general outline will perhaps suffice. If, then, as some of a man's own misadventures have a certain weight and influence on life while others are, as it were, lighter, so too there are differences among the misadventures of our friends taken as a whole, and it makes a difference whether the various sufferings befall the living or the dead (much more even than whether lawless and terrible deeds are presupposed in a tragedy or done on the stage), this difference also must be taken into account; or rather, perhaps, the fact that doubt is felt whether the dead share in any good or evil. For it seems, from these considerations, that even if anything whether good or evil penetrates to them, it must be something weak and negligible, either in itself or for them, or if not, at least it must be such in degree and kind as not to make happy those who are not happy nor to take away their blessedness from those who are. The good or bad fortunes of friends, then, seem to have some effects on the dead, but effects of such a kind and degree as neither to make the happy unhappy nor to produce any other change of the kind.

12. These questions having been definitely answered, let us consider whether happiness is among the things that are praised or rather among the things that are prized; for clearly it is not to be placed among *potentialities*.[17] Everything that is praised seems to be praised because it is of a certain kind and is related somehow to something else; for we praise the

---

* Aristotle now returns to the question stated in 1100ᵃ 18–30.
[17] Cf. *Top.* 126ᵇ 4; *M. M.* 1183ᵇ 20.

just or brave man and in general both the good man and virtue itself because of the actions and functions involved, and we praise the strong man, the good runner, and so on, because he is of a certain kind and is related in a certain way to something good and important. This is clear also from the praises of the gods; for it seems absurd that the gods should be referred to our standard, but this *is* done because praise involves a reference, as we said, to something else. But if praise is for things such as we have described, clearly what applies to the best things is not praise, but something greater and better, as is indeed obvious; for what we do to the gods and the most godlike of men is to call them blessed and happy. And so too with good *things;* no one praises happiness as he does justice, but rather calls it blessed, as being something more divine and better.

Eudoxus also seems to have been right in his method of advocating the supremacy of pleasure; he thought that the fact that, though a good, it is not praised indicated it to be better than the things that are praised, and that this is what God and the good are; for by reference to these all other things are judged. *Praise* is appropriate to virtue, for as a result of virtue men tend to do noble deeds; but *encomia* are bestowed on acts, whether of the body or of the soul. But perhaps nicety in these matters is more proper to those who have made a study of encomia; to us it is clear from what has been said that happiness is among the things that are prized and perfect. It seems to be so also from the fact that it is a first principle; for it is for the sake of this that we all do all that we do, and the first principle and cause of goods is, we claim, something prized and divine.

13. Since happiness is an activity of soul in accordance with perfect virtue, we must consider the nature of virtue; for perhaps we shall thus see better the nature of happiness. The true student of politics, too, is thought to have studied virtue above all things; for he wishes to make his fellow

citizens good and obedient to the laws. As an example of this we have the lawgivers of the Cretans and the Spartans, and any others of the kind that there may have been. And if this inquiry belongs to political science, clearly the pursuit of it will be in accordance with our original plan. But clearly the virtue we must study is human virtue; for the good we were seeking was human good and the happiness human happiness. By human virtue we mean not that of the body but that of the soul; and happiness also we call an activity of the soul. But if this is so, clearly the student of politics must know somehow the facts about the soul, as the man who is to heal the eyes or the body as a whole must know about the eyes or the body; and all the more since politics is more prized and better than medicine; but even among doctors the best educated spend much labour on acquiring knowledge of the body. The student of politics, then, must study the soul, and must study it with these objects in view, and do so just to the extent which is sufficient for the questions we are discussing; for further precision is perhaps something more laborious than our purposes require.

Some things are said about it, adequately enough, even in the discussions outside our school, and we must use these, e.g. that one element in the soul is irrational and one has a rational principle. Whether these are separated as the parts of the body or of anything divisible are, or are distinct by definition but by nature inseparable, like convex and concave in the circumference of a circle, does not affect the present question.

Of the irrational element one division seems to be widely distributed, and vegetative in its nature, I mean that which causes nutrition and growth; for it is this kind of power of the soul that one must assign to all nurslings and to embryos, and this same power to full-grown creatures; this is more reasonable than to assign some different power to them. Now the excellence of this seems to be common to all species and not specifically human; for this part or faculty seems to function most in sleep, while goodness and badness are least manifest in sleep (whence comes the saying that the happy are no better off than the wretched for half their lives; and this happens naturally enough, since sleep is an inactivity of the soul in that respect in which it is called good or bad), unless perhaps to a small extent some of the movements actually penetrate to the soul, and in this respect the dreams of good men are better than those of ordinary people. Enough of this subject, however; let us leave the nutritive faculty alone, since it has by its nature no share in human excellence.

There seems to be also another irrational element in the soul—one which in a sense, however, shares in a rational principle. For we praise the rational principle of the continent man and of the incontinent, and the part of their soul that has such a principle, since it urges them aright and towards the best objects; but there is found in them also another element naturally opposed to the rational principle which fights against and resists that principle. For exactly as paralysed limbs when we intend to move them to the right turn on the contrary to the left, so is it with the soul; the impulses of incontinent people move in contrary directions. But while in the body we see that which moves astray, in the soul we do not. No doubt, however, we must none the less suppose that in the soul too there is something contrary to the rational principle, resisting and opposing it. In what sense it is distinct from the other elements does not concern us. Now even this seems to have a share in a rational principle, as we said;[18] at any rate in the continent man it obeys the rational principle—and presumably in the temperate and brave man it is still more obedient; for in him it speaks, on all matters, with the same voice as the rational principle.

Therefore the irrational element also appears to be two-

[18] 1. 13.

fold. For the vegetative element in no way shares in a rational principle, but the appetitive and in general the desiring element in a sense shares in it, in so far as it listens to and obeys it; this is the sense in which we speak of "taking account" of one's father or one's friends, not that in which we speak of "accounting" for a mathematical property. That the irrational element is in some sense persuaded by a rational principle is indicated also by the giving of advice and by all reproof and exhortation. And if this element also must be said to have a rational principle, that which has a rational principle (as well as that which has not) will be twofold, one subdivision having it in the strict sense and in itself, and the other having a tendency to obey as one does one's father.

Virtue too is distinguished into kinds in accordance with this difference; for we say that some of the virtues are intellectual and others moral, philosophic wisdom and understanding and practical wisdom being intellectual, liberality and temperance moral. For in speaking about a man's character we do not say that he is wise or has understanding but that he is good-tempered or temperate; yet we praise the wise man also with respect to his state of mind; and of states of mind we call those which merit praise virtues.

BOOK X, CHAPTERS 6–8

Now that we have spoken of the virtues, the forms of friendship, and the varieties of pleasure, what remains is to discuss in outline the nature of happiness, since this is what we state the end of human nature to be. Our discussion will be the more concise if we first sum up what we have said already. We said,[1] then, that it is not a disposition; for if it were it might belong to some one who was asleep throughout his life, living the life of a plant, or, again, to some one

[1] 1095^b 31–1096^a 2, 1098^b 31–1099^a 7.

who was suffering the greatest misfortunes. If these implica-
tions are unacceptable, and we must rather class happiness
as an activity, as we have said before,[2] and if some activities
are necessary, and desirable for the sake of something else,
while others are so in themselves, evidently happiness must
be placed among those desirable in themselves, not among
those desirable for the sake of something else; for happiness
does not lack anything, but is self-sufficient. Now those
activities are desirable in themselves from which nothing is
sought beyond the activity. And of this nature virtuous
actions are thought to be; for to do noble and good deeds
is a thing desirable for its own sake.

Pleasant amusements also are thought to be of this nature;
we choose them not for the sake of other things; for we are
injured rather than benefited by them, since we are led to
neglect our bodies and our property. But most of the people
who are deemed happy take refuge in such pastimes, which
is the reason why those who are ready-witted at them are
highly esteemed at the courts of tyrants; they make themselves pleasant companions in the tyrants' favourite pursuits,
and that is the sort of man they want. Now these things are
thought to be of the nature of happiness because people in
despotic positions spend their leisure in them, but perhaps such people prove nothing; for virtue and reason, from
which good activities flow, do not depend on despotic position; nor, if these people, who have never tasted pure and
generous pleasure, take refuge in the bodily pleasures, should
these for that reason be thought more desirable; for boys,
too, think the things that are valued among themselves are
the best. It is to be expected, then, that, as different things
seem valuable to boys and to men, so they should to bad
men and to good. Now, as we have often maintained,[3] those

[2] 1098ᵃ 5–7.
[3] 1099ᵃ 13, 1113ᵃ 22–33, 1166ᵃ 12, 1170ᵃ 14–16, 1176ᵃ 15–22.

things are both valuable and pleasant which are such to the good man; and to each man the activity in accordance with his own disposition is most desirable, and, therefore, to the good man that which is in accordance with virtue. Happiness, therefore, does not lie in amusement; it would, indeed, be strange if the end were amusement, and one were to take trouble and suffer hardships all one's life in order to amuse oneself. For, in a word, everything that we choose we choose for the sake of something else—except happiness, which is an end. Now to exert oneself and work for the sake of amusement seems silly and utterly childish. But to amuse oneself in order that one may exert oneself, as Anacharsis[4] puts it, seems right; for amusement is a sort of relaxation, and we need relaxation because we cannot work continuously. Relaxation, then, is not an end; for it is taken for the sake of activity.

The happy life is thought to be virtuous; now a virtuous life requires exertion, and does not consist in amusement. And we say that serious things are better than laughable things and those connected with amusement, and that the activity of the better of any two things—whether it be two elements of our being or two men—is the more serious; but the activity of the better is *ipso facto* superior and more of the nature of happiness. And any chance person—even a slave—can enjoy the bodily pleasures no less than the best man; but no one assigns to a slave a share in happiness—unless he assigns to him also a share in human life. For happiness does not lie in such occupations, but, as we have said before,[5] in virtuous activities.

If happiness is activity in accordance with virtue, it is reasonable that it should be in accordance with the highest

[4] A Scythian prince who was believed to have travelled in Greece, and to have been the author of many aphorisms.
[5] 1098a 16, 1176a 35–b9.

virtue; and this will be that of the best thing in us. Whether it be reason or something else that is this element which is thought to be our natural ruler and guide and to take thought of things noble and divine, whether it be itself also divine or only the most divine element in us, the activity of this in accordance with its proper virtue will be perfect happiness. That this activity is contemplative we have already said.[6]

Now this would seem to be in agreement both with what we said before[7] and with the truth. For, firstly, this activity is the best (since not only is reason the best thing in us, but the objects of reason are the best of knowable objects); and, secondly, it is the most continuous, since we can contemplate truth more continuously than we can do anything. And we think happiness has pleasure mingled with it, but the activity of philosophic wisdom is admittedly the pleasantest of virtuous activities; at all events the pursuit of it is thought to offer pleasures marvellous for their purity and their enduringness, and it is to be expected that those who know will pass their time more pleasantly than those who inquire. And the self-sufficiency that is spoken of must belong most to the contemplative activity. For while a philosopher, as well as a just man or one possessing any other virtue, needs the necessaries of life, when they are sufficiently equipped with things of that sort the just man needs people towards whom and with whom he shall act justly, and the temperate man, the brave man, and each of the others is in the same case, but the philosopher, even when by himself, can contemplate truth, and the better the wiser he is; he can perhaps do so better if he has fellow-workers, but still he is the most self-sufficient. And this activity alone would seem to be loved for its own sake; for nothing arises from it apart from the

[6] This has not been said, but cf. 1095^b 14–1096^a 5, 1141^a 18–^{b}3, 1143^b 33–1144^a 6, 1145^a 6–11.

[7] 1097^a 25–^{b}21, 1099^a 7–21, 1173^b 15–19, 1174^b 20–23, 1175^b 36 1176^a 3.

contemplating, while from practical activities we gain more or less apart from the action. And happiness is thought to depend on leisure; for we are busy that we may have leisure, and make war that we may live in peace. Now the activity of the practical virtues is exhibited in political or military affairs, but the actions concerned with these seem to be unleisurely. Warlike actions are completely so (for no one chooses to be at war, or provokes war, for the sake of being at war; any one would seem absolutely murderous if he were to make enemies of his friends in order to bring about battle and slaughter); but the action of the statesman is also unleisurely, and—apart from the political action itself—aims at despotic power and honours, or at all events happiness, for him and his fellow citizens—a happiness different from political action, and evidently sought as being different. So if among virtuous actions political and military actions are distinguished by nobility and greatness, and these are unleisurely and aim at an end and are not desirable for their own sake, but the activity of reason, which is contemplative, seems both to be superior in serious worth and to aim at no end beyond itself, and to have its pleasure proper to itself (and this augments the activity), and the self-sufficiency, leisureliness, unweariedness (so far as this is possible for man), and all the other attributes ascribed to the supremely happy man are evidently those connected with this activity, it follows that this will be the complete happiness of man, if it be allowed a complete term of life (for none of the attributes of happiness is *in*complete).

But such a life would be too high for man; for it is not in so far as he is man that he will live so, but in so far as something divine is present in him; and by so much as this is superior to our composite nature is its activity superior to that which is the exercise of the other kind of virtue. If reason is divine, then, in comparison with man, the life according to it is divine in comparison with human life.

56

Nicomachean Ethics

But we must not follow those who advise us, being men to think of human things,[8] and, being mortal, of mortal things,[9] but must, so far as we can, make ourselves immortal, and strain every nerve to live in accordance with the best thing in us; for even if it be small in bulk, much more does it in power and worth surpass everything. This would seem, too, to be each man himself, since it is the authoritative and better part of him. It would be strange, then, if he were to choose not the life of his self but that of something else. And what we said[10] before will apply now; that which is proper to each thing is by nature best and most pleasant for each thing; for man, therefore, the life according to reason is best and pleasantest, since reason more than anything else is man. This life therefore is also the happiest.

But in a secondary degree the life in accordance with the other kind of virtue is happy; for the activities in accordance with this befit our human estate. Just and brave acts, and other virtuous acts, we do in relation to each other, observing our respective duties with regard to contracts and services and all manner of actions and with regard to passions; and all of these seem to be typically human. Some of them seem even to arise from the body, and virtue of character to be in many ways bound up with the passions. Practical wisdom, too, is linked to virtue of character, and this to practical wisdom, since the principles of practical wisdom are in accordance with the moral virtues and rightness in morals is in accordance with practical wisdom. Being connected with the passions also, the moral virtues must belong to our composite nature; and the virtues of our composite nature are human; so, therefore, are the life and the happi-

---

[8] Eur. fr. 1040 Nauck².

[9] Pind. *Isthm.* 5. 16 Schroeder; Soph. *(Tereus)* fr. 531 Nauck²; Antiphanes fr. 289 Kock.

[10] 1169ᵇ 33, 1176ᵇ 26.

ness which correspond to these. The excellence of the reason is a thing apart; we must be content to say this much about it, for to describe it precisely is a task greater than our purpose requires. It would seem, however, also to need external equipment but little, or less than moral virtue does. Grant that both need the necessaries, and do so equally, even if the statesman's work is the more concerned with the body and things of that sort; for there will be little difference there; but in what they need for the exercise of their activities there will be much difference. The liberal man will need money for the doing of his liberal deeds, and the just man too will need it for the returning of services (for wishes are hard to discern, and even people who are not just pretend to wish to act justly); and the brave man will need power if he is to accomplish any of the acts that correspond to his virtue, and the temperate man will need opportunity; for how else is either he or any of the others to be recognized? It is debated, too, whether the will or the deed is more essential to virtue, which is assumed to involve both; it is surely clear that its perfection involves both; but for deeds many things are needed, and more, the greater and nobler the deeds are. But the man who is contemplating the truth needs no such thing, at least with a view to the exercise of his inactivity; indeed they are, one may say, even hindrances, at all events to his contemplation; but in so far as he is a man and lives with a number of people, he chooses to do virtuous acts; he will therefore need such aids to living a human life.

But that perfect happiness is a contemplative activity will appear from the following consideration as well. We assume the gods to be above all other beings blessed and happy; but what sort of actions must we assign to them? Acts of justice? Will not the gods seem absurd if they make contracts and return deposits, and so on? Acts of a brave man, then, confronting dangers and running risks because it is noble to do so? Or liberal acts? To whom will they give? It will be strange if they are really to have money or anything of the kind. And what would their temperate acts be? Is not such praise tasteless, since they have no bad appetites? If we were to run through them all, the circumstances of action would be found trivial and unworthy of gods. Still, every one supposes that they *live* and therefore that they are active; we cannot suppose them to sleep like Endymion. Now if you take away from a living being action, and still more production, what is left but contemplation? Therefore the activity of God, which surpasses all others in blessedness, must be contemplative; and of human activities, therefore, that which is most akin to this must be most of the nature of happiness.

This is indicated, too, by the fact that the other animals have no share in happiness, being completely deprived of such activity. For while the whole life of the gods is blessed, and that of men too in so far as some likeness of such activity belongs to them, none of the other animals is happy, since they in no way share in contemplation. Happiness extends, then, just so far as contemplation does, and those to whom contemplation more fully belongs are more truly happy, not as a mere concomitant but in virtue of the contemplation; for this is in itself precious. Happiness, therefore, must be some form of contemplation.

But, being a man, one will also need external prosperity; for our nature is not self-sufficient for the purpose of contemplation, but our body also must be healthy and must have food and other attention. Still, we must not think that the man who is to be happy will need many things or great things, merely because he cannot be supremely happy without external goods; for self-sufficiency and action do not involve excess, and we can do noble acts without ruling earth and sea; for even with moderate advantages one can act virtuously (this is manifest enough; for private persons are thought to do worthy acts no less than despots—indeed even more); and it is enough that we should have so much as that; for the life of the man who is active in accordance with virtue will be happy. Solon, too, was perhaps sketching well the happy man when he described him[11] as moderately furnished with externals but as having done (as Solon thought) the noblest acts, and lived temperately; for one can with but moderate possessions do what one ought. Anaxagoras also seems to have supposed the happy man not to be rich, nor a despot, when he said[12] that he would not be surprised if the happy man were to seem to most people a strange person; for they judge by externals, since these are all they perceive. The opinions of the wise seem, then, to harmonize with our arguments. But while even such things carry some conviction, the truth in practical matters is discerned from the facts of life; for these are the decisive factor. We must therefore survey what we have already said, bringing it to the test of the facts of life, and if it harmonizes with the facts we must accept it, but if it clashes with them we must suppose it to be mere theory. Now he who exercises his reason and cultivates it seems to be both in the best state of mind and most dear to the gods. For if the gods have any care for human affairs, as they are thought to have, it would be reasonable both that they should delight in that which was best and most akin to them (i.e. reason) and that they should reward those who love and honour this most, as caring for the things that are dear to them and acting both rightly and nobly. And that all these attributes belong most of all to the philosopher is manifest. He, therefore, is the dearest to the gods. And he who is that will presumably be also the happiest; so that in this way too the philosopher will more than any other be happy.

[11] Hdt. i. 30.
[12] Diels, *Vors.* 46 A 30.

Lucretius (ca. 96-ca. 55 B.C.)

On the Nature of Things

BOOK III, VERSES 425–1107

In the first place, since I have shown that the *soul, being*
subtle, consists of minute particles, and is composed of much
smaller atoms than the clear fluid of water, or mist, or smoke;
(for it far surpasses *those bodies* in susceptibility-of motion,
and is more readily impelled when acted upon from a slight
cause; inasmuch as *both the mind and soul* are moved by the
mere images of smoke and mist; as when, lulled in sleep, we
see high altars exhale with vapour, and carry up smoke;
since doubtless these phantasms are produced in us;) now,
therefore, *I say*, since, when vessels are broken to pieces, you
see water flow about, and *any other* liquid run away; and
since, *also*, mist and smoke disperse into the air; *you must*
conclude that the soul is likewise scattered abroad, and is
dissipated much sooner *than mist and smoke*, and more easily
resolved into *its* original elements, when it *has* once *been*
withdrawn from the body of a man, *and* has taken its departure. For how can you believe that this *soul* can be held
together by any *combination of* air, when the body itself
(which is, as it were, its vessel) cannot contain it, *if it be*
convulsed by any violence, or rendered thin *and weak* by
blood being taken from the veins? How can *that air which is*
more rare than our body confine it?

Besides, we observe that the mind is produced together
with the body, and grows up along *with it,* and waxes old at

61

the same time *with it*. For as children wander *and totter* about with a weak and tender body, so the subtle sense of the mind follows *and corresponds to the weakness of their frame*. Then, when their age has grown up in robust vigour, their understanding is also greater, and their strength of mind more enlarged. Afterwards, when the body is shaken by the prevailing power of time, and, the strength being depressed, the limbs have sunk *into* infirmity, the understanding *then* halts, the tongue and the mind lose their sense, all *parts* fail and fade away at once. It is therefore natural that the whole substance of the soul should be dissolved, as smoke, into the sublime air of heaven; since we see that it is produced together with the body, and grows up together *with it,* and both, as I have shown, overcome by age, decay in concert.

To this is added, that as we observe the body itself to-be-subject-to violent diseases and severe pain, *so we see* the mind *to be susceptible* of sharp cares, and grief, and fear. For which cause it is reasonable that it should also be a partaker of death.

Moreover the mind, in diseases of the body, often wanders distracted; for it loses its faculties, and utters senseless words; and sometimes, by a heavy lethargy, is borne down into a deep and eternal sleep, the eyes and the nodding-head sinking; hence it neither hears the voice, nor can distinguish the countenances, of those who stand around recalling it to life, bedewing their faces and cheeks with tears. Wherefore you must necessarily admit that the mind is also dissolved, since the contagion of disease penetrates into it. For pain and disease are each the fabricator of death; a *truth* which we have been taught by the destruction of many *millions* in past times.

Further, when the violent power of wine has penetrated the heart of men, and its heat, being distributed, has spread into the veins, a heaviness of the limbs follows, the legs of

62

the tottering person are impeded, the tongue grows torpid, the mind is, *as it were,* drowned; the eyes swim; noise, hiccups, and quarrels arise, and other things of this kind, whatever are consequent *on intoxication.* Why do these *effects* happen, unless because the vehement force of the wine has exerted-its-customary-power to disturb the soul *as it is diffused* through the body itself? But whatsoever things can be *thus* disturbed and obstructed *in their operations,* show, that if a cause somewhat stronger shall spread within *them, the consequence* will be that they must perish, deprived of *all* future existence.

Moreover, frequently, overcome by the force of disease, a person suddenly falls down before our eyes, as *if struck* by the blow of a thunder-bolt, and foams *at the mouth,* groans, and trembles in his joints, loses his senses, stretches his nerves *to rigidity,* is distorted, pants with irregular *breathing,* and wearies his limbs with tossing about; evidently because the violence of the malady, dispersed throughout the body, *and* acting upon the soul, perturbs it, as the waves, on the foaming salt ocean, boil with the strong fury of the winds. Groans are then forced out, because the limbs are seized with pain, and especially because the particles of the voice are drawn forth, and carried, collected *in a body,* out of the mouth, *the way* by which they have, as it were, been accustomed *to pass,* and *where the course* of the road is paved *for them.* Loss of understanding takes place, because the *united* power of the mind and soul is disturbed, and, as I have shown, is divided *and* rent asunder, distracted by that same distemper. Afterwards, when the cause of the disease has given way, and the violent humour of the disordered body has retired into its hiding-place, then, as if staggering, *the person* first rises, and, by degrees, returns to all his senses, and re-possesses *the right state of* his soul.

When these *substances,* therefore, *the mind and the soul,* are shaken with such powerful diseases in the body itself,

63

and suffer, distracted in *such* miserable ways, why do you conceive that the same *mind and soul* can support an existence without a body, in the open air, *and* amidst strong winds?

And since we see that the mind may be healed, like a sick body, and wrought upon by means of medicine, this also signifies that the mind exists *only as a* mortal *substance.* For whoever attempts, and commences, to change the mind, or to alter any other nature *or substance* whatsoever, it is requisite *either* that he add *new* parts, or transpose *the parts* in *a new order,* or take away at least some small portion from the whole. But any *substance,* which is immortal, nei- ther allows its parts to be transposed, nor to-be-increased-by- addition, nor *permits* an atom to pass away from them. For whatever, being changed, goes beyond its own limits, this *change* is forthwith the death or *termination* of that which it was before.

The mind, therefore, whether it be diseased, or whether it be wrought upon by medicine, exhibits, as I have demon- strated, mortal symptoms: so far is the force of true reason seen to oppose false *reasoning,* and to cut off escape from him who shrinks *from its conclusions,* and to overthrow what is wrong by a double refutation.

Furthermore, we often see a man decay by degrees, and lose his vital power in one limb after another. On the feet *we observe* the toes and nails first grow livid; then the feet *them- selves* and the legs mortify; afterwards, throughout the other limbs, *we perceive* the traces of cold death thence proceed step by step. And since the substance of the soul is *thus* divided, and does not continue, *always and* at the same time, entire *and unimpaired,* it must be deemed mortal. But if perchance you think that *the soul* can itself contract itself internally throughout the limbs, and condense its parts into one *place,* and thus withdraw feeling from all the members successively, yet, *in such a case,* that place in which so great a mass of soul is collected, ought to seem in *possession of*

64

greater feeling. *But* since this *place of such increased feeling* is no where *apparent, the soul,* as we said before, is evidently, being separated-into-parts, scattered abroad, *and* therefore perishes.

Moreover, if we even consent to grant *that which* is false, and to allow that the soul may be *thus* concentrated in the bodies of those who leave light *and life* by dying part after part, you must still confess that the soul is mortal; *for* neither is it of any importance whether it perishes, being scattered throughout the air, or loses its sense when drawn together from *being dispersed in* its *several* parts, when animation steals away from the whole man more and more on all sides, and less and less of life is every where left.

And as the mind is one single part of a man, and remains fixed in a certain place, as the ears and eyes are, and the other *organs of* sense, whatsoever govern life; and as the hand, and the eye or nose, when detached from us, cannot, separately *of themselves,* have sensation or *even* existence, for, when cut off, they are in a short time wasted with putrefaction; so the mind cannot, of itself, exist without the body and the man himself, which *body* seems to be, as it were, its vessel, or whatsoever else you would imagine to be more closely united with it, since it adheres to the body by connexion.

Further, the animated powers of the body and mind are vigorous, and enjoy life, only when joined with one another; for neither can the nature *or substance* of the mind, without the body, alone, *and* of itself, produce vital motions; nor again, *can* the body, deprived of the soul, continue *its state of existence,* and use its faculties. Just, for example, as the eye itself, torn from its roots, can discern no object apart from the whole body, so the mind or soul seems to have no power in itself; evidently because when mingled throughout the veins and viscera, throughout the nerves and bones, they are held-in-close-confinement by the whole body, and their primary-particles, not being free, cannot fly asunder to great

65

distances; consequently, being thus confined, they move with sensitive motions, with which, after death, when cast forth beyond the body into the air of heaven, they cannot move; for this very reason, that they are not held-confined in a similar manner. For *surely* the air forms body and soul, if the soul shall be able to keep itself together *in the air,* and to contain itself for *exerting* those motions, which it before exercised amidst the nerves, and in the body itself. On which account, *I say* again and again, you must necessarily admit that when the whole enclosure of the body is dissolved, and the vital breath cast forth, the sentient-existence of the mind and the soul is dissolved; since there is common cause *and like fate* to both.

Besides, when the body cannot bear the dissociation of the soul, without putrifying with offensive odour, why do you doubt but that the essence of the soul, rising from the depths and innermost part *of the body,* has passed forth, *and has been* diffused abroad like smoke? and that for this reason the body, decaying with so great a dissolution, has utterly fallen away, because the foundations have been removed from their place, and the spirits pass out through the limbs, and through all the windings of the passages and ducts that are in the body? So that you may understand from many considerations, that the nature *or substance* of the soul, being disparted, has gone out through the members *of the body,* and that it was dissevered within the body itself, before, gliding outwards, it flowed forth into the air of heaven.

Moreover, whilst the soul dwells within the bounds of life, it yet frequently, when it has received a shock from some cause, seems to pass away, and *presents the appearance* that the mind is let loose from the whole body; and the countenance *then* seems to become inanimate as at the last hour, and all the relaxed members to fail the languid frame. Such is the case, when it is said that the mind has been damaged, or the vital power has suffered-syncope; while *all*

66

On the Nature of Things

is trepidation, and all are anxious to recover the last link of life. For then all the mind, and power of the soul, are shaken; and these, *it is evident,* sink with the body itself; *so* that a cause of somewhat greater force may bring *them* to dissolution.

Why *then* do you doubt, but that, *at the hour of death, the soul* driven forth at length, weak *and helpless,* out of the body, and being in the open air, with its covering removed, can not only not endure throughout all time, but cannot even maintain-its-existence for the smallest space whatsoever?

Nor does any one, when dying, appear to feel his soul go forth entire from his whole body, or come up first to his throat, and to his jaws above *it;* but *he finds that part of it which is* placed in any certain portion *of the body,* fail *and decay* in that part; as he is conscious of the other senses los-ing-their-power each in its own quarter; but if our soul were immortal, it would not so much complain that it suffers dis-solution when dying, but would rather rejoice to pass forth abroad, and to leave its covering, as a snake *delights to cast its skin,* or an old stag its too long antlers.

Again, why are the understanding and faculty of the mind never produced in the head, or the feet, or the hands, but remain-fixed, in all men alike, in their peculiar seats and definite quarters, if *it be not that* certain spots are assigned to each *part* to be born *in,* and where *each,* what-ever *it be,* may preserve-its-existence when born; and *if it be not* that such is the case with respect to the whole of the various members, so that there may no where arise an improper arrangement of the parts? So invariably, *in the operations of nature,* does one thing follow another; nor is fire wont to be produced from rivers, or cold to be generated in fire.

Besides, if the nature of the soul is immortal, and can have-a-sentient-existence, when separated from our body, we must consider it, as I suppose, to be endowed with the five senses; nor in any other way can we represent to ourselves the infernal souls as wandering on *the banks of* the Acheron. Accordingly painters, and the past generations of writers, have introduced *in their compositions* souls thus endowed with senses. But neither can the eyes, nor the nostrils, nor the hand itself, preserve-existence apart from the soul; nor *can* the tongue; nor can the ears perceive hearing, or even remain-in-being, apart *from the soul. How then can souls be possessed of the five senses, when all the organs of those senses have perished?*

And since we see that the vital sense spreads through the whole body, and that the whole is animated, if, on a sudden, any violence shall cut through *the body in the* middle, so as to sever the two parts asunder, the substance of the soul, also, without doubt, being disunited and divided together with the body, will be dispersed *and scattered abroad.* But that which is divided, and separates into any parts, evidently shows that it has not an ever-during nature.

People relate that chariots armed with scythes, warm with promiscuous slaughter, often cut off limbs with such suddenness, that the part which, being severed, has fallen from the body, is seen to quiver on the ground, when, notwithstanding, the mind and spirit of the man, from the quickness of the wound, cannot feel any pain. And because at the same time, the mind, in the ardour of battle, is given up *to action,* it pursues fighting and slaughter with the remainder of the body; nor is *one man* aware, frequently, in the midst of the horses, that the wheels and amputating scythes have carried away his left hand, which is lost together with its defence, nor *is* another *conscious,* while he climbs the wall and presses forward, that his right hand has dropped off. A third next attempts to rise after having lost his leg, while his dying foot, close by *him,* moves its toes on the ground. And the head *of a fourth,* severed from the warm and living trunk, keeps, *while lying* on the ground, its look of life and its eyes open, until it has yielded up all remains of the soul within it.

Moreover, if, when the tongue of a serpent vibrates *against you,* and his tail and long body threaten *you,* you may feel inclined to cut both *tail and body* into several parts with your sword, you will see all the parts separately, cut through with the recent wound, writhe about, and sprinkle the earth with blood; and *you will observe* the fore part, turning backward, seeking itself, *that is, the hinder part of the body,* with its mouth, so that, pierced with the burning anguish of the wound, it may seize it with its teeth.

Shall we then say that there are entire souls in all those several parts? But from that position it will follow that one living creature had several souls in its *single* body. *And since this is absurd, we must admit,* therefore, *that* that has been divided which was one with the body; wherefore both must be thought to be mortal; since *both* are equally divided into several portions.

Besides, if the nature of the soul exists imperishable, and is infused into men at their birth, why are we unable to remember the period-of-existence previously spent *by us,* nor retain any traces of past transactions? For if the power of the mind is so exceedingly changed, that all remembrance of past things has departed from it, that change, as I think, is not far removed from death *itself.* For which reason you must of necessity acknowledge, that whatever *soul* previously existed has perished, and that that which exists for the present has been produced for the present.

Again, if, after the body is completely formed, the vital power of the soul is wont to be introduced into us at the very time when we are born and when we cross the threshold of life, it would not be in accordance with this, that it should seem, *as it now seems,* to have grown up in the blood itself together with the body, and with its *several* members; but it would rather be natural that it should live alone, as in a cage, by itself *and* for itself; though *in such a manner,* that the whole body, *by its influence,* should abound with sense *and vitality.* For which reason, *I say* again and again, we must neither think that souls are without beginning, nor that they are exempt from the law of death. For neither must we deem that souls, *if* infused *into us* from without, could have been so completely united with our bodies; (which complete *union,* on the contrary, manifest experience proves to take place; for *the soul* is so combined *with the body* throughout the veins, viscera, nerves, and bones, that even the very teeth have a share of feeling; as their aching proves, and the acute-pain from cold water, and the crunching of a hard pebble suddenly among our food) nor, when they are so *completely* united, does it seem possible for them to come out entire, and to extricate themselves unharmed from all the nerves, and bones, and joints.

But if *still,* perchance, you think that a soul, infused from without, is wont to expand itself through our limbs, *yet to admit this, is only to admit that* every man's *soul,* being spread out with the body, will so much the more *certainly* perish *with it.* For that which is diffused *throughout the body,* is dissolved with it, *and* therefore perishes. Being distributed, then, through all the passages of the body—as food, when it is distributed through all the members and limbs, is dissolved, and takes of itself another nature—so the soul and the mind, although, *under this supposition,* they go whole into the body at first, yet are dissolved, *like digested food,* in diffusing themselves *through it,* while the particles are distributed, as if through tubes, into all the limbs; *the particles, I say,* of which is formed this substance of the mind, which now rules in our body, and which has been generated, *like the new nature of food,* from that which lost its consistence when it was spread throughout the limbs.

For which reasons, the nature *or substance* of the soul seems neither to have been without a natal day, nor to be exempt from death.

On the Nature of Things

Again, do any atoms of the soul remain in a dead body, or not? For if any remain and exist in *the body,* it will not be possible for *the soul* to be justly accounted immortal; since *when* she took her departure, *she was* diminished of *some* lost particles. But if, when removed, she fled with *all* her parts so entire, that she left no atoms of her substance in the body, whence do dead carcasses, when the viscera become putrid, send forth worms? And whence does such an abundance of living creatures, void of bones and blood, swarm over the swollen limbs?

But if, perchance, you think that *perfectly-formed* souls may be insinuated into those worms from without, and if *you suppose* that they may pass each into its own body, and *yet* omit to consider for what cause many thousands of souls should congregate *in the place* from which one soul has withdrawn, this point, however, *which you leave out of consideration,* is *of such a nature,* that it seems *especially* worthy to be sought into and brought under examination. *It is proper not only to reflect,* I say, whether souls hunt for particular atoms of worms, and build for themselves *carcasses* in which they may dwell, or whether they infuse themselves into bodies already made; but *also to consider that* there is no reason to be given why they should make bodies, or why they should labour *at all;* for, while they are without a body, they fly about undisturbed by diseases, and cold, and hunger; since *it is* the body *that* rather labours under these maladies (as well as from death) and the soul suffers all evils from contact with it. But, nevertheless, let it be as advantageous as you please for these *souls* to make a body which they may enter, there seems, however, to be no means by which they may make it. *It is fair,* therefore, *to conclude that* souls do not make for themselves bodies and limbs. Nor yet is there a possibility, *as it appears,* that they can be infused into bodies perfectly-formed; for neither *under that supposition* can they be

71

exactly fitted together; nor will their mutual-motions be carried on with sympathy.

Furthermore, why does violent rage attend upon the sullen breed of lions, and craft upon *that of* foxes; and why is flight communicated to stags from their sires, and *why* does hereditary fear add speed to their limbs? And as to other *qualities* of this sort, why do they all generate, in the body and temperament, from the earliest period of life, if *it be* not because a certain disposition of mind grows up together with each body from its own seed and stock? But if the soul were immortal, and were accustomed, *as the Pythagoreans think,* to change bodies, *surely* animals would *gradually alter,* and grow of mixed dispositions; the dog of Hyrcanian breed would often flee from the assault of the horned stag; the hawk, flying through the air of heaven, would tremble at the approach of the dove; men would lose their understanding, and the savage tribes of wild beasts become reasonable.

For that which *some* assert, *namely,* that an immortal soul is altered by a change of body, is advanced upon false reasoning; as that which is altered, loses its consistence, *and* therefore perishes; since the parts are transposed, and depart from their *original* arrangement; wherefore *the parts of the soul, under this hypothesis,* must also be subject to dissolution throughout the limbs; so that finally they may all perish together with the body.

But if they shall say that the souls of men always migrate into human bodies, I shall nevertheless ask, why a soul, from being wise *in a wise body,* should possibly become foolish *in the body of a fool;* why no child is *found* discreet, *or informed with a soul of mature understanding,* and why no foal of a mare is as skilful *in his paces* as the horse of full vigour? *Why, I say, is this,* if it be not because a certain temper of mind grows up with each body from its own seed and stock? These *philosophers,* forsooth, will take refuge in the assertion, that the mind becomes tender in a tender body;

72

On the Nature of Things

but if this be the case, you must admit that the soul is mortal, since, being so exceedingly changed in its new body, it loses its former vitality and powers.

Or in what way will the vigour of a soul, strenghtened in concert with each *particular* body, be able to reach *with it* the desired flower of mature age, unless it shall be joined to it in its first origin? Or with what motive does *the soul* go forth from limbs that are grown old? Does it fear to remain imprisoned in a decaying carcass, *lest it should decay with it?* Or *is it afraid* lest its tenement, shaken with a long course of life, should *fall and* overwhelm it? But to that which is immortal, there are no *such* dangers.

Moreover, to *imagine* that souls stand ready at the amorous intercourses, or parturitions, of beasts, *to enter into the young,* seems exceedingly ridiculous. *It appears too absurd to suppose* that immortal *beings,* in infinite numbers, should wait for mortal bodies, and contend emulously among themselves which shall be first and foremost to enter—unless perchance *you suppose that* agreements have been made among the souls, that the first which shall have come flying *to the body,* shall have first ingress, and that they may *thus* have no contest in strength with one another.

Again, neither can a tree exist in the sky, nor clouds in the deep sea; nor *can* fish live in the fields; nor blood be in wood, nor liquid in stones. It is fixed and arranged where every thing may grow and subsist; thus the nature *or substance* of the mind cannot spring up alone without the body, or exist apart from the nerves and the blood. Whereas if this could *happen,* the power of the mind might *at times* rather arise in the head or the shoulders, or the bottom of the heels, and might *rather* accustom itself to grow in any place, than to remain in the same man and in the same receptacle. But since it seems fixed and appointed also in our own body, where the soul and the mind may subsist and grow up by themselves, it is so much the more to be denied that they can endure and be produced out of the entire body. For which reason, when the body has perished, you must necessarily admit that the soul which is diffused throughout the body, has perished with it.

Besides, to join the mortal to the immortal, and to suppose that they can sympathize together, and perform mutual *operations,* is to think absurdly; for what can be conceived more at variance *with reason,* or more inconsistent and irreconcilable in itself, than that which is mortal, joined to that which is imperishable and eternal, should *submit to* endure violent storms *and troubles* in combination *with it?*

Further, whatsoever *bodies* remain eternal, must either, as being of a solid consistence, repel blows, and suffer nothing to penetrate them, that can disunite their compact parts within; *(such* as are the primary-particles of matter, the nature of which we have shown above) or they must be able to endure throughout all time, because they are free from blows, *or unsusceptible of them;* (as is a vacuum, which remains intangible, and suffers nothing from a stroke) *or they must be indestructible for this reason,* that there is no sufficiency of space round about, into which their *constituent* substances may, as it were, separate and be dissolved; (as the entire universe is eternal, *inasmuch as* there is neither any space without it into which *its parts* may disperse; nor are there any bodies which may fall upon it, and break it to pieces by a violent concussion) but, as I have shown, neither is the nature of the soul of a solid consistence, since with *all compound* bodies vacuum is mixed; nor is it like a vacuum *itself;* nor, again, are bodies wanting, which, rising fortuitously from the infinite *of things,* may overturn this frame of the mind with a violent tempest, or bring *upon it* some other kind of disaster and danger; nor, moreover, is vastness and profundity of space wanting, into which the substance of the soul may be dispersed, or may *otherwise* perish *and be*

On the Nature of Things

overwhelmed by any other kind of force. The gate of death,
therefore, is not shut against the mind *and soul*.

But if perchance *the soul, in the opinion of any,* is to be
accounted immortal the more on this account, that it is kept
fortified by things preservative of life; or because objects
adverse to its safety do not approach it; or because those that
do approach, being by some means diverted, retreat before
we can perceive what injury they inflict; the notion *of those
who think* thus is evidently far removed from just reasoning.
For besides that it sickens from diseases of the body, there
often happens something to trouble it concerning future
events, and keep it disquieted in fear, and harass it with
cares; while *remorse for* faults, from past acts wickedly *and
foolishly* committed, *torments and* distresses it. Join *to these
afflictions* the insanity peculiar to the mind, and the oblivion
of *all* things; *and* add, *besides,* that it is *often* sunk into the
black waves of lethargy.

Death, therefore, is nothing, nor at all concerns us, since
the nature *or substance* of the soul is *to be* accounted mortal.
And as, in past time, we felt no anxiety, when the Cartha-
ginians gathered on all sides to fight *with our forefathers,
and* when all things under the lofty air of heaven, shaken
with the dismaying tumult of war, trembled with dread; and
men were uncertain to the sway of which *power* every thing
human, by land and by sea, was to fall; so, when we shall
cease to be, when there shall be a separation of the body and
soul of which we are conjointly composed, it is certain that
to us, who shall not then exist, nothing will by any possibility happen, or excite our feeling, not even if the earth
shall be mingled with the sea, and the sea with the heaven.

And even if the substance of the mind, and the powers of
the soul, after they have been separated from our body, *still*
retain-their-faculties, it is nothing to us, who subsist *only as*
being conjointly constituted by an arrangement and union
of body and soul together. Nor, if time should collect our

75

material-atoms after death, and restore them again as they are now placed, and the light of life should be given back to us, would it yet at all concern us that this were done, when the recollection of our existence has once been interrupted. And it is now of no importance to us, in regard to ourselves, what we were before; nor does any solicitude affect us in reference to those whom a new age shall produce from our matter, *should it again be brought together as it is at present.* For when you consider the whole past space of infinite time, and *reflect* how various are the motions of matter, you may easily believe that *our* atoms have often been placed in the same order as *that in which* they now are. Yet we cannot revive that time in our memory; for a pause of life has been thrown between, and all the motions of *our atoms* have wandered hither and thither, far-away from sentient-movements. For he, *among men now living,* to whom misery and pain are to happen *after his death,* must himself exist *again, in his own identity,* at that very time on which the evil *which he is to suffer* may have power to fall; but since death, *which interrupts all consciousness, and prevents all memory of the past,* precludes *the possibility of* this; and *since the circumstance of* having previously existed, prohibits him *who lived before, and* with whom these calamities *which we suffer* might be associated, from existing *a second time, (with any recollection of his other life) as* the same *combination* of atoms of which we now consist, we may be assured that in death there is nothing to be dreaded by us; that he who does not exist, cannot become miserable; and that it makes not the least difference *to a man,* when immortal death has ended his mortal life, that he was ever born at all.

Whenever, therefore, you see a man express concern that it should be *his* lot after death either to putrefy *on the ground* when his body is laid aside, or to be destroyed by flames, or by the jaws of wild beasts, you may know that *his mind* is not in a healthy state, and that some secret dis-

76

quietude *as to his fate* is concealed in his breast, although he may himself deny that he believes any consciousness will remain to him after death. For, as I think, he does not make good what he professes, nor *speaks from conviction,* from which *he pretends to speak;* nor withdraws and removes himself, *in thought,* wholly out of life, but, foolish as he is, makes something of himself still to survive. For when any one *of such a character* represents to himself, while alive, that birds and beasts will tear his body at death, he is seized with commiseration for himself; for neither does he at all distinguish himself *dead from himself living,* nor sufficiently withdraw himself from his exposed carcass; but supposes it to be *still* himself, and standing by it, *in imagination,* communicates to it a portion of his own feeling. Hence he is concerned that he was born mortal, nor reflects that in real death there will remain of him no other self, which, surviving, may mourn for him that he has perished, and, standing upright, may lament that he, lying down, is torn in pieces or burnt to ashes. For if it is an evil at death, to be *ill*-treated by the jaws and teeth of wild beasts, I do not see how it can be otherwise than unpleasant *for a man,* being laid on a *funeral*-pyre, to burn in hot flames, or, placed in honey, to be suffocated, or to grow stiff with cold, when he is lying on the highest flat of a gelid rock, or to be pressed down and overwhelmed with the weight of superincumbent earth.

"For now," men say, "your pleasant home shall no more receive you, nor your excellent wife; nor shall your dear children run to snatch kisses, and touch your breast with secret delight. You will no more be able to be in flourishing circumstances, and to be a protection to your friends. Unhappily, one adverse day has taken from you, unfortunate *man,* all the numerous blessings of life." In such remarks they do not add this, "Nor now, moreover, does any regret for those things remain with you." Which *truth* if men would well consider in their thoughts, and adhere to it in their words, they would relieve themselves from much anxiety and fear of mind. "You, for your part," *says a mourner over a corpse,* "laid to sleep in your bed, will so remain as you are for whatever time is to come, released from all distressing griefs; but we, *standing* near you, shall inconsolably lament you reduced to ashes on the awful pyre; and no *lapse* of time shall remove our unfading sorrow from our hearts." Of him, however, *who makes such lamentations,* we may ask this *question,* "If the matter *of death* is reduced to sleep and rest, what can there be so bitter *in it,* that any one should pine in eternal grief *for the decease of a friend?"*

This also is often a practice among men, that when they have sat down *to a feast,* and hold their cups in their hands, and overshadow their faces with chaplets, they say *seriously and* from their hearts, "This enjoyment is but short *to us* little men; soon it will have passed; nor will it ever hereafter be possible to recall it." As if at their death this evil were to be dreaded above all, that parching thirst should scorch and burn up the wretches, or an *insatiable* longing for some other thing should settle on them. *Yet how different will be the fact!* Since not even when the mind and body are *merely* at rest together in sleep, will any one feel concern for himself and his life; for, for our parts, our sleep might thus be eternal; nor does any care for ourselves affect us; and yet, at that season, the atoms, throughout our limbs, withdraw to no great distance from sensible motions, and the man who is suddenly roused from sleep quickly recollects himself. Death, then, we must consider to be of far less concern to us, if less can be than that which we see to be nothing. For a greater separation of the atoms of matter takes place in death, nor does any man awake when once the cold pause of life has overtaken him.

Furthermore, if Universal Nature should suddenly utter a voice, and thus herself upbraid any one of us: "What mighty cause have you, O mortal, thus excessively to indulge in bitter grief? Why do you groan and weep, *at the thought of* death? For *if* your past and former life has been an *object* of gratification to you, and all your blessings have not, as if poured into a leaky vessel flowed away and been lost without pleasure, why do you not, O unreasonable man, retire like a guest satisfied with life, and take your undisturbed rest with resignation? But if those things, of which you have had the use, have been wasted and lost, and life is offensive to you, why do you seek to incur further trouble, which may all again pass away and end in dissatisfaction? *Why* do you not rather put an end to life and anxiety? For there is nothing further, which I can contrive and discover to please you; every thing is always the same. If your body is not yet withered with years, and your limbs are not worn out *and* grown feeble, yet all things remain the same, *even* if you should go on to out-last all ages of living; and still more *would you see them the same,* if you should never come to die." What do we answer *to this,* but that Nature brings a just charge *against us,* and sets forth in *her* words a true allegation?

But would she not more justly reproach and upbraid, in severe accents, him who, being miserable unreasonably, deplores death? "Away with thy tears, wretch," *she might well say,* "and forbear thy complaints." But if he *who is* older, and more advanced in years, complain, *she may retort thus:* "After having been possessed of all the most valuable things of life, thou pinest and wastest away *with age.* But, because thou always desirest what is absent, and despisest present *advantages,* life has passed from thee imperfect and unsatisfactory, and death has stood by thy head unawares, and before thou canst depart content and satisfied with thy circumstances. Now, however, resign all things unsuitable to thy age, and yield at once, with submissive feelings, to that which is stronger *than thou; for* it is necessary." *And* justly, as I think, would she address *him;* justly would she

79

LUCRETIUS

upbraid and reproach him; for that which is old, driven out by that which is new, always retires, and it is indispensable to repair one thing out of another; nor is any man consigned to the gulf of *Erebus,* or black Tartarus, *but allowed to retire peaceably to a dreamless sleep.* The matter, *of which thou art made,* is wanted *by nature* that succeeding generations may grow up from it; all which, however, when they have passed their *appointed term of life,* will follow thee: and so have *other generations,* before these, fallen *into destruction; and other generations,* not less *certainly* than thyself, will fall. Thus shall one thing never cease to rise from another; and *thus* is life given to none in possession, *but* to all *only* for use.

Consider, also, how utterly unimportant to us was the past antiquity of infinite time, *that elapsed* before we were born. This, then, nature exhibits to us as a specimen of the time which will be again after our death. For what does there appear terrible in it? Does any thing seem gloomy? Is not *all* more free from trouble than any sleep?

And of the souls likewise, whatever are said to be in the profundity of Acheron, all *the sufferings* happen to ourselves, *not in death, but* in life. Tantalus, torpid with vain terror, does not (as it is reported) fear the huge rock impending over him in the air; but *such terror* rather *dwells with us* in life; a groundless fear of the gods oppresses mortals, and they dread that fall which fortune may assign to each.

Nor do vultures penetrate into Tityus, lying in Hades; nor, however they might search in his huge breast, would they be able to find, through infinite time, any thing *to devour,* of however vast an extent of body he may be, *even though it be* such as may cover, with its limbs outspread, not merely nine acres, but the orb of the whole earth; nor yet would he be able to endure eternal pain, or to supply food incessantly from his own body; but he is a Tityus among us, whom, lying under *the influence of* love, the vul-

80

tures *of passion* tear, and anxious disquietude devours; or whom cares, with any other unbecoming-feeling lacerate.

A Sisyphus, likewise, is before our eyes in life, who sets his heart to solicit from the people the fasces and sharp axes, and always retires repulsed and disappointed. For to seek power, which is empty, nor is ever granted, and constantly to endure hard labour in *the pursuit of* it, this is to push with effort the stone up the hill, which yet is rolled down again from the summit, and impetuously seeks the level of the open plain.

To feed perpetually, moreover, an ungrateful nature, and to fill *it* with good things, and never to satisy *it; a kindness* which the seasons of the year do to us, as they come round *in their course,* and bring their fruits and various charms; whilst we, notwithstanding, are never satisfied with the blessings of life; this is, I think, that which they relate of the damsels in the flower of their youth, *that they* pour water into a punctured vessel, which, however, can by no means be filled.

But also Cerberus and the Furies *are mentioned,* and privation of light, and Tartarus, casting forth fires from its jaws, *objects* which are no where, nor indeed can be; but there is, in life, an eminent dread of punishment for enormous crimes; there is the prison, the reward of guilt, and the terrible precipitation, of those *who are condemned,* from the rock; *there are* stripes, executioners, the wooden-horse, pitch, *hot* iron, fire-brands; and though these may be absent, yet the mind, conscious of *evil* deeds, feeling dread in anticipation, applies *to itself* stings, and tortures *itself* with scourges, nor sees, in the mean time, what end there can be of its sufferings, nor what can be the limit of its punishment, and fears rather lest these same tortures should become heavier at death. Hence, in fine, the life of fools becomes, as it were, an existence in Tartarus.

This *reflection,* likewise, you may at times address to yourself. "Even the good Ancus," *as Ennius expresses it,* "has deserted the light with his eyes," who was much better in many things than thou, worthless *man!* Besides, many other kings, and rulers of affairs, who swayed mighty nations, have yielded up the ghost. *And what am I better than they?*

He, even, himself, who formerly paved a road over the vast sea, and afforded a way to his legions to pass through the deep, and taught them to walk on foot through salt gulfs, and despised the murmurs of the ocean, trampling on it with his cavalry; *even he, I say,* the light *of life* being withdrawn from him, poured forth his soul from his dying body.

Scipio, the thunderbolt of war, the dread of Carthage, gave his bones to the earth, just as if he had been the meanest slave.

Add *to these,* the inventors of the sciences and the graces; add the associates of the muses; over whom the unrivalled Homer having obtained the supremacy, has been laid to rest in the same sleep with others.

When mature old age, too, gave Democritus warning that the mindful motions of his intellect were languishing, he himself, of his own accord, offered his head to death.

Epicurus himself, having run through his light of life, is dead; Epicurus, who excelled the human race in genius, and threw all into the shade, as the ethereal sun, when rising, *obscures* the stars.

Wilt thou, then, hesitate, and grudge to die, in whom, even while living and seeing, life is almost dead? *Thou,* who wastest the greater part of existence in sleep, and snorest waking, nor ceasest to see dreams, and bearest a mind disturbed with empty terror; nor canst thou, frequently, discover what evil affects thee, when, stupified *and* wretched, thou art oppressed with numerous cares on all sides, and, fluctuating with uncertain thought, wanderest in error?

If men could feel, as they seem to feel, that there is an oppression on their minds, which wearies them with its weight, and could also perceive from what causes it arises, and whence so great a mass, as it were, of evil exists in their breasts, they would not live in the manner in which we generally see them *living; for we observe them* uncertain what they would have, and always inquiring *for something new;* and changing their place, as if *by the change* they could lay aside a load.

He, who has grown weary of remaining at home, often goes forth from his vast mansion, and suddenly returns, inasmuch as he perceives that he is nothing bettered by being abroad. He runs precipitately, hurrying on his horses, to his villa, as if he were eager to carry succour to an edifice on fire; but, as soon as he has touched the threshold of the building, he yawns, or falls heavily to sleep, and seeks forgetfulness *of himself,* or even with *equal* haste goes back and revisits the city.

In this way each man flees from himself; but *himself,* as it *always* happens, whom he cannot escape, and *whom he still* hates, adheres to him in spite *of his efforts; and* for this reason, that the sick man does not know the cause of his disease, which if every one could understand, he would, in the first place, having laid aside all other pursuits, study to learn the *Nature of Things;* since *in such inquiries* the state of eternity, not of one hour *merely,* is concerned; *a state* in which the whole age of mortals, whatever remains after death, must continue.

Besides, why does *so* pernicious *and* so strong desire of existence compel us to remain anxious in uncertain perils? A certain bound of life is fixed to mortals; nor can death be avoided, *or can we exempt ourselves* from undergoing it.

Moreover, we are continually engaged and fixed in the same occupations; nor, by the prolongation of life, is any new pleasure discovered. Yet that which we desire, seems, while it is distant *in the future,* to excel *all* other objects; *but* afterwards, when it has fallen to our lot, we covet something else; and thus a uniform thirst of life occupies us, longing earnestly *for that which is to come;* while what fate the last period may bring us, or what chance may throw in our way, or what death awaits us, still remains in uncertainty.

Nor, by protracting life, do we deduct a single moment from the duration of death; we cannot diminish aught *from its reign, or cause* that we may be for a less period sunk in non-existence. How many generations soever, therefore, we may pass in life, nevertheless that *same* eternal death will still await us. Nor will he be less long out of being, who terminated his life under this day's sun, than he who died many months and years ago.

Søren Kierkegaard (1813-1855)

Purity of Heart

What then must I do? Live as an "Individual."

The talk asks you then *whether you live in such a way that you are conscious of being an "individual."* The question is not of the inquisitive sort, as if one asked about that "individual" in some special sense, about the one whom admiration and envy unite in pointing out. No, it is the serious question of what each man really is according to his eternal vocation, so that he himself shall be conscious that he is following it; and what is even more serious, to ask it as if he were considering his life before God. This consciousness is the fundamental condition for truthfully willing only one thing. For he who is not himself a unity is never really anything wholly and decisively; he only exists in an external sense—as long as he lives as a numeral with the crowd, a fraction within the earthly conglomeration. Alas, how indeed should such a one decide to busy himself with the thought: truthfully to will only one thing!

Indeed it is precisely this consciousness that must be asked for. Just as if the talk could not ask in generalities, but rather asks you as an individual. Or, better still, my listener, if you would ask yourself, whether you have this consciousness, whether you are actively contemplating the occasion of this talk. For in the outside world, the crowd is busy making a noise. The one makes a noise because he heads the crowd, the many because they are members of the crowd. But the all-knowing One, who in spite of anyone is able to observe it all, does not desire the crowd. He desires the individual; He will deal only with the individual, quite unconcerned as to whether the individual be of high or low station, whether he be distinguished or wretched.

Each man himself, as an individual, should render his account to God. No third person dares venture to intrude upon this accounting between God and the individual. Yet the talk, by putting its question, dares and ought to dare to remind man, in a way never to be forgotten, that the most ruinous evasion of all is to be hidden in the crowd in an attempt to escape God's supervision of him as an individual, in an attempt to get away from hearing God's voice as an individual. Long ago, Adam attempted this same thing when his evil conscience led him to imagine that he could hide himself among the trees. It may even be easier and more convenient, and more cowardly, to hide oneself among the crowd in the hope that God should not be able to recognize one from the other. But in eternity each shall render account as an individual. That is, eternity will demand of him that he shall have lived as an individual. Eternity will draw out before his consciousness all that he has done as an individual, he who had forgotten himself in noisy self-conceit. In eternity, he shall be brought to account strictly as an individual, he who intended to be in the crowd where there should be no strict reckoning. Each one shall render account to God as an individual. The King shall render account as an individual; and the most wretched beggar, as an individual. No one may pride himself at being more than an individual and no one despondently think that he is not an individual, perhaps because here in earth's busyness he had not as much as a name, but was named after a number.

For, after all, what is eternity's accounting other than that the voice of conscience is forever installed with its eternal right to be the exclusive voice? What is it other than that throughout eternity an infinite stillness reigns wherein the

86

Purity of Heart

conscience may talk with the individual about what he, as an individual, of what he has done of good or of evil, about the fact that during his life he did not wish to be an individual? What is it other than that within eternity there is infinite space so that each person, as an individual, is apart with his conscience? For in eternity there is no mob pressure, no crowd, no hiding place in the crowd, as little as there are riots or street fights! Here in the temporal order conscience is prepared to make each person into an individual. But here in the temporal order, in the unrest, in the noise, in the pressure of the mob, in the crowd, in the primeval forest of evasion, alas, it is true, the calamity still happens, that someone completely stifles the voice of his conscience—his conscience, for he can never rid himself of it. It continues to belong to him, or more accurately, he continues to belong to it. Yet we are not now talking about this calamity, for even among the better persons it happens all too readily that the voice of conscience becomes merely one voice among many. Then it follows so easily that the isolated voice of conscience (as generally happens to a solitary one) becomes overruled—by the majority. But in eternity, conscience is the only voice that is heard. It must be heard by the individual, for the individual has become the eternal echo of this voice. It must be heard. There is no place to flee from it. For in the infinite there is no place, the individual is himself the place. It must be heard. In vain the individual looks about for the crowd. Alas, it is as if there were a world between him and the nearest individual, whose conscience is also speaking to him about what he as an individual has spoken, and done, and thought of good and of evil.

Do you now live so that you are conscious of yourself as an individual; that in each of your relations in which you come into touch with the outside world, you are conscious of yourself, and that at the same time you are related to yourself as an individual? Even in these relations which we men

87

so beautifully style the most intimate of all, do you remember that you have a still more intimate relation, namely, that in which you as an individual are related to yourself before God? If you are bound to another human being by the holy bond of matrimony, do you consider in this intimate relation that still more intimate relation in which you as an individual are related to yourself before God? The talk does not ask you whether you now love your wife: it hopes so; nor whether she is the apple of your eye and the desire of your heart: it wishes you this. It does not ask what you have done to make your wife happy, about how you both have arranged your household life, about what good advice you have been able to get from others, or what harmful influence others have had upon you. It does not ask whether your marital life is more commendable than that of many others, or whether it perhaps might be looked upon by some as a worthy example. No, the talk asks about none of these things. It asks you neither in congratulation, nor inquisitively, nor watchfully, nor apologetically, nor comparatively. It asks you only about the ultimate thing: whether you yourself are conscious of that most intimate relation to yourself as an individual. You do not carry the responsibility for your wife, nor for other men, nor by any comparative standard with other men, but only as an individual, before God, where it is not asked whether your marriage was in accordance with others, with the common practice, or better than others, but where you as an individual will be asked only whether it was in accordance with your responsibility as an individual. For common practice changes, and all comparison goes lame, or is only half truth. But eternity's practice, which never goes out of fashion, is that you are the individual, that you yourself in the intimate relation of marriage should have been conscious of this.

In truth, it is not divorce that eternity is aiming at; neither is it divorce that eternity does away with the difference between man and woman. Your wife will have no occasion to grieve because you are pondering this, your most intimate relation to God. And should she be so foolish as to desire for herself only that which is earthly or even foolish enough to desire as well to draw you down to the earthly, yet a woman's folly shall certainly not be able to change the law of eternity. In eternity it will not be asked whether your wife seduced you (eternity will talk with her about that), but simply as an individual you will be asked whether you allowed yourself to be seduced. If your marriage is so blessed that you see a family growing up around you, may you be conscious that while you have an intimate relation to your children you have a still more intimate relation to yourself as an individual. You share the responsibility with your wife, and hence eternity will also ask her as an individual about her share of the responsibility. For in eternity there is not a single complication that is able to make the accounting difficult and evasion easy. Eternity does not ask concerning how far you brought up your children in the way that you saw others do it. It simply asks you, as an individual, how you brought up your children. It does not talk with you in the manner that you would talk with a friend in confidence. For alas, even this confidence can all too easily accustom you to evasion. For even the most trustworthy friend still speaks as a third person. But in eternity, you are the individual, and conscience when it talks with you is no third person, any more than you are a third person when you talk with conscience. For you and conscience are one. It knows all that you know, and it knows that you know it. With respect to your children's upbringing you can weigh various matters with your wife, or your friends. But how you act and the responsibility for it is finally wholly and solely yours as an individual. And if you fail to act, hiding from yourself and from others behind a screen of deliberation, you bring down the responsibility solely upon yourself as an individual.

Yes, in the temporal order where in all directions both this and that are asked about in the manifold complex complications of their reciprocal action, there one may rightly enough believe that it was a fantasy of the imagination, a chimera, that each one among these countless millions of people should be convinced accurately down to the least trifle of what his life consisted. But in eternity this is possible, because each becomes an individual. And this applies to every relation of your life.

If you do not live in some out-of-the-way place in the world, if you live in a populous city, and you direct your attention outwards, sympathetically engrossing yourself in the people and in what is going on, do you remember each time you throw yourself in this way into the world around you that in this relation you relate yourself to yourself as an individual with eternal responsibility? Or do you press yourself into the crowd, where the one excuses himself with the others, where at one moment there are, so to speak, many, and where in the next moment each time that the talk touches upon responsibility, there is no one? Do you judge like the crowd, in its capacity as a crowd? You are not obliged to have an opinion about what you do not understand. No, on the contrary, you are eternally excused from that. But you are eternally responsible as an individual to render an account for your opinion, and for your judgment. And in eternity, you will not be asked inquisitively and professionally, as though by a newspaper reporter, whether there were many that had the same—wrong opinion. You will be asked only whether you have held it, whether you have spoiled your soul by joining in this frivolous and thoughtless judging, because the others, because the many judged thoughtlessly. You will be asked only whether you may not have ruined the best within you by joining the crowd in its defiance, thinking that you were many and therefore you had the prerogative, because you were many, that is, because you were many who were wrong. In eternity it will be asked whether you may not have damaged a good thing, in order that you also might judge with them that did not know how to judge, but who possessed the crowd's strength, which in the temporal sense is significant but to which eternity is wholly indifferent.

You see, in the temporal order, a man counts and says: "One more or less, it makes no difference"—and he applies this even to himself! In the temporal order a man counts and says: "One over against a hundred, after all what can come of that?" So he grows cowardly in the face of—number. And numbers are usually false. Truth is content to be a unity. But a man wins something by this cowardly indulgence. He does not win a bed in a hospital. No, but he wins the amazing thing of becoming the strongest of all, because the crowd is always the strongest. Eternity, on the other hand, never counts. The individual is always only one and conscience in its meticulous way concerns itself with the individual. In eternity you will look in vain for the crowd. You will listen in vain to find whether you cannot hear where the noise and the gathering is, so that you may run to it. In eternity you, too, will be forsaken by the crowd. And this is terrifying. Yet in the temporal order to be forsaken by the crowd, provided that the Eternal comforts, may be something blessed, and the pain of it, a mere jest. What then in eternity will conscience demand of you by the consciousness that you are an individual? It will teach you that if you judge (for in very many cases it will restrain you from judging), you must bear the responsibility for your judgment. It will teach you that you should examine what you understand and what you do not understand as if you stood trembling in the presence of a departed one; it wishes to frighten you from resorting to the brilliant flights into wretchedness to which you are often subject. For many fools do not make a wise man, and the crowd is doubtful recommendation for a cause. Yes,

SØREN KIERKEGAARD

the larger the crowd, the more probable that that which it praises is folly, and the more improbable that it is truth, and the most improbable of all that it is any eternal truth. For in eternity crowds simply do not exist. The truth is not such that it at once pleases the frivolous crowd—and at bottom it never does; to such a multitude the truth must appear as simply absurd. But the man who, conscious of himself as an individual, judges with eternal responsibility, he is slow to pass judgment upon the unusual. For it is possible that it is falsehood and deceit and illusion and vanity. But it is also possible that it is true. He remembers the word of the simple sage of ancient times: "This, that a man's eye cannot see by the light by which the majority see could be because he is used to darkness; but it could also be because he is used to a still clearer light, and when this is so, it is no laughing matter."[1]

No, it is no laughing matter, but it is laughable, or it is pitiable, that the frivolous ones laugh at a man because he is wiser or better than they. For even laughter calls for a reasonable ground, and when this is absent, the laughter becomes the very thing that is laughable. But here in the temporal order, in the midst of earth's appalling prodigality with human beings, here number tempts. It tempts a man to count, to count himself in with the crowd. Here, by the use of round numbers, everything can be manipulated with ease. Yes, here in the temporal order it is possible that no individual can ever succeed, even if it were true that he sincerely willed the Good, in dispersing the crowd. But eternity can do it. Eternity seizes each one by the strong arm of conscience, holding him as an individual. Eternity sets him apart with his conscience. Woe unto him, if he is left to this judge alone! For in that case eternity will set him apart with his conscience in that place where there is pressure, to

[1] Socrates in Plato's *Republic* VII. 518 A.

92

be sure, but not as in the temporal order where the pressure is the excuse, yes, the victory. No, eternity places him where to be under pressure is to be alone, stripped of every excuse; to be alone and to be lost. The royal psalm singer says that while the heathen clamor, God sits in his heaven and laughs at them.[2] I dare not believe this. It would seem to be preferable to say that while the crowd clamors and shouts and triumphs and celebrates; while one individual after another hastens to the place of tumult, where it is good to be if one is in search of oblivion and indulgence from that which is eternal; while at the same time the crowd shouts mockingly at God. "Yes, now see whether you can get hold of us"; yet since it is difficult in the rush of the crowd to distinguish the individual, difficult to see the single tree when one is looking at the wood, the sober countenance of eternity quietly waits. And if all the generations that have lived on earth rose up and gathered themselves in a single crowd in order to loose a storm against eternity, in order to coerce eternity by their colossal majority, eternity would scatter them as easily as the firmness of an immovable rock would scatter frothy scum; as easily as the wind when it rushes forward scatters chaff. Just as easily, but not in the same way. For the wind scatters the chaff, but then turns around and drifts it together again. Eternity scatters the crowd by giving each an infinite weight, by making him heavy—as an individual. For what in eternity is the highest blessing is also the deepest seriousness. What, there, is the most blessed comfort, is also the most appalling responsibility.

In eternity there are chambers enough so that each may be placed alone in one. For wherever conscience is present, and it is and shall be present in each person, there exists in eternity a lonely prison, or the blessed chamber of salvation. On that account this consciousness of being an individual

[2] Psalms 2:4.

is the primary consciousness in a man, which is his eternal consciousness. But that man is slow to pass judgment who bears in mind that he is an individual, and that the final and highest responsibility for the judgment rests solely upon him. For even the most trusted friend in passing judgment as an impartial observer must necessarily leave out what is crucial. To be the party directly concerned, the one to whom conscience in this affair speaks the intimate "thou," is another matter, for conscience only speaks this intimate "thou" to your friend in regard to the manner in which he is to give counsel. Such a thoughtful one does not willingly pass judgment on many things, and just this helps him to will only one thing. He thinks it is not altogether an advantage to live in a populous city where because of the swiftness of the means of communication almost everyone can easily have a hasty and superficial judgment about everything possible. On the contrary, he looks upon this easiness as a temptation and a snare, and he learns earnestness in order as an individual to be concerned about his eternal responsibility.

"Even a fool might be a wise man if he could keep silent," says the proverb.[3] And this is so, not merely because then he would not betray his foolishness, but also because this self-control would help him to become conscious of himself as an individual, and would prevent him from adopting the crowd's opinion. Or if he had an opinion of his own, it would prevent him from hastening to get the crowd to adopt it. The one who is conscious of himself as an individual has his vision trained to look upon everything as inverted. His sense becomes familiar with eternity's true thought: that everything in this life appears in inverted form. The purely momentary, in the next moment, to say nothing of eternity, becomes nonsense and vanity: the fiery moment of lust (and

[3] The Latin proverb "Tu si tacuisses, philosophus mansisses." See Boethius, *Consolatio philos.* II. 17.

what is so strong for the moment as lust!) is loathsome in memory; the fiery moment of anger, revenge, and passion whose gratification seems an irresistible impulse is horrible to remember. For the angry one, the vengeful one, the passionate one, thinks in the moment of passion that he revenges himself. But in the moment of remembrance, when the act of revenge comes back to him, he loathes himself, for he sees that precisely in that moment of revenge he lost himself. The purely momentary seems to be profitable. Yet in the next moment its deception becomes apparent and, eternally understood, calls for repentance. So it is with all things of the moment, and hence with the crowd's opinion or with membership in the crowd in so far as this opinion and this membership is a thing of the moment.

My listeners, do you at present live in such a way that you are yourself clearly and eternally conscious of being an individual? This was the question the address was to ask, or rather that you are to ask yourself, if you actively consider this occasion. The talk should not tell you only that which will disturb you, even though many are of the conviction that a man ought ever to live in such an aroused state of consciousness. Nor is it concerned how many or how few hold that conviction. The speaker will not attempt to win you to this conviction, even if he does as a rule hold it himself. He does not wish to force it upon you any more than you would desire to force it upon him if you were of this conviction. For the exalted earnestness of the Eternal wishes neither the commendation of the majority nor the commendation of eloquence. One thing alone the talk does not dare to promise you—nor does it wish to insult you. It does not dare to promise you earthly gain if you enter upon and in dedication persevere in this conviction. On the contrary, if persevered in, it will make your life more taxing, and frequently perhaps wearisome. If persevered in, it may make you the target of others' ridicule, not to mention even greater sacrifices that perseverance might choose to require of you. Of course, the ridicule does not distract you if you continue to persist in your conviction. Ridicule will even be a help to you, in the sense that it is a further proof to you that you are on the right path. For the judgment of the crowd has its significance. One should not remain proudly ignorant of it, no, one should be attentive to it. If after this he sees to it that he does the opposite from the judgment of the crowd, then he, for the most part, does the right thing. Or if at the outset a man does the opposite, and he is then so fortunate as to have the judgment of the crowd express itself to the contrary, then he can be fairly certain that he has laid hold of the right thing. Then he has not only himself inwardly weighed and tested the conviction properly, but he has also the advantage of having it tested a second time by the help of ridicule. Ridicule may wound his feelings but just by that wound it shows that he is on the right path—the path of honor and of victory, like a warrior's wound, when it is on the breast where both the wound and the badge of honor are to be borne.

You have surely noticed among schoolboys that the one that is regarded by all as the boldest is the one who has no fear of his father, who dares to say to the others, "Do you think I am afraid of him?" On the other hand, if they sense that one of their number is actually and literally afraid of his father, they will readily ridicule him a little. Alas, in men's fear-ridden rushing together into a crowd (for why indeed does a man rush into a crowd except because he is afraid!) there, too, it is a mark of boldness not to be afraid, not even of God. And if someone notes that there is an individual outside the crowd who is really and truly afraid, not of the crowd, but of God, he is sure to be the target of some ridicule. The ridicule is usually glossed over somewhat and it is said: a man should *love* God.

Yes, to be sure, God knows that man's highest consolation

96

Purity of Heart

is that God is love and that man is permitted to love Him. But let us not become too forward, and foolishly, yes, blasphemously, dismiss the tradition of our fathers, established by God Himself: that really and truly a man should fear God. This fear is known to the man who is himself conscious of being an individual, and thereby is conscious of his eternal responsibility before God. For he knows that even if he could with the help of evasions and excuses get on well in this life, and even if he could by this shady path have gained the whole world, yet there is still a place in the next world where there is no more evasion than there is shade in the scorching desert.

The talk will not go into this further. It will only ask you again and again, do you now live so that you are conscious of being an individual and thereby that you are conscious of your eternal responsibility before God? Do you live in such a way that this consciousness is able to secure the time and quiet and liberty of action to penetrate every relation of your life? This does not demand that you withdraw from life, from an honorable calling, from a happy domestic life. On the contrary, it is precisely that consciousness which will sustain and clarify and illuminate what you are to do in the relations of life. You should not withdraw and sit brooding over your eternal accounting. To do this is to deserve something further to account for. You will more and more readily find time to perform your duty and your task, while concern over your eternal responsibility will hinder you from being "busy" and busily having a hand in everything possible— and activity that can best be called: time wasting.

Arthur Schopenhauer (1788-1860)

The World as Will and Idea

Characterisation of the Will to Live

Our second book closed with the question as to the goal
and aim of that will which had shown itself to be the inner
nature of all things in the world. The following remarks
may serve to supplement the answer to this question given
there in general terms, for they lay down the character of the
will as a whole.

Such a characterisation is possible because we have recognized as the inner nature of the world something thoroughly
real and empirically given. On the other hand, the very name
"world-soul," by which many have denoted that inner being,
gives instead of this a mere *ens rationis;* for "soul" signifies
an individual unity of consciousness which clearly does not
belong to that nature, and in general, since the conception
"soul" supposes knowing and willing in inseparable connection and yet independent of the animal organism, it is not
to be justified, and therefore not to be used. The word
should never be applied except in a metaphorical sense, for
it is much more insidious than psyche or anima, which
signify breath.

Much more unsuitable, however, is the way in which so-
called pantheists express themselves, whose whole philosophy
consists chiefly in this, that they call the inner nature of the
world, which is unknown to them, "God"; by which indeed
they imagine they have achieved much. According to this,

then, the world would be a theophany. But let one only look at it. This world of constantly needy creatures, who continue for a time only by devouring one another, fulfill their existence in anxiety and want, and often suffer terrible miseries, till at last they fall into the arms of death; whoever distinctly looks upon this will be obliged to confess that a God who could think of changing Himself into such a world as this must certainly have been tormented by the devil. I know well that the pretended philosophers of this century follow Spinoza in this, and think themselves thereby justified. But Spinoza had special reasons for thus naming his one substance, in order, namely, to preserve at least the word, although not the thing. The stake of Giordano Bruno and of Vanini was still fresh in the memory; they also had been sacrificed to that God for whose honour incomparably more human sacrifices have bled than the altars of all heathen gods of both hemispheres together. If, then, Spinoza calls the world God, it is exactly the same thing as when Rousseau, in the *"Contrat social,"* constantly and throughout denotes the people by the word *le souverain;* we might also compare it with this, that once a prince who intended to abolish the nobility in his land, in order to rob no one of his own, hit upon the idea of ennobling all his subjects. Those philosophers of our day have certainly one other ground for the nomenclature we are speaking of, but it is no more substantial. In their philosophising they all start, not from the world of our consciousness of it, but from God, as something given and known; He is not their *quaesitum,* but their *datum.* If they were boys I would then explain to them that this is a *petitio principii,* but they know this as well as I do. But since Kant has shown that the path of the earlier dogmatism, which proceeded honestly, the path from the world to a God, does not lead there, these gentlemen now imagine they have found a fine way of escape and made it cunningly. Will the reader of a later age pardon me for detaining him with persons of whom he has never heard.

Every glance at the world, to explain which is the task of the philosopher, confirms and proves that *will to live,* far from being an arbitrary hypostasis or an empty word, is the only true expression of its inmost nature. Everything presses and strives toward *existence,* if possible *organized existence,* i.e., *life,* and after that to the highest possible grade of it. In animal nature it then becomes apparent that *will to live* is the keynote of its being, its one unchangeable and unconditioned quality. Let any one consider this universal desire for life, let him see the infinite willingness, facility, and exuberance with which the will to live presses impetuously into existence under a million forms everywhere and at every moment, by means of fructification and of germs, nay, when these are wanting, by means of *generatio aequivoca,* seizing every opportunity, eagerly grasping for itself every material capable of life; and then again let him cast a glance at its fearful alarm and wild rebellion when in any particular phenomenon it must pass out of existence, especially when this takes place with distinct consciousness. Then it is precisely the same as if in this single phenomenon the whole world be annihilated for ever, and the whole being of this threatened living thing is at once transformed into the most desperate struggle against death and resistance to it. Look, for example, at the incredible anxiety of a man in danger of his life, the rapid and serious participation in this of every witness of it, and the boundless rejoicing at his deliverance. Look at the rigid terror with which a sentence of death is heard, the profound awe with which we regard the preparations for carrying it out, and the heartrending compassion which seizes us at the execution itself. We would then suppose there was something quite different in question than a few less years of an empty, sad existence, embittered by troubles of every kind, and always uncertain: we would rather be amazed that it was a matter of any consequence whether one attained a few years earlier to the place where after an ephemeral exist ence he has billions of years to be. In such phenomena, then, it becomes visible that I am right in declaring that the *will to live* is that which cannot be further explained, but lies at the foundation of all explanation, and that this, far from being an empty word, like the absolute, the infinite, the idea, and similar expressions, is the most real thing we know, nay, the kernel of reality itself.

But if now, abstracting for a while from this interpretation drawn from our inner being, we place ourselves as strangers over against nature, in order to comprehend it objectively, we find that from the grade of organized life upwards it has only one intention—that of the *maintenance of the species*. To this end it works, through the immense superfluity of germs, through the urgent vehemence of the sexual instinct, through its willingness to adapt itself to all circumstances and opportunities, even to the production of bastards, and through the instinctive maternal affection, the strength of which is so great that in many kinds of animals it even out- weighs self-love, so that the mother sacrifices her life in order to preserve that of the young. The individual, on the con- trary, has for nature only an indirect value, only so far as it is the means of maintaining the species. Apart from this its existence is to nature a matter of indifference; indeed nature even leads it to destruction as soon as it has ceased to be use- ful for this end. Why the individual exists would thus be clear; but why does the species itself exist? That is a ques- tion which nature when considered merely objectively can- not answer. For in vain do we seek by contemplating her for an end of this restless striving, this ceaseless pressing into existence, this anxious care for the maintenance of the spe- cies. The strength and time of the individuals are consumed in the effort to procure sustenance for themselves and their young, and are only just sufficient, sometimes even not suffi cient, for this. Even if here and there a surplus of strength, and therefore of comfort—in the case of the one rational species also of knowledge—remains, this is much too insignificant to pass for the end of that whole process of nature. The whole thing, when regarded thus purely objectively, and indeed as extraneous to us, looks as if nature was only concerned that of all her (Platonic) *Ideas,* i.e., permanent forms, none should be lost. Accordingly, as if she had so thoroughly satisfied herself with the fortunate discovery and combination of these Ideas (for which the three preceding occasions on which she stocked the earth's surface with animals were only the preparation), that now here only fear is lest any one of these beautiful fancies should be lost, i.e., lest any one of these forms should disappear from time and the causal series. For the individuals are fleeting as the water in the brook; the Ideas, on the contrary, are permanent, like its eddies. But the exhaustion of the water would also do away with the eddies. We would have to stop at this unintelligible view if nature were known to us only from without, thus were given us merely *objectively,* and we accepted it as it is comprehended by knowledge, and also as sprung from knowledge, i.e., in the sphere of the idea, and were obliged to confine ourselves to this province in solving it. But the case is otherwise, and a glance at any rate is afforded us into the *interior of nature;* inasmuch as this is nothing else than *our own inner being,* which is precisely where nature, arrived at the highest grade to which its striving could work itself up, is now by the light of knowledge found directly in self-consciousness. Here the will shows itself to us as something *toto genere* different from the idea, in which nature appears unfolded in all her (Platonic) Ideas; and it now gives us, at one stroke, the explanation which could never be found upon the objective path of the idea. Thus the subjective here gives the key for the exposition of the objective. In order to recognize, as something original and uncondi-

102

tioned, that exceedingly strong tendency of all animals and men to retain life and carry it on as long as possible—a tendency which was set forth above as characteristic of the subjective, or of the will—it is necessary to make clear to ourselves that this is by no means the result of any objective *knowledge* of the worth of life, but is independent of all knowledge; or, in other words, that those beings exhibit themselves, not as drawn from in front, but as impelled from behind.

If with this intention we first of all review the interminable series of animals, consider the infinite variety of their forms, as they exhibit themselves always differently modified according to their element and manner of life, and also ponder the inimitable ingenuity of their structure and mechanism, which is carried out with equal perfection in every individual; and finally, if we take into consideration the incredible expenditure of strength, dexterity, prudence, and activity which every animal has ceaselessly to make through its whole life; if, approaching the matter more closely, we contemplate the untiring diligence of wretched little ants, the marvellous and ingenious industry of the bees, or observe how a single burying-beetle (*Necrophorus vespillo*) buries a mole forty times its own size in two days in order to deposit its eggs in it and insure nourishment for the future brood (*Gleditsch, Physik. Bot. Ekon. Abhandl.,* iii. 220), at the same time calling to mind how the life of most insects is nothing but ceaseless labour to prepare food and an abode for the future brood which will arise from their eggs, and which then, after they have consumed the food and passed through the chrysalis state, enter upon life merely to begin again from the beginning the same labour; then also how, like this, the life of the birds is for the most part taken up with their distant and laborious migrations, then with the building of their nests and the collecting of food for the brood, which itself has to play the same role the following year; and so all

103

work constantly for the future, which afterwards makes bankrupt; then we cannot avoid looking round for the reward of all this skill and trouble, for the end which these animals have before their eyes, which strive so ceaselessly—in short, we are driven to ask: What is the result? What is attained by the animal existence which demands such infinite preparation? And there is nothing to point to but the satisfaction of hunger and the sexual instinct, or in any case a little momentary comfort, as it falls to the lot of each animal individual, now and then in the intervals of its endless need and struggle. If we place the two together, the indescribable ingenuity of the preparations, the enormous abundance of the means, and the insufficiency of what is thereby aimed at and attained, the insight presses itself upon us that life is a business, the proceeds of which are very far from covering the cost of it. This becomes most evident in some animals of a specially simple manner of life. Take, for example, the mole, that unwearied worker. To dig with all its might with its enormous shovel claws is the occupation of its whole life; constant night surrounds it; its embryo eyes only make it avoid the light. It alone is truly an *animal nocturnum;* not cats, owls, and bats, who see by night. But what, now, does it attain by this life, full of trouble and devoid of pleasure? Food and the begetting of its kind; thus only the means of carrying on and beginning anew the same doleful course in new individuals. In such examples it becomes clear that there is no proportion between the cares and troubles of life and the results or gain of it. The consciousness of the world of perception gives a certain appearance of objective worth of existence to the life of those animals which can see, although in their case this consciousness is entirely subjective and limited to the influence of motives upon them. But the *blind* mole, with its perfect organization and ceaseless activity, limited to the alternation of insect larvae and hunger, makes the disproportion of the means to the end appar-

104

ent. In this respect the consideration of the animal world
left to itself in lands uninhabited by men is also specially
instructive. A beautiful picture of this, and of the suffering
which nature prepares for herself without the interference
of man, is given by Humboldt in his *Ansichten der Natur*
(second edition, p. 30 *et seq.*); nor does he neglect to cast a
glance (p. 44) at the analogous suffering of the human race,
always and everywhere at variance with itself. Yet in the
simple and easily surveyed life of the brutes the emptiness
and vanity of the struggle of the whole phenomenon is more
easily grasped. The variety of the organizations, the ingenuity of the means, whereby each is adapted to its element and
its prey contrasts here distinctly with the want of any lasting
final aim; instead of which there presents itself only momentary comfort, fleeting pleasure conditioned by wants, much
and long suffering, constant strife, *bellum omnium,* each one
both a hunter and hunted, pressure, want, need, and anxiety,
shrieking and howling; and this goes on *in secula seculorum,*
or till once again the crust of the planet breaks. Yunghahn
relates that he saw in Java a plain far as the eye could reach
entirely covered with skeletons, and took it for a battlefield;
they were, however, merely the skeletons of large turtles, five
feet long and three feet broad, and the same height, which
come this way out of the sea in order to lay their eggs, and
are then attacked by wild dogs (*Canis rutilans*), who with
their united strength lay them on their backs, strip off their
lower armour, that is, the small shell of the stomach, and
so devour them alive. But often then a tiger pounces upon
the dogs. Now all this misery repeats itself thousands and
thousands of times, year out, year in. For this, then, these
turtles are born. For whose guilt must they suffer this torment? Wherefore the whole scene of horror? To this the only
answer is: it is thus that the will to live objectifies itself.
Let one consider it well and comprehend it in all its objec-
tifications; and then one will arrive at an understanding of

its nature and of the world; but not if one frames general conceptions and builds card houses out of them. The comprehension of the great drama of the objectification of the will to live, and the characterisation of its nature, certainly demands somewhat more accurate consideration and greater thoroughness than the dismissal of the world by attributing to it the title of God, or, with a silliness which only the German fatherland offers and knows how to enjoy, explaining it as the "Idea in its other being," in which for twenty years the simpletons of my time have found their unutterable delight. Certainly, according to pantheism or Spinozism, of which the systems of our century are mere travesties, all that sort of thing reels itself off actually without end, straight on through all eternity. For then the world is a God, *ens perfectissimum,* i.e., nothing better can be or be conceived. Thus there is no need of deliverance from it; and consequently there is none. But why the whole tragi-comedy exists cannot in the least be seen; for it has no spectators, and the actors themselves undergo infinite trouble, with little and merely negative pleasure.

Let us now add the consideration of the human race. The matter indeed becomes more complicated, and assumes a certain seriousness of aspects; but the fundamental character remains unaltered. Here also life presents itself by no means as a gift for enjoyment, but as a task, a drudgery to be performed; and in accordance with this we see, in great and small, universal need, ceaseless cares, constant pressure, endless strife, compulsory activity, with extreme exertion of all the powers of body and mind. Many millions, united into nations, strive for the common good, each individual on account of his own; but many thousands fall as a sacrifice for it. Now senseless delusions, now intriguing politics, incite them to wars with each other; then the sweat and the blood of the great multitude must flow, to carry out the ideas of individuals, or to expiate their faults. In peace industry and trade are active, inventions work miracles, seas are navigated, delicacies are collected from all ends of the world, the waves engulf thousands. All strive, some planning, others acting; the tumult is indescribable. But the ultimate aim of it all, what is it? To sustain ephemeral and tormented individuals through a short span of time in the most fortunate case with endurable want and comparative freedom from pain, which, however, is at once attended with ennui; then the reproduction of this race and its striving. In this evident disproportion between the trouble and the reward, the will to live appears to us from this point of view, if taken objectively, as a fool, or subjectively, as a delusion, seized by which everything living works with the utmost exertion of its strength for something that is of no value. But when we consider it more closely, we shall find here also that it is rather a blind pressure, a tendency entirely without ground or motive.

The law of motivation, as was shown in section 29 of *The World as Will and Idea* only extends to the particular actions, not to willing *as a whole and in general*. It depends upon this, that if we conceive of the human race and its action *as a whole and universally,* it does not present itself to us, as when we contemplate the particular actions, as a play of puppets who are pulled after the ordinary manner by threads outside them; but from this point of view, as puppets which are set in motion by internal clockwork. For if, as we have done above, one compares the ceaseless, serious, and laborious striving of men with what they gain by it, nay, even with what they ever can gain, the disproportion we have pointed out becomes apparent, for one recognizes that that which is to be gained, taken as the motive-power, is entirely insufficient for the explanation of that movement and that ceaseless striving. What, then, is a short postponement of death, a slight easing of misery or deferment of pain, a momentary stilling of desire, compared with such an abundant and certain victory over them all as death? What could such advantages accomplish taken as actual moving causes of a human race, innumerable because constantly renewed, which unceasingly moves, strives, struggles, grieves, writhes, and performs the whole tragi-comedy of the history of the world, nay, what says more than all, *perseveres* in such a mock-existence as long as each one possibly can? Clearly this is all inexplicable if we seek the moving causes outside the figures and conceive the human race as striving, in consequence of rational reflection, or something analogous to this (as moving threads), after those good things held out to it, the attainment of which would be a sufficient reward for its ceaseless cares and troubles. The matter being taken thus, every one would rather have long ago said, *"Le jeu ne vaut pas la chandelle,"* and have gone out. But, on the contrary, every one guards and defends his life, like a precious pledge intrusted to him under heavy responsibility, under infinite cares and abundant misery, even under which life is tolerable. The wherefore and the why, the reward for this, certainly he does not see; but he has accepted the worth of that pledge without seeing it, upon trust and faith, and does not know what it consists in. Hence, I have said that these puppets are not pulled from without, but each bears in itself the clockwork from which its movements result. This is *the will to live,* manifesting itself as an untiring machine, an irrational tendency, which has not its sufficient reason in the external world. It holds the individuals firmly upon the scene and is the *primum mobile* of their movements, while the external objects, the motives, only determine their direction in the particular case; otherwise the cause would not be at all suitable to the effect. For, as every manifestation of a force of nature has a cause, but the force of nature itself none, so every particular act of will has a motive, but the will in general has none: indeed at bottom these two are one and the same. The will, as that which is metaphysical, is everywhere the boundary-stone of every investigation, beyond which it cannot go. From the original and unconditioned nature of the will, which has been proved, it is explicable that man loves beyond everything else an existence full of misery, trouble, pain, and anxiety, and again, full of ennui, which, if he considered and weighed it purely objectively, he would certainly abhor, and fears above all things the end of it, which is yet for him the one thing certain.[1] Accordingly we often see a miserable figure, deformed and shrunk with age, want, and disease, implore our help from the bottom of his heart for the prolongation of an existence, the end of which would necessarily appear altogether desirable if it were an objective judgment that determined here. Thus instead of this it is the blind will, appearing as the tendency to life, the love of life, and the sense of life; it is the same which makes the plants grow. This sense of life may be compared to a rope which is stretched above the puppet-show of the world of men, and on which the puppets hang by invisible threads, while apparently they are supported only by the ground beneath them (the objective value of life). But if the rope becomes weak the puppet sinks; if it breaks the puppet must fall, for the ground beneath it only seemed to support it: i.e., the weakening of that love of life shows itself as hypochondria, spleen, melancholy; its entire exhaustion as the inclination to suicide, which now takes place on the slightest occasion, nay, for a merely imaginary reason, for now, as it were, the man seeks a quarrel with himself, in order to shoot himself dead, as many do with others for a like purpose; indeed, upon necessity, suicide is resorted to without any special occasion. (Evidence of this will be found in Esquirol. *Des maladies mentales,* 1838.) And as with the persistence in life, so is it also with its action and movement.

---

[1] "Augustini de civit. Dei," L. xi. c. 27, deserves to be compared as an interesting commentary on what is said here.

This is not something freely chosen; but while every one would really gladly rest, want and ennui are the whips that keep the top spinning. Therefore, the whole and every individual bears the stamp of a forced condition; and every one, in that, inwardly weary, he longs for rest, but yet must press forward, is like his planet, which does not fall into the sun only because a force driving it forward prevents it. Therefore everything is in continual strain and forced movement. Men are only apparently drawn from in front; really they are pushed from behind; it is not life that tempts them on but necessity that drives them forward. The law of motivation is, like all causality, merely the form of the phenomenon. We may remark in passing that this is the source of the comical, the burlesque, the grotesque, the ridiculous side of life; for, urged forward against his will, every one bears himself as best he can, and the straits that thus arise often look comical enough, serious as is the misery which underlies them.

In all these considerations, then, it becomes clear to us that the will to live is not a consequence of the knowledge of life, is in no way a *conclusio ex praemissis,* and in general is nothing secondary. Rather, it is that which is first and unconditioned, the premiss of all premisses, and just on that account that from which philosophy must *start,* for the will to live does not appear in consequence of the world, but the world in consequence of the will to live.

I scarcely need to draw attention to the fact that the considerations with which we now conclude the second book already point forcibly to the serious theme of the fourth book, indeed would pass over into it directly if it were not that my architectonic symmetry makes it necessary that the third book, with its fair contents, should come between, as a second consideration of *the world as idea,* the conclusion of which, however, again points in the same direction.

Arthur Schopenhauer

Parerga

The Vanity of Existence

This vanity finds expression in the whole way in which things exist; in the infinite nature of Time and Space, as opposed to the finite nature of the individual in both; in the ever-passing present moment as the only mode of actual existence; in the interdependence and relativity of all things; in continual Becoming without ever Being; in constant wishing and never being satisfied; in the long battle which forms the history of life, where every effort is checked by difficulties, and stopped until they are overcome. Time is that in which all things pass away; it is merely the form under which the will to live—the thing-in-itself and therefore imperishable—has revealed to it that its efforts are in vain; it is that agent by which at every moment all things in our hands become as nothing, and lose any real value they possess.

That which *has been* exists no more; it exists as little as that which has *never been*. But of everything that exists you must say, in the next moment, that it has been. Hence something of great importance now present, in that the latter is a *reality*, and related to the former as something to nothing.

A man finds himself, to his great astonishment, suddenly existing, after thousands and thousands of years of non-existence: he lives for a little while; and then, again, comes an equally long period when he must exist no more. The heart rebels against this, and feels that it cannot be true.

111

The crudest intellect cannot speculate on such a subject without having a presentiment that Time is something ideal in its nature. This ideality of Time and Space is the key to every true system of metaphysics, because it provides for quite another order of things than is to be met within the domain of nature. This is why Kant is so great. Of every event in our life we can say only for one moment that it *is;* for ever after, that it *was.* Every evening we are poorer by a day. It might, perhaps, make us mad to see how rapidly our short span of time ebbs away; if it were not that in the furthest depths of our being we are secretly conscious of our share in the exhaustible spring of eternity, so that we can always hope to find life in it again.

Consideration of the kind, touched on above, might, indeed, lead us to embrace the belief that the greatest *wisdom* is to make the enjoyment of the present the supreme object of life; because that is the only reality, all else being merely the play of thought. On the other hand, such a course might just as well be called the greatest *folly:* for that which in the next moment exists no more, and vanishes utterly, like a dream, can never be worth a serious effort.

The whole foundation on which our existence rests is the present—the ever-fleeting present. It lies, then, in the very nature of our existence to take the form of constant motion, and to offer no possibility of our ever attaining the rest for which we are always striving. We are like a man running downhill, who cannot keep on his legs unless he runs on, and will inevitably fall if he stops; or, again, like a pole balanced on the tip of one's finger; or like a planet, which would fall into its sun the moment it ceased to hurry forward on its way. Unrest is the mark of existence.

In a world where all is unstable, and nought can endure, but is swept onwards at once in the hurrying whirlpool of changes; where a man, if he is to keep erect at all, must always be advancing and moving, like an acrobat on a rope—

in such a world, happiness is inconceivable. How can it
dwell where, as Plato says, *continual Becoming and never
Being* is the sole form of existence? In the first place, a man
never is happy, but spends his whole life in striving after
something which he thinks will make him so; he seldom
attains his goal, and when he does, it is only to be disappointed; he is mostly shipwrecked in the end, and comes
into harbor with masts and rigging gone. And then, it is all
one whether he has been happy or miserable; for his life
was never anything more than a present moment always
vanishing; and now it is over.

At the same time it is a wonderful thing that, in the world
of human beings as in that of animals in general, this manifold restless motion is produced and kept up by the agency
of two simple impulses—hunger and the sexual instinct;
aided a little, perhaps, by the influence of boredom, but by
nothing else; and that, in the theatre of life, these suffice to
form the *primum mobile* of how complicated a machinery,
setting in motion how strange and varied a scene!

On looking a little closer, we find that inorganic matter
presents a constant conflict between chemical forces, which
eventually works dissolution; and on the other hand, that
organic life is impossible without continual change of matter, and cannot exist if it does not receive perpetual help
from without. This is the realm of *finality;* and its opposite
would be *an infinite existence,* exposed to no attack from
without, and needing nothing to support it; the realm of
eternal peace; some timeless, changeless state, one and undi-
versified; the negative knowledge of which forms the domi-
nant note of the Platonic philosophy. It is to some such state
as this that the denial of the will to live opens up the way.

The scenes of our life are like pictures done in rough
mosaic. Looked at close, they produce no effect. There is
nothing beautiful to be found in them, unless you stand
some distance off. So, to gain anything we have longed for is

only to discover how vain and empty it is; and even though we are always living in expectation of better things, at the same time we often repent and long to have the past back again. We look upon the present as something to be put up with while it lasts, and serving only as the way towards our goal. Hence most people, if they glance back when they come to the end of life, will find that all along they have been living *ad interim:* they will be surprised to find that the very thing they disregarded and let slip by unenjoyed, was just the life in the expectation of which they passed all their time. Of how many a man may it not be said that hope made a fool of him until he danced into the arms of death!

Then again, how insatiable a creature is man! Every satisfaction he attains lays the seeds of some new desire, so that there is no end to the wishes of each individual will. And why is this? The real reason is simply that, taken in itself, Will is the lord of all worlds: everything belongs to it, and therefore no one single thing can ever give it satisfaction, but only the whole, which is endless. For all that, it must rouse our sympathy to think how very little the Will, this lord of the world, really gets when it takes the form of an individual; usually only just enough to keep the body together. This is why man is so very miserable.

Life presents itself chiefly as a task—the task, I mean, of subsisting at all, *gagner sa vie.* If this is accomplished, life is a burden, and then there comes the second task of doing something with that which has been won—of warding off boredom, which, like a bird of prey, hovers over us, ready to fall wherever it sees a life secure from need. The first task is to win something; the second, to banish the feeling that it has been won; otherwise it is a burden.

Human life must be some kind of mistake. The truth of this will be sufficiently obvious if we only remember that man is a compound of needs and necessities hard to satisfy; and that even when they are satisfied, all he obtains is a state

114

of painlessness, where nothing remains to him but abandon-
ment to boredom. This is direct proof that existence has no
real value in itself; for what is boredom but the feeling of
the emptiness of life? If life—the craving for which is the
very essence of our being—were possessed of any positive
intrinsic value, there would be no such thing as boredom at
all: mere existence would satisfy us in itself, and we should
want for nothing. But as it is, we take no delight in existence
except when we are struggling for something; and then distance and difficulties to be overcome make our goal look as
though it would satisfy us—an illusion which vanishes when
we reach it; or else when we are occupied with some purely
intellectual interest—when in reality we have stepped forth
from life to look upon it from the outside, much after the
manner of spectators at a play. And even sensual pleasure
itself means nothing but a struggle and aspiration, ceasing
the moment its aim is attained. Whenever we are not occupied in one of these ways, but gaze upon existence itself, its
vain and worthless nature is brought home to us; and this
is what we mean by boredom. The hankering after what
is strange and uncommon—an innate and ineradicable tendency of human nature—shows how glad we are in any interruption of that natural course of affairs which is so very
tedious.

That this most perfect manifestation of the will to live,
the human organism, with the cunning and complex working of its machinery, must fall to dust and yield up itself
and all its strivings to extinction—this is the naive way in
which Nature, who is always so true and sincere in what she
says, proclaims the whole struggle of this will as in its very
essence barren and unprofitable. Were it of any value in
itself, anything unconditioned and absolute, it could not
thus end in mere nothing.

If we turn from contemplating the world as a whole, and,
in particular, the generations of men as they live their little

hour of mock-existence and then are swept away in rapid succession; if we turn from this, and look at life in its small details, as presented, say, in a comedy, how ridiculous it all seems! It is like a drop of water seen through a microscope, a single drop teeming with *infusoria;* or a speck of cheese full of mites invisible to the naked eye. How we laugh as they bustle about so eagerly, and struggle with one another in so tiny a space! And whether here, or in the little span of human life, this terrible activity produces a comic effect.

It is only in the microscope that our life looks so big. It is an indivisible point, drawn out and magnified by the powerful lenses of Time and Space.

Gabriel Marcel (1889-   )

Homo Viator. Introduction to a Metaphysics of Hope

The Ego and Its Relation to Others *

In our subject today we shall find that the distinction, in any case uncertain, between child psychology and psychology pure and simple has practically no importance. If we forget, as I think we should, the theories and definitions of philosophy in order to learn all we can from direct experience, we are led to the conclusion that the act which establishes the *ego,* or rather by which the *ego* establishes itself, is always identically the same: it is this act which we must try to grasp without allowing ourselves to be led astray by the fictitious speculations which throughout human history have been accumulating in this field. I think that we should employ current forms of ordinary language which distort our experiences far less than the elaborate expressions in which philosophical language is crystallised. The most elementary example, the closest to earth, is also the most instructive. Take, for instance, the child who brings his mother flowers he has just been gathering in the meadow. "Look," he cries, "I picked these." Mark the triumph in his voice and above all the gesture, simple and rapid enough, perhaps, which accompanies his announcement. The child points himself out for admiration and gratitude: "It was I, I who am with

* Lecture given to the *Institut Supérieur de Pedagogie* at Lyons, December 13, 1942.

you here, who picked these lovely flowers, don't go thinking it was Nanny or my sister; it was I and *no one else.*" This exclusion is of the greatest importance: it seems that the child wants to attract attention almost materially. He claims enthusiastic praise, and it would be the most calamitous thing in the world if by mistake it was bestowed on someone who did not deserve it. Thus the child draws attention to himself, he offers himself to the other in order to receive a special tribute. I do not believe it is possible to insist too much upon the presence of the other, or more exactly others, involved in the statement: "It is I who. . . ." It implies that "There are, on the one hand, those who are excluded about whom you must be careful not to think, and, on the other, there is the *you* to whom the child speaks and whom he wants as a witness."

The same affirmation on the part of an adult would be less openly advertised; it would be enveloped in a halo of false modesty where the complexities of the game of social hypocrisy are discernible. Think of the amateur composer who has just been singing an unknown melody in some drawing-room. People exclaim: "What is that? Is it an unpublished song by Faure?" etc. "No, as a matter of fact, it is my own . . ." etc. If we leave on one side, as we should, all the elaborations of social convention, we shall recognise the fundamental identity of the act. The difference has only to do with the attitude adopted or simulated regarding the expected tribute.

To go on with our analysis, we observe that this ego here before us, considered as a centre of magnetism, cannot be reduced to certain parts which can be specified such as "my body, my hands, my brain"; it is a global presence—a presence which gains glory from the magnificent bouquet which I myself have picked, which I have brought you; and I do not know whether you should admire more the artistic taste of which it is a proof or the generosity which I have shown

118

in giving it to you, I, who might so easily have kept it for myself. Thus the beauty of the object is in a fashion reflected upon me, and if I appeal to you, then, I repeat, I do so as to a qualified witness whom I invite to wonder at the *whole* we form—the bouquet and I.

But we must not fail to notice that the admiration which I expect from you, which you give me, can only confirm and heighten the satisfaction I feel in recognising my own merits. Why should we not conclude from this that the *ego here present* certainly involves a reference to someone else, only this other someone is treated as a foil or amplifier for my own self-satisfaction.

"But," you will object, "self-satisfaction, self-confidence, self-love: all this takes for granted a self already established which it is necessary to define." I think that here we must be careful not to fall into a trap of language. This pre-existent *ego* can only be postulated, and if we try to describe it, we can only do so negatively, by way of exclusion. On the other hand, it is very instructive to give a careful account of the act which establishes what I call myself, the act, for instance, by which I attract the attention of others so that they may praise me, maybe, or blame me, but at all events so that they notice me. In every case *I produce* myself, in the etymological sense of the word, that is to say I put myself forward.

Other examples bring us to the same conclusion. Let us keep to the level of a child's experience. A little stranger stretches out his hand to take the ball which I have left on the ground; I jump up; the ball is mine. Here again the relationship with others is at the root of the matter, but it takes the form of an order: *Do not touch*. I have no hesitation in saying that the instantaneous claiming of our own property is one of the most significant of our experiences. Here again I "produce" myself. I warn the other person that he must conform his conduct to the rule I have given him. It can be observed without any great subtlety that the sense

119

of possession was already implicit in the previous examples, only it was possession of a virtue rather than a thing. Here, however, more clearly than just now, the ego is seen as a global and indefinable presence. I, here before you, possess the ball, perhaps I might consent to lend it to you for a few moments, but you must quite understand that it is I who am very kindly lending it to you and that, in consequence, I can take it back from you at any minute if I so wish; I the despot, I the autocrat.

I have used the term presence several times; now I will try as far as possible to define what I mean by it. Presence denotes something rather different and more comprehensive than the fact of just being there; to be quite exact one should not actually say that an object is present. We might say that presence is always dependent on an experience which is at the same time irreducible and vague, the sense of existing, of being in the world. Very early in the development of a human being this consciousness of existing, which we surely have no reason to doubt is common also to animals, is linked up with the urge to make ourselves *recognised* by some other person, some witness, helper, rival or adversary who, whatever may be said, is needed to integrate the self, but whose place in the field of consciousness can vary almost indefinitely.

If this analysis as a whole is correct, it is necessary to see what I call my *ego* in no way as an isolated reality, whether it be an element or a principle, but as *an emphasis* which I give, not of course to the whole of my experience, but to that part of it which I want to safeguard in a special manner against some attack or possible infringement. It is in this sense that the impossibility of establishing any precise frontiers of the *ego* has been often and rightly pointed out. This becomes clear as soon as one understands that the *ego* can never be thought of as a portion of space. On the other hand, it cannot be repeated often enough that, after all, the self is *here, now;* or at any rate there are such close affinities between these facts that we really cannot separate them. I own that I cannot in any way conceive how a being for whom there was neither a here nor a now could nevertheless appear as "I." From this it follows paradoxically enough that the emphasis of which I have spoken cannot avoid tending to conceive of itself as an enclosure, that is to say as exactly the thing it is not; and it is only on deeper reflection that it will be possible to detect what is deceptive in this localisation.

I spoke of an enclosure, but it is an enclosure which moves, and what is even more essential, it is vulnerable: a *highly sensitive enclosure.* The incomparable analyses of Meredith in *The Egoist* would fit in very naturally here. Nobody, perhaps, has ever gone so far in the analysis of a susceptibility for which the term self-love is manifestly incomplete. Actually, this susceptibility is rooted in anguish rather than in love. Burdened with myself, plunged in this disturbing world, sometimes threatening me, sometimes my accomplice, I keep an eager look-out for everything emanating from it which might either soothe or ulcerate the wound I bear within me, which is my *ego.* This state is strikingly analogous to that of a man who has an abscess at the root of his tooth and who experiments cautiously with heat and cold, acid and sugar, to get relief. What then is this anguish, this wound? The answer is that it is above all the experience of being torn by a contradiction between the all which I aspire to possess, to annex, or, still more absurd, to monopolise, and the obscure consciousness that after all I am nothing but an empty void; for, still, I can affirm nothing about myself which would be permanent; nothing which would be secure against criticism and the passage of time. Hence the craving to be confirmed from outside, by another; this paradox, by virtue of which even the most self-centered among us looks to others and only to others for his final investiture.

This contradiction is constantly appearing here. Nowhere

121

does it show up in greater relief than in the attitude which our everyday language so aptly terms pose. The *poseur* who seems only to be preoccupied with others is in reality entirely taken up with himself. Indeed, the person he is with only interests him in so far as he is likely to form a favourable picture of him which in turn he will receive back. The other person reflects him, returns to him this picture which he finds so enchanting. It would be interesting to find out what social climate is most favourable for posing, and what on the other hand are the conditions most likely to discourage it. It might generally be said that in a virile atmosphere posing is unmasked immediately and made fun of. At school or in barracks the *poseur* has practically no chance of success. A consensus of opinion is almost certain to be formed against him, his companions see through him at once, each one of them accuses him of infringing a certain implicit pact, that of the little community to which he belongs. It is not easy to formulate it exactly, but it is a distinct perception of the incompatibility between a certain reality in which each one participates and this play-acting which degrades and betrays it. On the other hand, the more artificial, unreal and, in a certain sense, effeminate the environment, the less the incompatibility will be felt. This is because in such circles everything depends upon opinions and appearances, from which it follows that seduction and flattery have the last word.

Now, posing is a form of flattery, a manner of paying court while seeming to obtrude oneself. Beneath it all we invariably find self-love and, I might add, pretension. This last, by its very ambiguity, is particularly instructive. To pretend is not only to aspire or to aim high, it is also to simulate, and actually there is simulation in all posing. To realise this we only need to recall what affectation is in all its forms. From the moment that I become preoccupied about the effect I want to produce on the other person, my every act, word and attitude loses its authenticity; and we all know what even a studied or affected simplicity can be.

Homo Viator

Here, however, we must note something of capital importance. From the very fact that I treat the other person merely as a means of resonance or an amplifier, I tend to consider him as a sort of apparatus which I can, or think I can, manipulate, or of which I can dispose at will. I form my own idea of him and, strangely enough, this idea can become a substitute for the real person, a shadow to which I shall come to refer my acts and words. The truth of the matter is that to pose is always to pose before oneself. "To play to the gallery . . .," we are accustomed to say, but the gallery is still the self. To be more exact, we might say that the other person is the provisional and as it were accessory medium, through which I can arrive at forming a certain image, or idol of myself; the work of stylisation by which each of us fashions this image might be traced step by step. This work is helped by social failure as much as by success. When he who poses is scoffed at by his companions, he decides, more often than not, that he has to do with imbeciles and shuts himself up with jealous care in a little private sanctuary where he can be alone with his idol.

Here we are in line with the merciless analyses to which the anti-romantics have subjected the cult of the *ego*. "But," you may ask, "should we not take care not to go too far? Is there not a normal condition of the *ego* which should not be confused with its abnormalities or perversions?" The question is a very delicate one. It must in no way be mistaken for a problem of technical philosophy, with which we are not dealing here and which involves the question of the very existence of a superior principle of unity which guides our personal development. What concerns us here is only to know under what conditions I become conscious of myself as a person. It must be repeated that these conditions are essentially social. There is, in particular, every reason to think that the system of perpetual competition to which the individual is subjected in the world of today cannot fail to increase and exasperate this consciousness of the *ego*. I have

123

no hesitation in saying that if we want to fight effectively against individualism in its most harmful form, we must find some way of breaking free from the asphyxiating atmosphere of examinations and competition in which our young people are struggling. "I must win, not you! I must get above you!" We can never insist enough upon how the real sense of fellowship which shows itself in such striking contrast among any team worthy of the name, has been rendered weak and anaemic by the competitive system. This system does in fact encourage each one to compare himself with his neighbour, to give himself a mark or a number by which he can be measured against him. Moreover, we must notice a thing which is essential in our argument: such a system, which makes self-consciousness or, if you prefer to call it so, self-love ten times worse, is at the same time the most depersonalising process possible; for the thing in us which has real value cannot be judged by comparison, having no common measure with anything else. Unfortunately, however, it seems as though people have taken a delight in accumulating every possible confusion concerning this point, and I have no hesitation in saying that the responsibilities of those who claim to celebrate the cult of the individual are overwhelming. Maybe there is no more fatal error than that which conceives of the *ego* as the secret abode of originality. To get a better idea of this we must here introduce the wrongly discredited notion of gifts. The best part of my personality does not belong to me. I am in no sense the owner, only the trustee. Except in the realm of metaphysics, with which we are not dealing today, there is no sense in enquiring into the origin of these gifts. On the other hand, it is very important to know what my attitude should be with regard to them. If I consider myself as their guardian, responsible for their fruitfulness, that is to say if I recognise in them a call or even perhaps a question to which I must respond, it will not occur to me to be proud about them and to parade them before an audience, which, I repeat, really means myself. Indeed, if we come to think of it, there is nothing in me which cannot or should not be regarded as a gift. It is pure fiction to imagine a pre-existent self on whom these gifts were bestowed in virtue of certain rights, or as a recompense for some former merit.

This surely means that I must puncture the illusion, infinitely persistent it is true, that I am possessed of unquestionable privileges which make me the centre of my universe, while other people are either mere obstructions to be removed or circumvented, or else those echoing amplifiers, whose purpose is to foster my self-complacency. I propose to call this illusion moral egocentricity, thus marking clearly how deeply it has become rooted in our very nature. In fact, just as any notions we may have of cosmography do not rid us from the immediate impression that the sun and stars go round the earth, so it is not possible for us to escape completely here below from the preconceived idea which makes each one tend to establish himself as the centre around which all the rest have no other function but to gravitate. It is equally true that this idea or prejudice, no matter how becomingly it may be adorned in the case of great egoists, appears, when we come down to a final analysis, to be merely another expression of a purely biological and animal claim. Moreover, the ill-starred philosophies which, particularly in the nineteenth century, attempted to justify this position not only marked a retrogression as far as the secular wisdom of civilised humanity was concerned, but, it cannot be disputed for a moment, have directly helped to precipitate mankind into the chaos where it is struggling at the present time.

Does it, however, follow that this *egolatry*, this idolatry of the self, must necessarily be met by a rationalistic and impersonal doctrine? Nothing, I believe, would be farther from the truth. Whenever men have tried to put such a doctrine into practice we must own that it has proved itself extremely disappointing. To be more exact, such an experiment has never been and never could be effective. Actually it is of the very essence of this doctrine that it cannot be really put into practice, except perhaps by a few theorists who are only at ease among abstractions, paying for this faculty by the loss of all real contact with living beings, and, I might add, with the great simplicities of existence. For the immense majority of human beings, the entities which such a rationalism claims to set up as the object of everybody's reverent attention are only shams behind which passions incapable of recognising themselves take cover. It has been given to our generation, as to that of the end of the eighteenth century and that of the Second Empire, not only to observe but to suffer the disastrous effects of the sin of the ideologists. This consists, above all perhaps, of infinitely intensifying the inner-falsehood, of thickening the film which is interposed between a human being and his true nature until it is almost impossible to destroy it.

Moreover, this same point will enable us to understand the most characteristic elements in what to-day is commonly accepted as the meaning of the term "person." Nowadays, the individual allows himself, legitimately enough, to be likened to an atom caught up in a whirlwind, or, if you wish, a mere statistical unit; because most of the time he is simply a specimen among an infinity of others, since the opinions, which he thinks are his own, are merely reflections of the ideas accepted in the circles he frequents and handed round in the press which he reads daily. Thus he is only, as I have had occasion to write, an anonymous unit of that anonymous entity "one." But he almost inevitably has the illusion that his reactions are authentic, so that he *submits,* while all the time he imagines he is taking action. It is, on the contrary, in the nature of a person to face any given situation directly and, I should add, to make an effective decision upon it. But, it may be asked, is not this the *ego* appearing once more? I think not. Let us understand each other. There could naturally be no question of conceiving of the person as of something distinct from that other thing, the *ego;* as if they were in separate compartments. Such an idea would be completely fictitious. We must go further. The person cannot be regarded as an element or attribute of the *ego* either. It would be better to say that it is something compelling, which most certainly takes its birth in what appears to me to be mine, or to be me myself, but this compelling force only becomes conscious of itself when it becomes a reality. It can thus in no way be compared with a slight desire. Let us say that it is of the order of "I will" and not of "I would like. . . ." I claim to be a person in so far as I assume responsibility for what I do and what I say. But to whom am I responsible, to whom do I acknowledge my responsibility? We must reply that I am conjointly responsible both to myself and to everyone else, and that this conjunction is precisely characteristic of an engagement of the person, that it is the mark proper to the person. We will not stay any longer among abstractions where there is always a risk of becoming imprisoned by words. Supposing that I wish or feel bound to put a certain person on his guard against someone else. I decide to write him a letter to this effect. If I do not sign my letter I am still as it were moving in a realm of play, of pastimes, and I might readily add mystification; I reserve to myself the possibility of denying my action; I deliberately maintain my position in a zone as it were halfway between dreams and reality, where self-complacency triumphs, the chosen land of those who, in our time, have made themselves the champions of the gratuitous act. From the moment that I sign my letter, on the contrary, I have taken on the responsibility for it, that is to say I have shouldered the consequences in advance. I have created the irrevocable not only for the other person but for myself. Of my own free will I have brought into existence new decisions which will bear upon my own life with all their weight. This, of course, does not exclude the possibility that it was a reprehensible, perhaps even a criminal action to write the letter. There is nevertheless a radical difference of quality, or more exactly of weight, between this action and that of writing a letter without signing it. Let us repeat that I tend to establish myself as a person in so far as I assume responsibility for my acts and so behave as a real being (rather than a dreamer who reserves the strange power of modifying his dreams, without having to trouble whether this modification has any repercussions in the hypothetical outside world in which everybody else dwells). From the same point of view we might also say that I establish myself as a person in so far as I really believe in the existence of others and allow this belief to influence my conduct. What is the actual meaning of *believing* here? It means to realise or acknowledge their existence in itself, and not only through those points of intersection which bring it into relation with my own.

Person—engagement—community—reality: there we have a sort of chain of notions, which, to be exact, do not readily follow from each other by deduction (actually there is nothing more fallacious than a belief in the value of deduction) but of which the union can be grasped by an act of the mind. It would be better not to call this act by the much abused term of intuition, but by one which on the contrary is too little used—that of synopsis, the act by which a group is held together under the mind's comprehensive gaze.

As I hinted just now, one cannot strictly say that personality is good in itself, or that it is an element of goodness: the truth is much more that it controls the existence of a world where there is good and evil. I should be inclined to think that the *ego,* so long as it remains shut up within itself, that is to say the prisoner of its own feelings, of its covetous desires, and of that dull anxiety which works upon it, is really beyond the reach of evil as well as of good. It literally

128

has not yet awakened to reality. Indeed, it is to be wondered whether there does not exist an infinite number of beings for whom this awakening has never truly taken place. There is no doubt that direct judgment cannot be applied to such beings. I would go further: it seems to me that each of us, in a considerable part of his life or his being, is still unawakened, that is to say that he moves on the margin of reality like a sleepwalker. Let us say that the *ego,* as such, is ruled by a sort of vague fascination, which is localised, almost by chance, in objects arousing sometimes desire, sometimes terror. It is, however, precisely against such a condition that what I consider the essential characteristic of the person is opposed, the characteristic, that is to say of availability (*disponibilité*).

This, of course, does not mean emptiness, as in the case of an available dwelling (*local disponible*), but it means much rather an aptitude to give oneself to anything which offers, and to bind oneself by the gift. Again, it means to transform circumstances into opportunities, we might even say favours, thus participating in the shaping of our own destiny and marking it with our seal. It has sometimes been said of late, "Personality is vocation." It is true if we restore its true value to the term vocation, which is in reality a call, or more precisely the response to a call. We must not, however, be led astray here by any mythological conception. It depends, in fact, on me whether the call is recognized as a call, and, strange as it may seem, in this matter it is true to say that it comes both from me and from outside me at one and the same time; or rather, in it we become aware of that most intimate connection between what comes from me and what comes from outside, a connection which is nourishing or constructive and cannot be relinquished without the ego wasting and tending towards death.

Perhaps we might make this clearer by pointing out that each of us from the very beginning appears to himself and to others as a particular problem for which the circumstances, whatever they may be, are not enough to provide a solution. I use the term problem absolutely against my will, for it seems to be quite inadequate. Is it not obvious that if I consider the other person as a sort of mechanism exterior to my own *ego,* a mechanism of which I must discover the spring or manner of working, even supposing I manage to take him to pieces in the process, I shall never succeed in obtaining anything but a completely exterior knowledge of him, which is in a way the very denial of his real being? We must even go further and say that such a knowledge is in reality sacrilegious and destructive, it does no less than denude its object of the one thing he has which is of value and so it *degrades him effectively.* That means—and there is nothing which is more important to keep in view—that the knowledge of an individual being cannot be separated from the act of love or charity by which this being is accepted in all which makes of him a unique creature or, if you like, the image of God. There is no doubt that this expression borrowed from the language of religion renders more exactly than any other the truth I have in view at the moment. It is, however, none the less necessary to remember that the truth can be actively misunderstood by each one of us at any time and that there will always be something in experience which seems to provide an argument for him who, following in the footsteps of the cynics of all time, claims to reduce his fellows to little machines whose every movement it is only too easy for him to examine and even to regulate according to his fancy.

It must be understood that these observations are just as directly applicable to the relationship which binds me to myself, the manner in which it is given me to apprehend my own being. It is indeed a fact that I also can conceive of myself as a pure piece of mechanism and make it my chief business to control the machine as well as possible. From the same standpoint, I can regard the problem of my life purely as a problem of tangible results. All that is perfectly consistent. The simplest reflection, however, shows that this mechanism must inevitably serve some purpose which I am at liberty to choose and which is recognised and established as a purpose by my own act. We know from experience, however, that this act can remain practically unsuspected by the very one who has made it. If, indeed, I passively accept a group of regulations which seem to be imposed upon me by the circle to which I belong by birth, by the party to which I have allowed myself to be attached without any genuine thought on my part, everything goes on as though I were really nothing but an instrument, a mere cog in the wheel, as if, in short, the supreme human gift of free action had been refused me. Nevertheless, on reflection we see that all the time this presupposes the act by which the person has failed to recognise himself, or more exactly, has alienated that which alone could confer the dignity which is proper to his nature.

What then is this principle which it is given him thus to fail to recognise or on the contrary to guard and promote? It is easy to discover it if we penetrate the meaning of the notion of availability to which I referred a little way back. The being who is ready for anything is the opposite of him who is occupied or cluttered up with himself. He reaches out, on the contrary, beyond his narrow self, prepared to consecrate his being to a cause which is greater than he is, but which at the same time he makes his own. Here, moreover, it is the order of creation, of power, and of creative fidelity which is borne in upon us. We go wrong when we confuse creating with producing. That which is essential in the creator is the act by which he places himself at the disposal of something which, no doubt in one sense depends upon him for its existence, but which at the same time appears to him to be beyond what he is and what he judged

131

himself capable of drawing directly and immediately from himself. This obviously applies to the case of the artist and to the mysterious gestation which alone makes the appearance of a work of art possible. It is not necessary to insist on this. We must remember, however, that the creative process, though less apparent, is none the less effective wherever there is personal development of any kind. Only here what the person has to create is not some work in a way outside himself and capable of assuming an independent existence, it is his own self in very truth. How can we help seeing that the personality is not to be conceived of apart from the act by which it creates itself, yet at the same time this creation depends in some way upon a superior order? It will seem to the person that sometimes he invents the order, sometimes he discovers it, and reflection will moreover show that there is always a continuity between the invention and the discovery, and that no line of demarcation as definite as that ordinarily accepted by common sense can be established between the one and the other.

If this is so, it must be seen that the personality cannot in any way be compared to an object of which we can say *it is there,* in other words that it is part of a collection of things which can, of their essence, be counted, or again, that it is a statistical unity which can be noted in the calculations of a sociologist employing the methods of an engineer. Or again, if we no longer consider things from outside but from within, that is to say from the point of view of the person himself, it does not seem that strictly speaking he can say "I am" of himself. He is aware of himself far less as a being than as a desire to rise above everything which he is and is not, above the actuality in which he really feels he is involved and has a part to play, but which does not satisfy him, for it falls short of the aspiration with which he identifies himself. His motto is not *sum* but *sursum.*

We must be on our guard here. It certainly would not

do to underestimate the danger of a certain romanticism which belongs to every age. This consists of systematically depreciating that which is, in favour of some vaguely imagined and wished-for possibility, of which the transcendent appeal seems to be bound up with the fact that it is not and perhaps never can be fully realised. There can be no question here of an aspiration of that kind, for such an aspiration really springs from the *ego* and not from the personality, it is still a mere form of self-complacency. Here, and indeed everywhere as I see it, the necessity for incarnation must be given an important place. What I have been trying to say is that the personality is only realised in the act by which it tends to become incarnate (in a book, for instance, or an action or in a complete life), but at the same time it is of its very essence never to fix itself or crystallise itself finally in this particular incarnation. Why? Because it participates in the inexhaustible fullness of the being from which it emanates. There lies the deep reason for which it is impossible to think of personality or the personal order without at the same time thinking of that which reaches beyond them both, a supra-personal reality, presiding over all their initiative, which is both their beginning and their end. Here it would be well, if I had the time, to mark as clearly as possible the opposition—difference is not a strong enough word —between this supra-personal reality and its rivals, I should rather say its caricatures, which are no more than idols, and have led to the incredibly numerous false religions so prevalent, alas, in our time.

Here comes the great question to which I would draw your attention in ending this paper: What is the sign by which we can discover whether the personality is indeed surpassing and transcending itself or whether, on the contrary, it is falling back in some degree and sinking below its true level? This question is tragically acute today in presence of the fascinated and fanatical multitudes who, taking their

orders without a shadow of enquiry or reflection, rush singing to their death. Can we really speak of a transcendence
in this case? Has that which is personal reached its fulfilment
in the supra-personal? I do not think we can reply by a pure
and simple yes or no to this question. Most certainly there
is as it were a promise or aspiration in this sacrifice which
confers an undeniable nobility upon it and places it infinitely above any conduct based on selfish calculations. Yet,
at the same time, we cannot avoid seeing that this sort of col-
lective heroism, in so far as it partakes of the nature of an
intoxication, looks most disquietingly like various kinds of
sub-human behaviour, and as such falls outside the order
in which any true values find their expression. It seems to
me that it is precisely from the point of view of these values
—and of these values alone—that the indispensable discrimi-
nation, of which I just now pointed out the necessity, can
be made. It is the property of these values, however, to be universal, and, if for the moment we do not consider the case of
the artist as such, for he must be judged by a special metaphysical set of rules, we shall notice that among these universal values there are two which stand out above the rest.
They are the value of truth and that of justice. Equally, I
dare to claim that any "religion" which tends to obliterate
them, even momentarily, proves by that very fact that it is
tending to be degraded into idolatry. I scarcely need to insist
upon the terribly concrete corollaries following from these
propositions, which bear the stamp of such harmless generalities. It is clear in particular, that every concession made
either to racialism or to the Nietzschean or pseudo-Nietzs-
chean ideology which grants the *masters* the supreme right
of treating facts like a plastic substance, easy to manipulate
to suit their will, it is clear, I repeat, that every step taken
in such a direction would be in no way a transcendence but
a retrogression. We cannot be severe enough towards those
who at the present time have thus confused men's minds.

Of course, you must not misunderstand these suggestions.

134

Homo Viator

There is no question of returning to the dismal and bare rationalism which, alas, has for some forty years formed our official gospel. The claim of universality is impossible to define. True Christian philosophy and theology have the imperishable glory, not only of having never been mistaken about it, but of having honoured it and established it in the indefeasible foundations of our being. It is merely a question of incorporating this claim in the most concrete forms of human experience, without ever despising them, but, on the contrary, recognising that the most humble of them, if it is fully lived, can go immeasurably deep. You will, I know, allow me to end this lecture with some words of Gustave Thibon whom you heard in this very place only a few days ago, and who seems to me to have admirably expressed the need for incarnation from which the personality cannot escape without betraying its true mission, without losing itself among the mirages of abstraction, without paradoxically reducing itself to one impoverished indigent form of the very *ego* it falsely claimed to surpass in every way.

"You feel you are hedged in; you dream of escape; but beware of mirages. Do not run or fly away in order to get free: rather dig in the narrow place which has been given you; you will find God there and everything. God does not float on your horizon, he sleeps in your substance. Vanity runs, love digs. If you fly away from yourself, your prison will run with you and will close in because of the wind of your flight; if you go deep down into yourself it will disappear in paradise."

Le Peuch.
November, 1941.

SUGGESTIONS FOR FURTHER READING

Aristotle, *De Anima*.
Albert Camus, *The Myth of Sisyphus*, *The Rebel*.
Ernst Cassirer, *Essay on Man*.

GABRIEL MARCEL

G. K. Chesterton, *The Everlasting Man.*
Geoffrey Clive, *The Romantic Enlightenments.*
S. Kierkegaard, *The Sickness Unto Death.*
Friedrich Nietzsche, *Ecce Homo, The Will to Power.*
Plato, *The Republic, Symposium, Phaedo.*
Jean-Paul Sartre, *Being and Nothingness, Existentialism is a Humanism.*
Teilhard de Chardin, *The Phenomenon of Man.*

PART TWO
The Shared World

Introduction

Although an occasional philosopher may voice doubts about the existence of other people, for nearly all men the sharedness of the world is a primary datum of life. Only by means of a strenuous act of abstraction can a person view his own existence without constant reference to other humans who taught him his language, instructed him in telling good from evil, gave him his first character-profiles of himself, and interact with him daily. However, the fact that a thinker accepts this datum does not determine what he will say next about community or coexistence. The philosophers of human nature in part two of these readings express a wide range of positions concerning the bonds which relate oneself to another and the degrees of dependency between individual and community.

Several human relationships are interwoven in the opening selection from Plato. The young man Euthyphro has set out to bring his own father to trial for the murder of a servant. Now a father in trouble with the law might ordinarily expect sympathy and refuge from his children, but Euthyphro has made himself deaf to any appeal of that sort. Socrates asks about the notion of piety or rectitude that stands behind the young man's plan. Surely a man who coolly hails his own flesh and blood into court must have a firmer grip on that notion than most of us, or else be driven out of his mind

139

by the tension between civil law and family loyalty. As the questioning proceeds, Socrates talks as though the only thing he cares about is finding the elusive definition of "piety," but the context of his search suggests a quite different aim: to remind Euthyphro that tension, objective uncertainty, and self-examination belong to the ethical sphere of life. It comes out in the dialogue that Euthyphro has his share of uncertainty, but the tension typically present in grave ethical decisions is missing. Therefore his inner situation of uncertainty does not agree with his breezy and confident outward behavior. The real force of the dialogue appears not in the unsuccessful search for a definition but in the Socratic technique of leading Euthyphro to examine himself and notice the rift between his inner and outer conditions. This self-examination takes place not in the dialogue but afterwards, as Euthyphro collects his bewildered thoughts.

In Aristotle's *Politics* the emphasis falls on the community and the social nature of man. Many thoughts flow from his observation that a man living apart from society must be either a beast or a god. The state as such ought to be honored as a benefaction, but particular governments differ in the proportion of their concern for the happiness and virtue of their citizens. The state ought to concern itself with those matters, according to Aristotle. This may sound obvious and bromidic in a country where various governmental agencies are constituted expressly to serve the individual's well-being and, indirectly at least, his virtue. However, a good many states in the past and a number today are very far from Aristotelian in their conceptions of their reciprocal relation to the citizen. A case-history may be studied in William L. Shirer's *The Rise and Fall of the Third Reich*.

St. Augustine, too, writes about politics, war and peace,

Introduction

happiness and human woe, but in a later age, after Christ and the apostles have died proclaiming the paradox of victory over death. If God has founded a city whose members are his saints, how shall these saints walk in earthly cities such as "the great Babylon of the West," imperial Rome? On the premise that Christianity has overcome the Socratic unknowings by means of revelation, Augustine shows how the Christian conception of human life crosses swords with that of secular philosophies, for instance Stoicism. To be a new man leavening an old world—this task requires a welding together of divine and human wisdom which *The City of God* attempts on a scale not to be equaled until the thirteenth century, when St. Thomas Aquinas produced his *Summa Theologica.*

The selection by Paracelsus (Philip Aureolus Theophrastus Bombastus von Hohenheim, 1490–1541) combines elements of a Judaeo-Christian view of man with a strong dose of nature—mysticism reminiscent of paganism. Curious ambiguities come into play as the author attempts to fuse these into a single conception of human nature. The result represents an early stage in the development of naturalistic modes of thought that were to emerge fully in the later Renaissance and after.

Plato and Aristotle are centrally concerned with the existing man's happiness and virtue, Augustine with his salvation, and Paracelsus with the dignity of his cosmic standing. Among those who take a wholly naturalistic view of human life are Karl Marx and his collaborator Friedrich Engels. The task of the rightly oriented human, as they see it, is to obey Party leadership for the sake of an eventual classless society and an idyllic life for men who do not yet exist, i.e., for future generations. Men who do exist are expendable in

141

this cause. Marxist social science declares the inevitability of world communism. The man of today, properly instructed, will recognize that inevitability and align his energies with it. Social-minded hope, scientific certitude, and ennobling seriousness of purpose are the primary selling points in Marxist self-advertising. The last has been perhaps its strongest attraction for educated persons troubled by vagueness of purpose. However, the instant or overnight seriousness one can acquire by offering oneself to the revolutionary cause is a suspicious commodity. Does it show genuine seriousness or not if someone uses violent means to make others take his presence seriously? Is an individual's deepest responsibility to humans who have yet to be born? This is the sort of question which the man-breaking tyrannies of actual communist governments have prompted in the minds of their subjects and the watching world. The readings by Engels, sometimes on the surface and more often between the lines, reveal a profound contrast with Socratic and Christian conceptions of what it means to be human.

The closing selection in part two criticizes certain tendencies in contemporary Western civilization. Ortega y Gasset, in *The Revolt of the Masses,* notes that the sheer increase in numbers has brought with it a new phenomenon, the mass man. Every man living is an heir to the accumulations of centuries of civilization. Ortega's concern is with the man who behaves as "mere heir" and with the signs by which one can recognize such behavior.

142

Plato

Euthyphro

PERSONS OF THE DIALOGUE
SOCRATES   EUTHYPHRO

Scene: The Porch of the King Archon

Euthyphro. Why have you left the Lyceum, Socrates? and what are you doing in the Porch of the King Archon? Surely you cannot be concerned in a suit before the King, like myself?

Socrates. Not in a suit, Euthyphro, impeachment is the word which the Athenians use.

Euth. What! I suppose that some one has been prosecuting you, for I cannot believe that you are the prosecutor of another.

Soc. Certainly not.

Euth. Then someone else has been prosecuting you?

Soc. Yes.

Euth. And who is he?

Soc. A young man who is little known, Euthyphro; and I hardly know him: his name is Meletus, and he is of the deme of Pitthis. Perhaps you may remember his appearance; he has a beak, and long straight hair, and a beard which is ill grown.

Euth. No, I do not remember him, Socrates. But what is the charge which he brings against you?

Soc. What is the charge? Well, a very serious charge, which shows a good deal of character in the young man, and for which he is certainly not to be despised. He says he knows how the youth are corrupted and who are their corruptors. I fancy that he must be a wise man, and seeing that I am the reverse of a wise man, he has found me out, and is going to accuse me of corrupting his young friends. And of this our mother the state is to be the judge. Of all our political men he is the only one who seems to me to begin in the right way, with the cultivation of virtue in youth; like a good husbandman, he makes the young shoots his first care, and clears away us who are the destroyers of them. This is only the first step; he will afterwards attend to the elder branches; and if he goes on as he has begun, he will be a very great public benefactor.

Euth. I hope that he may; but I rather fear, Socrates, that the opposite will turn out to be the truth. My opinion is that in attacking you he is simply aiming a blow at the foundation of the state. But in what way does he say that you corrupt the young?

Soc. He brings a wonderful accusation against me, which at first hearing excites surprise: he says that I am a poet or maker of gods, and that I invent new gods and deny the existence of old ones; this is the ground of his indictment.

Euth. I understand, Socrates; he means to attack you about the familiar sign which occasionally, as you say, comes to you. He thinks that you are a neologian, and he is going to have you up before the court for this. He knows that such a charge is readily received by the world, as I myself know too well; for when I speak in the assembly about divine things, and foretell the future to them, they laugh at me and think me a madman. Yet every word that I say is true. But they are jealous of us all; and we must be brave and go at them.

Soc. Their laughter, friend Euthyphro, is not a matter of much consequence. For a man may be thought wise; but the Athenians, I suspect, do not much trouble themselves about him until he begins to impart his wisdom to others; and then for some reason or other, perhaps, as you say, from jealousy, they are angry.

Euth. I am never likely to try their temper in this way.

Soc. I dare say not, for you are reserved in your behaviour, and seldom impart your wisdom. But I have a benevolent habit of pouring out myself to everybody, and would even pay for a listener, and I am afraid that the Athenians may think me too talkative. Now if, as I was saying, they would only laugh at me, as you say that they laugh at you, the time might pass gaily enough in the court; but perhaps they may be in earnest, and then what the end will be you soothsayers only can predict.

Euth. I dare say that the affair will end in nothing, Socrates, and that you will win your cause; and I think that I shall win my own.

Soc. And what is your suit, Euthyphro? are you the pursuer or the defendant?

Euth. I am the pursuer.

Soc. Of whom?

Euth. You will think me mad when I tell you.

Soc. Why, has the fugitive wings?

Euth. Nay, he is not very volatile at his time of life.

Soc. Who is he?

Euth. My father.

Soc. Your father! my good man?

Euth. Yes.

Soc. And of what is he accused?

Euth. Of murder, Socrates.

Soc. By the powers, Euthyphro! how little does the common herd know of the nature of right and truth. A man must be an extraordinary man, and have made great strides in wisdom, before he could have seen his way to bring such an action.

Euth. Indeed, Socrates, he must.

Soc. I suppose that the man whom your father murdered

was one of your relatives—clearly he was; for if he had been a stranger you would never have thought of prosecuting him.

Euth. I am amused, Socrates, at your making a distinction between one who is a relation and one who is not a relation; for surely the pollution is the same in either case, if you knowingly associate with the murderer when you ought to clear youself and him by proceeding against him. The real question is whether the murdered man has been justly slain. If justly, then your duty is to let the matter alone; but if unjustly, then even if the murderer lives under the same roof with you and eats at the same table, proceed against him. Now the man who is dead was a poor dependent of mine who worked for us as a field labourer on our farm in Naxos, and one day in a fit of drunken passion he got into a quarrel with one of our domestic servants and slew him. My father bound him hand and foot and threw him into a ditch, and then sent to Athens to ask of a diviner what he should do with him. Meanwhile he never attended to him and took no care about him, for he regarded him as a murderer; and thought that no great harm would be done even if he did die. Now this was just what happened. For such was the effect of cold and hunger and chains upon him, that before the messenger returned from the diviner, he was dead. And my father and family are angry with me for taking the part of the murderer and prosecuting my father. They say that he did not kill him, and that if he did, the dead man was but a murderer, and I ought not to take any notice, for that a son is impious who prosecutes a father. Which shows, Socrates, how little they know what the gods think about piety and impiety.

Soc. Good heavens, Euthyphro! and is your knowledge of religion and of things pious and impious so very exact, that, supposing the circumstances to be as you state them, you are not afraid lest you too may be doing an impious thing in bringing an action against your father?

Euthyphro

Euth. The best of Euthyphro, and that which distinguishes him, Socrates, from other men, is his exact knowledge of all such matters. What should I be good for without it?

Soc. Rare friend! I think that I cannot do better than be your disciple. Then before the trial with Meletus comes on I shall challenge him, and say that I have always had a great interest in religious questions, and now, as he charges me with rash imaginations and innovations in religion, I have become your disciple. You, Meletus, as I shall say to him, acknowledge Euthyphro to be a great theologian, and sound in his opinions; and if you approve of him you ought to approve of me, and not have me into court; but if you disapprove, you should begin by indicting him who is my teacher, and who will be the ruin, not of the young, but of the old; that is to say, of myself whom he instructs, and of his old father whom he admonishes and chastises. And if Meletus refuses to listen to me, but will go on, and will not shift the indictment from me to you, I cannot do better than repeat this challenge in the court.

Euth. Yes, indeed, Socrates; and if he attempts to indict me I am mistaken if I do not find a flaw in him; The court shall have a great deal more to say to him than to me.

Soc. And I, my dear friend, knowing this, am desirous of becoming your disciple. For I observe that no one appears to notice you—not even this Meletus; but his sharp eyes have found me out at once, and he has indicted me for impiety. And therefore, I adjure you to tell me the nature of piety and impiety, which you said that you knew so well, and of murder, and of other offences against the gods. What are they? Is not piety in every action always the same? and impiety, again—is it not always the opposite of piety, and also the same with itself, having, as impiety, one notion which includes whatever is impious?

Euth. To be sure, Socrates.

Soc. And what is piety, and what is impiety?

PLATO

Euth. Piety is doing as I am doing; that is to say, prosecuting any one who is guilty of murder, sacrilege, or of any similar crime—whether he be your father or mother, or whoever he may be—that makes no difference; and not to prosecute them is impiety. And please to consider, Socrates, what a notable proof I will give you of the truth of my words, a proof which I have already given to others:—of the principle, I mean, that the impious, whoever he may be, ought not to go unpunished. For do not men regard Zeus as the best and most righteous of the gods?—and yet they admit that he bound his father (Cronos) because he wickedly devoured his sons, and that he too had punished his own father (Uranus) for a similar reason, in a nameless manner. And yet when I proceed against my father, they are angry with me. So inconsistent are they in their way of talking when the gods are concerned, and when I am concerned.

Soc. May not this be the reason, Euthyphro, why I am charged with impiety—that I cannot away with these stories about the gods? and therefore I suppose that people think me wrong. But, as you who are well informed about them approve of them, I cannot do better than assent to your superior wisdom. What else can I say, confessing as I do, that I know nothing about them? Tell me, for the love of Zeus, whether you really believe that they are true.

Euth. Yes, Socrates; and things more wonderful still, of which the world is in ignorance.

Soc. And do you really believe that the gods fought with one another, and had dire quarrels, battles, and the like, as the poets say, and as you may see represented in the works of great artists? The temples are full of them; and notably the robe of Athene, which is carried up to the Acropolis at the great Panathenaea, is embroidered with them. Are all these tales of the gods true, Euthyphro?

Euth. Yes, Socrates; and as I was saying, I can tell you, if you would like to hear them, many other things about the gods which would quite amaze you.

148

Soc. I dare say; and you shall tell me them at some other time when I have leisure. But just at present I would rather hear from you a more precise answer, which you have not as yet given, my friend, to the question, What is "piety"? When asked, you only replied, Doing as you do, charging your father with murder.

Euth. And what I said was true, Socrates.

Soc. No doubt, Euthyphro; but you would admit that there are many other pious acts?

Euth. There are.

Soc. Remember that I did not ask you to give me two or three examples of piety, but to explain the general idea which makes all pious things to be pious. Do you not recollect that there was one idea which made the impious impious, and the pious pious?

Euth. I remember.

Soc. Tell me what is the nature of this idea, and then I shall have a standard to which I may look, and by which I may measure actions, whether yours or those of any one else, and then I shall be able to say that such and such an action is pious, such another impious.

Euth. I will tell you, if you like.

Soc. I should very much like.

Euth. Piety, then, is that which is dear to the gods, and impiety is that which is not dear to them.

Soc. Very good, Euthyphro; you have now given me the sort of answer which I wanted. But whether what you say is true or not I cannot as yet tell, although I make no doubt that you will prove the truth of your words.

Euth. Of course.

Soc. Come, then, and let us examine what we are saying. That thing or person which is dear to the gods is pious, and that thing or person which is hateful to the gods is impious, these two being the extreme opposites of one another. Was not that said?

Euth. It was.

Soc. And well said?

Euth. Yes, Socrates, I thought so; it was certainly said.

Soc. And further, Euthyphro, the gods were admitted to have enmities and hatreds and differences?

Euth. Yes, that was also said.

Soc. And what sort of difference creates enmity and anger? Suppose for example that you and I, my good friend, differ about a number; do differences of this sort make us enemies and set us at variance with one another? Do we not go at once to arithmetic, and put an end to them by a sum?

Euth. True.

Soc. Or suppose that we differ about magnitudes, do we not quickly end the differences by measuring?

Euth. Very true.

Soc. And we end a controversy about heavy and light by resorting to a weighing machine?

Euth. To be sure.

Soc. But what differences are there which cannot be thus decided, and which therefore make us angry and set us at enmity with one another? I dare say the answer does not occur to you at the moment, and therefore I will suggest that these enmities arise when the matters of difference are the just and unjust, good and evil, honourable and dishonourable. Are not these the points about which men differ, and about which when we are unable satisfactorily to decide our differences, you and I and all of us quarrel, when we do quarrel?[1]

Euth. Yes, Socrates, the nature of the differences about which we quarrel is such as you describe.

Soc. And the quarrels of the gods, noble Euthyphro, when they occur, are of a like nature?

Euth. Certainly they are.

Soc. They have differences of opinion, as you say, about

[1] Cp. 1 Alcib. 111 foll.

Euthyphro

good and evil, just and unjust, honourable and dishonourable; there would have been no quarrels among them, if there had been no such differences—would there now?

Euth. You are quite right.

Soc. Does not every man love that which he deems noble and just and good, and hate the opposite of them?

Euth. Very true.

Soc. But, as you say, people regard the same things, some as just and others as unjust—about these they dispute; and so there arise wars and fighting among them.

Euth. Very true.

Soc. Then the same things are hated by the gods and loved by the gods, and are both hateful and dear to them?

Euth. True.

Soc. And upon this view the same things, Euthyphro, will be pious and also impious?

Euth. So I should suppose.

Soc. Then, my friend, I remark with surprise that you have not answered the question which I asked. For I certainly did not ask you to tell me what action is both pious and impious: but now it would seem that what is loved by the gods is also hated by them. And therefore, Euthyphro, in thus chastising your father you may very likely be doing what is agreeable to Zeus but disagreeable to Cronos or Uranus, and what is acceptable to Hephaestus but unacceptable to Here, and there may be other gods who have similar differences of opinion.

Euth. But I believe, Socrates, that all the gods would be agreed as to the propriety of punishing a murderer: there would be no difference of opinion about that.

Soc. Well, but speaking of men, Euthyphro, did you ever hear any one arguing that a murderer or any sort of evil-doer ought to be let off?

Euth. I should rather say that these are the questions which they are always arguing, especially in courts of law:

they commit all sorts of crimes, and there is nothing which they will not do or say in their own defence.

Soc. But do they admit their guilt, Euthyphro, and yet say that they ought not to be punished?

Euth. No; they do not.

Soc. Then there are some things which they do not venture to say and do: for they do not venture to argue that the guilty are to be unpunished, but they deny their guilt, do they not?

Euth. Yes.

Soc. Then they do not argue that the evil-doer should not be punished, but they argue about the fact of who the evil-doer is, and what he did and when?

Euth. True.

Soc. And the gods are in the same case, if as you assert they quarrel about just and unjust, and some of them say while others deny that injustice is done among them. For surely neither God nor man will ever venture to say that the doer of injustice is not to be punished?

Euth. That is true, Socrates, in the main.

Soc. But they join issue about the particulars—gods and men alike; and, if they dispute at all, they dispute about some act which is called in question, and which by some is affirmed to be just, by others to be unjust. Is not that true?

Euth. Quite true.

Soc. Well then, my dear friend Euthyphro, do tell me, for my better instruction and information, what proof have you that in the opinion of all the gods a servant who is guilty of murder, and is put in chains by the master of the dead man, and dies because he is put in chains before he who bound him can learn from the interpreters of the gods what he ought to do with him, dies unjustly; and that on behalf of such a one a son ought to proceed against his father and accuse him of murder. How would you show that all the gods absolutely agree in approving of his act? Prove to me

Euthyphro

that they do, and I will applaud your wisdom as long as I live.

Euth. It will be a difficult task; but I could make the matter very clear indeed to you.

Soc. I understand; you mean to say that I am not so quick of apprehension as the judges: for to them you will be sure to prove that the act is unjust, and hateful to the gods.

Euth. Yes indeed, Socrates; at least if they will listen to me.

Soc. But they will be sure to listen if they find that you are a good speaker. There was a notion that came into my mind while you were speaking; I said to myself: "Well, and what if Euthyphro does prove to me that all the gods regarded the death of the serf as unjust, how do I know anything more of the nature of piety and impiety? for granting that this action may be hateful to the gods, still piety and impiety are not adequately defined by these distinctions, for that which is hateful to the gods has been shown to be also pleasing and dear to them." And therefore, Euthyphro, I do not ask you to prove this; I will suppose, if you like, that all the gods condemn and abominate such an action. But I will amend the definition so far as to say that what all the gods hate is impious, and what they love pious or holy; and what some of them love and others hate is both or neither. Shall this be our definition of piety and impiety?

Euth. Why not, Socrates?

Soc. Why not! certainly, as far as I am concerned, Euthyphro, there is no reason why not. But whether this admission will greatly assist you in the task of instructing me as you promised, is a matter for you to consider.

Euth. Yes, I should say that what all the gods love is pious and holy, and the opposite which they all hate, impious.

Soc. Ought we to enquire into the truth of this, Euthyphro, or simply to accept the mere statement on our own authority and that of others? What do you say?

153

Euth. We should enquire; and I believe that the statement will stand the test of enquiry.

Soc. We shall know better, my good friend, in a little while. The point which I should first wish to understand is whether the pious or holy is beloved by the gods because it is holy, or holy because it is beloved of the gods.

Euth. I do not understand your meaning, Socrates.

Soc. I will endeavour to explain: we speak of carrying and we speak of being carried, of leading and being led, seeing and being seen. You know that in all such cases there is a difference, and you know also in what the difference lies?

Euth. I think that I understand.

Soc. And is not that which is beloved distinct from that which loves?

Euth. Certainly.

Soc. Well; and now tell me, is that which is carried in this state of carrying because it is carried, or for some other reason?

Euth. No; that is the reason.

Soc. And the same is true of what is led and of what is seen?

Euth. True.

Soc. And a thing is not seen because it is visible, but conversely, visible because it is seen; nor is a thing led because it is in the state of being led, or carried because it is in the state of being carried, but the converse of this. And now I think, Euthyphro, that my meaning will be intelligible; and my meaning is, that any state of action or passion implies previous action or passion. It does not become because it is becoming, but it is in a state of becoming because it becomes; neither does it suffer because it is in a state of suffering, but it is in a state of suffering because it suffers. Do you not agree?

Euth. Yes.

Euthyphro

Soc. Is not that which is loved in some state either of becoming or suffering?

Euth. Yes.

Soc. And the same holds as in the previous instances; the state of being loved follows the act of being loved, and not the act the state.

Euth. Certainly.

Soc. And what do you say of piety, Euthyphro: is not piety, according to your definition, loved by all the gods?

Euth. Yes.

Soc. Because it is pious or holy, or for some other reason?

Euth. No, that is the reason.

Soc. It is loved because it is holy, not holy because it is loved?

Euth. Yes.

Soc. And that which is dear to the gods is loved by them, and is in a state to be loved of them because it is loved of them?

Euth. Certainly.

Soc. Then that which is dear to the gods, Euthyphro, is not holy, nor is that which is holy loved of God, as you affirm; but they are two different things.

Euth. How do you mean, Socrates?

Soc. I mean to say that the holy has been acknowledged by us to be loved of God because it is holy, not to be holy because it is loved.

Euth. Yes.

Soc. But that which is dear to the gods is dear to them because it is loved by them, not loved by them because it is dear to them.

Euth. True.

Soc. But, friend Euthyphro, if that which is holy is the same with that which is dear to God, and is loved because it is holy, then that which is dear to God would have been loved as being dear to God; but if that which is dear to God is dear to him because loved by him, then that which is holy would have been holy because loved by him. But now you see that the reverse is the case, and that they are quite different from one another. For one (θεοφιλὲς) is of a kind to be loved because it is loved, and the other (ὅσιον) is loved because it is of a kind to be loved. Thus you appear to me, Euthyphro, when I ask you what is the essence of holiness, to offer an attribute only, and not the essence—the attribute of being loved by all the gods. But you still refuse to explain to me the nature of holiness. And therefore, if you please, I will ask you not to hide your treasure, but to tell me once more what holiness or piety really is, whether dear to the gods or not (for that is a matter about which we will not quarrel); and what is impiety?

Euth. I really do not know, Socrates, how to express what I mean. For somehow or other our arguments, on whatever ground we rest them, seem to turn round and walk away from us.

Soc. Your words, Euthyphro, are like the handiwork of my ancestor Daedalus; and if I were the sayer or propounder of them, you might say that my arguments walk away and will not remain fixed where they are placed because I am a descendant of his. But now, since these notions are your own, you must find some other gibe, for they certainly, as you yourself allow, show an inclination to be on the move.

Euth. Nay, Socrates, I shall still say that you are the Daedalus who sets arguments in motion; not I, certainly, but you make them move or go round, for they would never have stirred, as far as I am concerned.

Soc. Then I must be a greater than Daedalus: for whereas he only made his own inventions to move, I move those of other people as well. And the beauty of it is, that I would rather not. For I would give the wisdom of Daedalus, and the wealth of Tantalus, to be able to detain them and keep them fixed. But enough of this. As I perceive that you are

Euthyphro

lazy, I will myself endeavor to show you how you might instruct me in the nature of piety; and I hope that you will not grudge your labour. Tell me, then—Is not that which is pious necessarily just?

Euth. Yes.

Soc. And is, then, all which is just pious? or, is that which is pious all just, but that which is just, only in part and not all, pious?

Euth. I do not understand you, Socrates.

Soc. And yet I know that you are as much wiser than I am, as you are younger. But, as I was saying, revered friend, the abundance of your wisdom makes you lazy. Please to exert yourself, for there is no real difficulty in understanding me. What I mean I may explain by an illustration of what I do not mean. The poet (Stasinus) sings—

Of Zeus, the author and creator of all these things,
You will not tell: for where there is fear there is also reverence.

Now I disagree with this poet. Shall I tell you in what respect?

Euth. By all means.

Soc. I should not say that where there is fear there is also reverence; for I am sure that many persons fear poverty and disease, and the like evils, but I do not perceive that they reverence the objects of their fear.

Euth. Very true.

Soc. But where reverence is, there is fear; for he who has a feeling of reverence and shame about the commission of any action, fears and is afraid of an ill reputation.

Euth. No doubt.

Soc. Then we are wrong in saying that where there is fear there is also reverence; and we should say, where there is reverence there is also fear. But there is not always reverence where there is fear; for fear is a more extended notion, and reverence is a part of fear, just as the odd is a part of number,

157

and number is a more extended notion than the odd. I suppose that you follow me now?

Euth. Quite well.

Soc. That was the sort of question which I meant to raise when I asked whether the just is always the pious, or the pious always the just; and whether there may not be justice where there is not piety; for justice is the more extended notion of which piety is only a part. Do you dissent?

Euth. No, I think that you are quite right.

Soc. Then, if piety is a part of justice, I suppose that we should enquire what part? If you had pursued the enquiry in the previous cases; for instance, if you had asked me what is an even number, and what part of number the even is, I should have had no difficulty in replying, a number which represents a figure having two equal sides. Do you not agree?

Euth. Yes, I quite agree.

Soc. In like manner, I want you to tell me what part of justice is piety or holiness, that I may be able to tell Meletus not to do me injustice, or indict me for impiety, as I am now adequately instructed by you in the nature of piety or holiness, and their opposites.

Euth. Piety or holiness, Socrates, appears to me to be that part of justice which attends to the gods, as there is the other part of justice which attends to men.

Soc. That is good, Euthyphro; yet still there is a little point about which I should like to have further information, What is the meaning of "attention"? For attention can hardly be used in the same sense when applied to the gods as when applied to other things. For instance, horses are said to require attention, and not every person is able to attend to them, but only a person skilled in horsemanship. Is it not so?

Euth. Certainly.

Soc. I should suppose that the art of horsemanship is the art of attending to horses?

Euth. Yes.

158

Euthyphro

Soc. Nor is every one qualified to attend to dogs, but only the huntsman?

Euth. True.

Soc. And I should also conceive that the art of the huntsman is the art of attending to dogs?

Euth. Yes.

Soc. As the art of the oxherd is the art of attending to oxen?

Euth. Very true.

Soc. In like manner holiness or piety is the art of attending to the gods?—that would be your meaning, Euthyphro?

Euth. Yes.

Soc. And is not attention always designed for the good or benefit of that to which the attention is given? As in the case of horses, you may observe that when attended to by the horseman's art they are benefited and improved, are they not?

Euth. True.

Soc. As the dogs are benefited by the huntsman's art, and the oxen by the art of the oxherd, and all other things are tended or attended for their good and not for their hurt?

Euth. Certainly, not for their hurt.

Soc. But for their good?

Euth. Of course.

Soc. And does piety or holiness, which has been defined to be the art of attending to the gods, benefit or improve them? Would you say that when you do a holy act you make any of the gods better?

Euth. No, no; that was certainly not what I meant.

Soc. And I, Euthyphro, never supposed that you did. I asked you the question about the nature of the attention, because I thought that you did not.

Euth. You do me justice, Socrates; that is not the sort of attention which I mean.

Soc. Good: but I must still ask what is this attention to the gods which is called piety?

159

Euth. It is such, Socrates, as servants show to their masters.

Soc. I understand—a sort of ministration to the gods.

Euth. Exactly.

Soc. Medicine is also a sort of ministration or service, having in view the attainment of some object—would you not say of health?

Euth. I should.

Soc. Again, there is an art which ministers to the shipbuilder with a view to the attainment of some result?

Euth. Yes, Socrates, with a view to the building of a ship.

Soc. As there is an art which ministers to the housebuilder with a view to the building of a house?

Euth. Yes.

Soc. And now tell me, my good friend, about the art which ministers to the gods: what work does that help to accomplish? For you must surely know if, as you say, you are of all men living the one who is best instructed in religion.

Euth. And I speak the truth, Socrates.

Soc. Tell me then, oh tell me—what is that fair work which the gods do by the help of our ministrations?

Euth. Many and fair, Socrates, are the works which they do.

Soc. Why, my friend, and so are those of a general. But the chief of them is easily told. Would you not say that victory in war is the chief of them?

Euth. Certainly.

Soc. Many and fair, too, are the works of the husbandman, if I am not mistaken; but his chief work is the production of food from the earth?

Euth. Exactly.

Soc. And of the many and fair things done by the gods, which is the chief or principal one?

Euth. I have told you already, Socrates, that to learn all these things accurately will be very tiresome. Let me simply say that piety or holiness is learning how to please the gods in word and deed, by prayers and sacrifices. Such piety is the salvation of families and states, just as the impious, which is unpleasing to the gods, is their ruin and destruction.

Soc. I think that you could have answered in much fewer words the chief question which I asked, Euthyphro, if you had chosen. But I see plainly that you are not disposed to instruct me—clearly not: else why, when we reached the point, did you turn aside? Had you only answered me I should have truly learned of you by this time the nature of piety. Now, as the asker of a question is necessarily dependent on the answerer, whither he leads I must follow; and can only ask again, what is the pious and what is piety? Do you mean that they are a sort of science of praying and sacrificing?

Euth. Yes, I do.

Soc. And sacrificing is giving to the gods, and prayer is asking of the gods?

Euth. Yes, Socrates.

Soc. Upon this view, then, piety is a science of asking and giving?

Euth. You understand me capitally, Socrates.

Soc. Yes, my friend; the reason is that I am a votary of your science, and give my mind to it, and therefore nothing which you say will be thrown away upon me. Please then to tell me, what is the nature of this service to the gods? Do you mean that we prefer requests and give gifts to them?

Euth. Yes, I do.

Soc. Is not the right way of asking to ask of them what we want?

Euth. Certainly.

Soc. And the right way of giving is to give to them in return. Men give what they want of us. There would be no meaning in an art which gives to any one that which he does not want.

Euth. Very true, Socrates.

Soc. Then piety, Euthyphro, is an art which gods and men have of doing business with one another?

Euth. That is an expression which you may use, if you like.

Soc. But I have no particular liking for anything but the truth. I wish, however, that you would tell me what benefit accrues to the gods from our gifts. There is no doubt about what they give to us; for there is no good thing which they do not give; but how we can give any good thing to them in return is far from being equally clear. If they give everything and we give nothing, that must be an affair of business in which we have very greatly the advantage of them.

Euth. And do you imagine, Socrates, that any benefit accrues to the gods from our gifts?

Soc. But if not, Euthyphro, what is the meaning of gifts which are conferred by us upon the gods?

Euth. What else, but tributes of honour; and, as I was just now saying, what pleases them?

Soc. Piety, then, is pleasing to the gods, but not beneficial or dear to them?

Euth. I should say that nothing could be dearer.

Soc. Then once more the assertion is repeated that piety is dear to the gods?

Euth. Certainly.

Soc. And when you say this, can you wonder at your words not standing firm, but walking away? Will you accuse me of being the Daedalus who makes them walk away, not perceiving that there is another and far greater artist than Daedalus who makes them go round in a circle, and he is yourself; for the argument, as you will perceive, comes round to the same point. Were we not saying that the holy or pious was not the same with that which is loved of the gods? Have you forgotten?

Euth. I quite remember.

Soc. And are you not saying that what is loved of the gods

Euthyphro

is holy; and is not this the same as what is dear to them—do you see?

Euth. True.

Soc. Then either we were wrong in our former assertion; or, if we were right then, we are wrong now.

Euth. One of the two must be true.

Soc. Then we must begin again and ask, What is piety? That is an enquiry which I shall never be weary of pursuing as far as in me lies; and I entreat you not to scorn me, but to apply your mind to the utmost, and tell me the truth. For, if any man knows, you are he; and therefore I must detain you, like Proteus, until you tell. If you had not certainly known the nature of piety and impiety, I am confident that you would never, on behalf of a serf, have charged your aged father with murder. You would not have run such a risk of doing wrong in the sight of the gods, and you would have had too much respect for the opinions of men. I am sure, therefore, that you know the nature of piety and impiety. Speak out then, my dear Euthyphro, and do not hide your knowledge.

Euth. Another time, Socrates; for I am in a hurry, and must go now.

Soc. Alas! my companion, and will you leave me in despair? I was hoping that you would instruct me in the nature of piety and impiety; and then I might have cleared myself of Meletus and his indictment. I would have told him that I had been enlightened by Euthyphro, and had given up rash innovations and speculations, in which I indulged only through ignorance, and that now I am about to lead a better life.

Aristotle

Politics

BOOK I, CHAPTERS 1, 2

Every state is a community of some kind, and every community is established with a view to some good; for mankind always act in order to obtain that which they think good. But, if all communities aim at some good, the state or political community, which is the highest of all, and which embraces all the rest, aims, and in a greater degree than any other, at the highest good.

Some people think[1] that the qualifications of a statesman, king, householder, and master are the same, and that they differ, not in kind, but only in the number of their subjects. For example, the ruler over a few is called a master; over more, the manager of a household; over a still larger number, a statesman or king, as if there were no difference between a great household and a small state. The distinction which is made between the king and the statesman is as follows: When the government is personal, the ruler is a king; when, according to the rules of political science, the citizens rule and are ruled in turn, then he is called a statesman.

But all this is a mistake; for governments differ in kind, as will be evident to any one who considers the matter according to the method[2] which has hitherto guided us. As in

[1] Cp. Plato, Politicus, 258 E-259 D.
[2] Cp. 1256ᵃ 2.

other departments of science, so in politics, the compound should always be resolved into the simple elements or at least parts of the whole. We must therefore look at the elements of which the state is composed, in order that we may see in what the different kinds of rule differ from one another, and whether any scientific result can be attained about each one of them.

He who thus considers things in their first growth and origin, whether a state or anything else, will obtain the clearest view of them. In the first place there must be a union of those who cannot exist without each other, namely, of male and female, that the race may continue (and this is a union which is formed, not of deliberate purpose, but because, in common with other animals and with plants, mankind have a natural desire to leave behind them an image of themselves), and of natural ruler and subject, that both may be preserved. For that which can foresee by the exercise of the mind is by nature intended to be lord and master, and that which can with its body give effect to such foresight is a subject, and by nature a slave; hence master and slave have the same interest. Now nature has distinguished between the female and the slave. For she is not niggardly, like the smith who fashions the Delphian knife for many uses; she makes each thing for a single use, and every instrument is best when intended for one and not for many uses. But among barbarians no distinction is made between women and slaves, because there is no natural ruler among them: they are a community of slaves, male and female. Wherefore the poets say—

It is meet that Hellenes should rule over barbarians;[3]
as if they thought that the barbarian and the slave were by nature one.

Out of these two relationships between man and woman,

---

[3] Eurip. *Iphig. in Aul.* 1400.

master and slave, the first thing to arise is the family, and
Hesiod is right when he says—

First house and wife and an ox for the plough,[4]

for the ox is the poor man's slave. The family is the association established by nature for the supply of men's everyday
wants, and the members of it are called by Charondas "companions of the cupboard," and by Epimenides the Cretan,"
"companions of the manger." But when several families are
united, and the association aims at something more than the
supply of daily needs, the first society to be formed is the village. And the most natural form of the village appears to be
that of a colony from the family, composed of the children
and grandchildren, who are said to be "suckled with the same
milk." And this is the reason why Hellenic states were originally governed by kings; because the Hellenes were under
royal rule before they came together, as the barbarians still
are. Every family is ruled by the eldest, and therefore in the
colonies of the family the kingly form of government prevailed because they were of the same blood. As Homer says:[5]

Each one gives law to his children and to his wives.

For they lived dispersedly, as was the manner in ancient
times. Wherefore men say that the Gods have a king, because
they themselves either are or were in ancient times under the
rule of a king. For they imagine, not only the forms of the
Gods, but their ways of life to be like their own.

When several villages are united in a single complete community, large enough to be nearly or quite self-sufficing, the
state comes into existence, originating in the bare needs of
life, and continuing in existence for the sake of a good life.

[4] *Op. et Di.* 405.
[5] *Od.* ix. 114, quoted by Plato, *Laws,* iii. 680 B, and in N. Eth. x.
1180ᵃ 28.

And therefore, if the earlier forms of society are natural, so is the state, for it is the end of them, and the nature of a thing is its end. For what each thing is when fully developed, we call its nature, whether we are speaking of a man, a horse, or a family. Besides, the final cause and end of a thing is the best, and to be self-sufficing is the end and the best.

Hence it is evident that the state is a creation of nature, and that man is by nature a political animal. And he who by nature and not by mere accident is without a state, is either a bad man or above humanity; he is like the

> Tribeless, lawless, heartless one,

whom Homer[6] denounces—the natural outcast is forthwith a lover of war; he may be compared to an isolated piece at draughts.

Now, that man is more of a political animal than bees or any other gregarious animals is evident. Nature, as we often say, makes nothing in vain,[7] and man is the only animal whom she has endowed with the gift of speech.[8] And whereas mere voice is but an indication of pleasure or pain, and is therefore found in other animals (for their nature attains to the perception of pleasure and pain and the intimation of them to one another, and no further), the power of speech is intended to set forth the expedient and inexpedient, and therefore likewise the just and the unjust. And it is a characteristic of man that he alone has any sense of good and evil, of just and unjust, and the like, and the association of living beings who have this sense makes a family and a state.

Further, the state is by nature clearly prior to the family and to the individual, since the whole is of necessity prior

---

[6] Il. ix. 63.
[7] Co. 1256ᵇ 20.
[8] Cp. vii. 1332ᵇ 5.

to the part; for example, if the whole body be destroyed, there will be no foot or hand, except in an equivocal sense, as we might speak of a stone hand; for when destroyed the hand will be no better than that. But things are defined by their working and power; and we ought not to say that they are the same when they no longer have their proper quality, but only that they have the same name. The proof that the state is a creation of nature and prior to the individual is that the individual, when isolated, is not self-sufficing; and therefore he is like a part in relation to the whole. But he who is unable to live in society, or who has no need because he is sufficient for himself, must be either a beast or a god: he is no part of a state. A social instinct is implanted in all men by nature, and yet he who first founded the state was the greatest of benefactors. For man, when perfected, is the best of animals, but, when separated from law and justice, he is the worst of all; since armed injustice is the more dangerous, and he is equipped at birth with arms, meant to be used by intelligence and virtue, which he may use for the worst ends. Wherefore, if he have not virtue, he is the most unholy and the most savage of animals, and the most full of lust and gluttony. But justice is the bond of men in states, for the administration of justice, which is the determination of what is just,[9] is the principle of order in political society.

BOOK VII, CHAPTERS 1, 3

He who would duly inquire about the best form of a state ought first to determine which is the most eligible life; while this remains uncertain the best form of the state must also be uncertain; for, in the natural order of things, those may be expected to lead the best life who are governed in the best manner of which their circumstances admit. We ought

[9] Cp. N. Eth. v. 1134² 31.

therefore to ascertain, first of all, which is the most generally eligible life, and then whether the same life is or is not best for the state and for individuals.

Assuming that enough has been already said in discussions outside the school concerning the best life, we will now only repeat what is contained in them. Certainly no one will dispute the propriety of that partition of goods which separates them into three classes,[1] viz. external goods, goods of the body, and goods of the soul, or deny that the happy man must have all three. For no one would maintain that he is happy who has not in him a particle of courage or temperance or justice or prudence, who is afraid of every insect which flutters past him, and will commit any crime, however great, in order to gratify his lust of meat and drink, who will sacrifice his dearest friend for the sake of a half-a-farthing, and is as feeble and false in mind as a child or a madman. These propositions are almost universally acknowledged as soon as they are uttered, but men differ about the degree or relative superiority of this or that good. Some think that a very moderate amount of virtue is enough, but set no limit to their desires of wealth, property, power, reputation, and the like. To whom we reply by an appeal to facts, which easily prove that mankind do not acquire or preserve virtue by the help of external goods, but external goods by the help of virtue, and that happiness, whether consisting in pleasure or virtue, or both, is more often found with those who are most highly cultivated in their mind and in their character, and have only a moderate share of external goods, than among those who possess external goods to a useless extent, but are deficient in higher qualities; and this is not only matter of experience, but, if reflected upon, will easily appear to be in accordance with reason. For, whereas external goods

[1] Cp. *Laws,* iii. 697 B, V. 713 E; *N. Eth.* i. 1098[b] 12.

ARISTOTLE

have a limit, like any other instrument,[2] and all things useful
are of such a nature that where there is too much of them
they must either do harm, or at any rate be of no use, to their
possessors, every good of the soul, the greater it is, is also
of greater use, if the epithet useful as well as noble is appropriate to such subjects. No proof is required to show that
the best state of one thing in relation to another corresponds
in degree of excellence to the interval between the natures
of which we say that these very states are states: so that, if
the soul is more noble than our possessions or our bodies,
both absolutely and in relation to us, it must be admitted
that the best state of either has a similar ratio to the other.
Again, it is for the sake of the soul that goods external and
goods of the body are eligible at all, and all wise men ought
to choose them for the sake of the soul, and not the soul
for the sake of them.

Let us acknowledge then that each one has just so much
of happiness as he has of virtue and wisdom, and of virtuous
and wise action. God is a witness to us of this truth, for he
is happy and blessed, not by reason of any external good, but
in himself and by reason of his own nature. And herein of
necessity lies the difference between good fortune and happiness; for external goods come of themselves, and chance is
the author of them, but no one is just or temperate by or
through chance. In like manner, and by a similar train of
argument, the happy state may be shown to be that which is
best and which acts rightly; and rightly it cannot act without
doing right actions, and neither individual nor state can do
right actions without virtue and wisdom. Thus the courage,
justice, and wisdom of a state have the same form and nature
as the qualities which give the individual who possesses them
the name of just, wise, or temperate.

Thus much may suffice by way of preface: for I could

[2] Cp. i. 1256[b] 35.

170

not avoid touching upon these questions, neither could I go through all the arguments affecting them; these are the business of another science.

Let us assume then that the best life, both for individuals and states, is the life of virtue, when virtue has external goods enough for the performance of good actions. If there are any who controvert our assertion, we will in this treatise pass them over, and consider their objections hereafter.

There remains to be discussed the question, Whether the happiness of the individual is the same as that of the state, or different? Here again there can be no doubt—no one denies that they are the same. For those who hold that the well-being of the individual consists in his wealth, also think that riches make the happiness of the whole state, and those who value most highly the life of a tyrant deem that city the happiest which rules over the greatest number; while they who approve an individual for his virtue say that the more virtuous a city is, the happier it is. Two points here present themselves for consideration: first (1), which is the more eligible life, that of a citizen who is a member of a state, or that of an alien who has no political ties; and again (2), which is the best form of constitution or the best condition of a state, either on the supposition that political privileges are desirable for all, or for a majority only? Since the good of the state and not of the individual is the proper subject of political thought and speculation, and we are engaged in political discussion, while the first of these two points has a secondary interest for us, the latter will be the main subject of the inquiry.

Now it is evident that the form of government is best in which every man, whoever he is, can act for the best and live happily. But even those who agree in thinking that the life of virtue is the most eligible raise a question, whether the life of business and politics is or is not more eligible than one which is wholly independent of external goods, I mean

171

than a contemplative life, which by some is maintained to be the only one worthy of a philosopher. For these two lives —the life of the philosopher and the life of the statesman— appear to have been preferred by those who have been most keen in the pursuit of virtue, both in our own and in other ages. Which is the better is a question of no small moment; for the wise man, like the wise state, will necessarily regulate his life according to the best end. There are some who think that while a despotic rule over others is the greatest injustice, to exercise a constitutional rule over them, even though not unjust, is a great impediment to a man's individual well-being. Others take an opposite view; they maintain that the true life of man is the practical and political, and that every virtue admits of being practiced, quite as much by statesmen and rulers as by private individuals. Others, again, are of the opinion that arbitrary and tyrannical rule alone consists with happiness; indeed, in some states the entire aim both of the laws and of the constitution is to give men despotic power over their neighbors. And, therefore, although in most cities the laws may be said generally to be in a chaotic state, still, if they aim at anything, they aim at the maintenance of power: thus in Lacedaemon and Crete the system of education and the greater part of the laws are framed with a view to war.[3] And in all nations which are able to gratify their ambition military power is held in esteem, for example among the Scythians and Persians and Thracians and Celts. In some nations there are even laws tending to stimulate the warlike virtues, as at Carthage, where we are told that men obtain the honour of wearing as many armlets as they have served campaigns. There was once a law in Macedonia that he who had not killed an enemy should wear a halter, and among the Scythians no one who had not slain his man was allowed to drink out of the cup which was handed round at

[3] Cp. Plato, Laws, i. 633 ff.

a certain feast. Among the Iberians, a warlike nation, the number of enemies whom a man has slain is indicated by the number of obelisks which are fixed in the earth round his tomb; and there are numerous practices among other nations of a like kind, some of them established by law and others by custom. Yet to a reflecting mind it must appear very strange that the statesman should be always considering how he can dominate and tyrannize over others, whether they will or not. How can that which is not even lawful be the business of the statesman or the legislator? Unlawful it certainly is to rule without regard to justice, for there may be might where there is no right. The other arts and sciences offer no parallel; a physician is not expected to persuade or coerce his patients, nor a pilot the passengers in his ship. Yet most men appear to think that the art of despotic government is statesmanship, and what men affirm to be unjust and inexpedient in their own case they are not ashamed of practicing towards others; they demand just rule for themselves, but where other men are concerned they care nothing about it. Such behaviour is irrational; unless the one party is, and the other is not, born to serve, in which case men have a right to command, not indeed all their fellows, but only those who are intended to be subjects; just as we ought not to hunt mankind, whether for food or sacrifice, but only the animals which may be hunted for food or sacrifice, that is to say, such wild animals as are eatable. And surely there may be a city happy in isolation, which we will assume to be well-governed (for it is quite possible that a city thus isolated might be well-administered and have good laws); but such a city would not be constituted with any view to war or the conquest of enemies—all that sort of thing must be excluded. Hence we see very plainly that warlike pursuits, although generally to be deemed honourable, are not the supreme end of all things, but only means. And the good lawgiver should inquire how states and races of men and communities may

173

participate in a good life, and in the happiness which is attainable by them. His enactments will not be always the same; and where there are neighbours[1] he will have to see what sort of studies should be practiced in relation to their several characters, or how the measures appropriate in relation to each are to be adopted. The end at which the best form of government should aim may be properly made a matter of future consideration.[2]

Let us now address those who, while they agree that the life of virtue is the most eligible, differ about the manner of practicing it. For some renounce political power, and think that the life of the free man is different from the life of the statesman and the best of all; but others think the life of the statesman best. The argument of the latter is that he who does nothing cannot do well, and that virtuous activity is identical with happiness. To both we say: "you are partly right and partly wrong." The first class are right in affirming that the life of the freeman is better than the life of the despot; for there is nothing grand or noble in having the use of a slave, in so far as he is a slave; or in issuing commands about necessary things. But it is an error to suppose that every sort of rule is despotic like that of a master over slaves, for there is as great a difference between the rule over freemen and the rule over slaves as there is between slavery by nature and freedom by nature, about which I have said enough at the commencement of this treatise.[3] And it is equally a mistake to place inactivity above action, for happiness is activity, and the actions of the just and wise are the realization of much that is noble.

But perhaps some one, accepting these premises, may still maintain that supreme power is the best of all things, because

[1] Cp. ii. 1265a 20, 1267a 19.
[2] 1333a 11 sqq.
[3] i. 4–7.

174

the possessors of it are able to perform the greatest number of noble actions. If so, the man who is able to rule, instead of giving up anything to his neighbour, ought rather to take away his power; and the father should make no account of his son, nor the son of his father, nor friend of friend; they should not bestow a thought on one another in comparison with this higher object, for the best is the most eligible and "doing well" is the best. There might be some truth in such a view if we assume that robbers and plunderers attain the chief good. But this can never be; their hypothesis is false. For the actions of a ruler cannot really be honourable, unless he is as much superior to other men as a husband is to a wife, or a father to his children, or a master to his slaves. And therefore he who violates the law can never recover by any success, however great, what he has already lost in departing from virtue. For equals share alike in the honourable and the just, as is just and equal. But that the unequal should be given to equals, and the unlike to those who are like, is contrary to nature, and nothing which is contrary to nature is good. If, therefore, there is any one[4] superior in virtue and in the power of performing the best actions, him we ought to follow and obey, but he must have the capacity for action as well as virtue.

If we are right in our view, and happiness is assumed to be virtuous activity, the active life will be the best, both for every city collectively, and for individuals. Not that a life of action must necessarily have relation to others, as some persons think, nor are those ideas only to be regarded as practical which are pursued for the sake of practical results, but much more the thoughts and contemplations which are independent and complete in themselves; since virtuous activity, and therefore a certain kind of action, is an end, and even in the case of external actions the directing mind is most truly

[4] Cp. iii. 1284^a 32 and 1288^a 28.

ARISTOTLE

said to act. Neither, again, is it necessary that states which are cut off from others and choose to live alone should be inactive; for activity, as well as other things, may take place by sections; there are many ways in which the sections of a state act upon one another. The same thing is equally true of every individual. If this were otherwise, God and the universe, who have no external actions over and above their own energies, would be far enough from perfection. Hence it is evident that the same life is best for each individual, and for states and for mankind collectively.

Saint Augustine (354-430)

The City of God

BOOK XIX

IV

WHAT THE CHRISTIANS BELIEVE REGARDING THE SUPREME
GOOD AND EVIL, IN OPPOSITION TO THE PHILOSOPHERS, WHO
HAVE MAINTAINED THAT THE SUPREME GOOD
IS IN THEMSELVES

If, then, we be asked what the city of God has to say upon
these points, and, in the first place, what its opinion regarding
the supreme good and evil is, it will reply that life eternal
is the supreme good, death eternal the supreme evil, and that
to obtain the one and escape the other we must live rightly.
And thus it is written, "The just lives by faith,"[5] for we do
not as yet see our good, and must therefore live by faith;
neither have we in ourselves power to live rightly, but can
do so only if He who has given us faith to believe in His
help does help us when we believe and pray. As for those
who have supposed that the sovereign good and evil are to be
found in this life, and have placed it either in the soul or
the body, or in both, or, to speak more explicitly, either in
pleasure or in virtue, or in both; in repose or in virtue, or
in both; in pleasure and repose, or in virtue, or in all combined; in the primary objects of nature, or in virtue, or in
both—all these have, with a marvelous shallowness, sought

[5] Hab. ii. 4.

to find their blessedness in this life and in themselves. Contempt has been poured upon such ideas by the Truth, saying by the prophet, "The Lord knoweth the thoughts of men" (or, as the Apostle Paul cites the passage, "The Lord knoweth the thoughts of the *wise*") "that they are vain."[6]

For what flood of eloquence can suffice to detail the miseries of this life? Cicero, in the *Consolation* on the death of his daughter, has spent all his ability in lamentation; but how inadequate was even his ability here? For when, where, how, in this life can these primary objects of nature be possessed so that they may not be assailed by unforeseen accidents? Is the body of the wise man exempt from any pain which may dispel pleasure, from any disquietude which may banish repose? The amputation or decay of the members of the body puts an end to its integrity, deformity blights its beauty, weakness its health, lassitude its vigor, sleepiness or sluggishness its activity—and which of these is it that may not assail the flesh of the wise man? Comely and fitting attitudes and movements of the body are numbered among the prime natural blessings; but what if some sickness makes the members tremble? what if a man suffers from curvature of the spine to such an extent that his hands reach the ground, and he goes upon all-fours like a quadruped? Does not this destroy all beauty and grace in the body, whether at rest or in motion? What shall I say of the fundamental blessings of the soul, sense and intellect, of which the one is given for the perception, and the other for the comprehension of truth? But what kind of sense is it that remains when a man becomes deaf and blind? where are reason and intellect when disease makes a man delirious? We can scarcely, or not at all, refrain from tears, when we think of or see the actions and words of such frantic persons, and consider how different from and even opposed to their own sober judgment and

[6] Ps. xciv. II, and I Cor. iii. 20.

ordinary conduct their present demeanor is. And what shall I say of those who suffer from demoniacal possession? Where is their own intelligence hidden and buried while the malignant spirit is using their body and soul according to his own will? And who is quite sure that no such thing can happen to the wise man in this life? Then, as to the perception of truth, what can we hope for even in this way while in the body, as we read in the true book of Wisdom, "The corruptible body weigheth down the soul, and the earthly tabernacle presseth down the mind that museth upon many things?"[7] And eagerness, or desire of action, if this is the right meaning to put upon the Greek ὁρμή, is also reckoned among the primary advantages of nature; and yet is it not this which produces those pitiable movements of the insane, and those actions which we shudder to see, when sense is deceived and reason deranged?

In fine, virtue itself, which is not among the primary objects of nature, but succeeds to them as the result of learning, though it holds the highest place among human good things, what is its occupation save to wage perpetual war with vices—not those that are outside of us, but within; not other men's, but our own—a war which is waged especially by that virtue which the Greeks call σωφροσύνη, and we temperance,[8] and which bridles carnal lusts, and prevents them from winning the consent of the spirit to wicked deeds? For we must not fancy that there is no vice in us, when, as the Apostle says, "The flesh lusteth against the spirit;"[9] for to this vice there is a contrary virtue, when, as the same writer says, "The spirit lusteth against the flesh." "For these two," he says, "are contrary one to the other, so that you cannot do the things which you would." But what is it we wish to do when we seek

[7] Wisdom ix. 15.
[8] Cicero, *Tusc. Quaest.* iii. 8.
[9] Gal. V. 17.

to attain the supreme good, unless that the flesh should cease to lust against the spirit, and that there be no vice in us against which the spirit may lust? And as we cannot attain to this in the present life, however ardently we desire it, let us by God's help accomplish at least this, to preserve the soul from succumbing and yielding to the flesh that lusts against it, and to refuse our consent to the perpetration of sin. Far be it from us, then, to fancy that while we are still engaged in this intestine war, we have already found the happiness which we seek to reach by victory. And who is there so wise that he has no conflict at all to maintain against his vices?

What shall I say of that virtue which is called prudence? Is not all its vigilance spent in the discernment of good from evil things, so that no mistake may be admitted about what we should desire and what avoid? And thus it is itself a proof that we are in the midst of evils, or that evils are in us; for it teaches us that it is an evil to consent to sin, and a good to refuse this consent. And yet this evil, to which prudence teaches and temperance enables us not to consent, is removed from this life neither by prudence nor by temperance. And justice, whose office it is to render to every man his due, whereby there is in man himself a certain just order of nature, so that the soul is subjected to God, and the flesh to the soul, and consequently both soul and flesh to God—does not this virtue demonstrate that it is as yet rather laboring towards its end than resting in its finished work? For the soul is so much the less subjected to God as it is less occupied with the thought of God; and the flesh is so much the less subjected to the spirit as it lusts more vehemently against the spirit. So long, therefore, as we are beset by this weakness, this plague, this disease, how shall we dare to say that we are safe? and if not safe, then how can we be already enjoying our final beatitude? Then that virtue which goes by the name of fortitude is the plainest proof of the ills of life, for it is these ills which it is compelled to bear patiently. And

180

this holds good, no matter though the ripest wisdom co-exists with it. And I am at a loss to understand how the Stoic philosophers can presume to say that these are no ills, though at the same time they allow the wise man to commit suicide and pass out of this life if they become so grievous that he cannot or ought not to endure them. But such is the stupid pride of these men who fancy that the supreme good can be found in this life, and that they can become happy by their own resources, that their wise man, or at least the man whom they fancifully depict as such, is always happy, even though he become blind, deaf, dumb, mutilated, racked with pains, or suffer any conceivable calamity such as may compel him to make away with himself; and they are not ashamed to call the life that is beset with these evils happy. O happy life, which seeks the aid of death to end it? If it is happy, let the wise man remain in it; but if these ills drive him out of it, in what sense is it happy? Or how can they say that these are not evils which conquer the virtue of fortitude, and force it not only to yield, but so to rave that it in one breath calls life happy and recommends it to be given up? For who is so blind as not to see that if it were happy it would not be fled from? And if they say we should flee from it on account of the infirmities that beset it, why then do they not lower their pride and acknowledge that it is miserable? Was it, I would ask, fortitude or weakness which prompted Cato to kill himself? for he would not have done so had he not been too weak to endure Caesar's victory. Where, then, is his fortitude? It has yielded, it has succumbed, it has been so thoroughly overcome as to abandon, forsake, flee this happy life. Or was it no longer happy? Then it was miserable. How, then, were these not evils which made life miserable, and a thing to be escaped from?

And therefore those who admit that these are evils, as the Peripatetics do, and the Old Academy, the sect which Varro advocates, express a more intelligible doctrine; but theirs also is a surprising mistake, for they contend that this is a happy life which is beset by these evils, even though they be so great that he who endures them should commit suicide to escape them. "Pains and anguish of body," says Varro, "are evils, and so much the worse in proportion to their severity; and to escape them you must quit this life." What life, I pray? This life, he says, which is oppressed by such evils. Then it is happy in the midst of these very evils on account of which you say we must quit it? Or do you call it happy because you are at liberty to escape these evils by death? What, then, if by some secret judgment of God you were held fast and not permitted to die, nor suffered to live without these evils? In that case, at least, you would say that such a life was miserable. It is soon relinquished, no doubt, but this does not make it not miserable; for were it eternal, you yourself would pronounce it miserable. Its brevity, therefore, does not clear it of misery; neither ought it to be called happiness because it is a brief misery. Certainly there is a mighty force in these evils which compel a man—according to them, even a wise man—to cease to be a man that he may escape them, though they say, and say truly, that it is as it were the first and strongest demand of nature that a man cherish himself, and naturally therefore avoid death, and should so stand his own friend as to wish and vehemently aim at continuing to exist as a living creature, and subsisting in this union of soul and body. There is a mighty force in these evils to overcome this natural instinct by which death is by every means and with all a man's efforts avoided, and to overcome it so completely that what was avoided is desired, sought after, and if it cannot in any other way be obtained, is inflicted by the man on himself. There is a mighty force in these evils which make fortitude a homicide—if, indeed, that is to be called fortitude which is so thoroughly overcome by these evils, that it not only cannot preserve by patience the man whom it undertook to govern

182

and defend, but is itself obliged to kill him. The wise man, I admit, ought to bear death with patience, but when it is inflicted by another. If, then, as these men maintain, he is obliged to inflict it on himself, certainly it must be owned that the ills, which compel him to this are not only evils, but intolerable evils. The life, then, which is either subject to accidents, or environed with evils so considerable and grievous, could never have been called happy, if the men who give it this name had condescended to yield to the truth, and to be conquered by valid arguments, when they inquired after the happy life, as they yield to unhappiness, and are overcome by overwhelming evils, when they put themselves to death, and if they had not fancied that the supreme good was to be found in this mortal life; for the very virtues of this life, which are certainly its best and most useful possessions, are all the more telling proofs of its miseries in proportion as they are helpful against the violence of its dangers, toils, and woes. For if these are true virtues—and such cannot exist save in those who have true piety—they do not profess to be able to deliver the men who possess them from all miseries; for true virtues tell no such lies, but they profess that by the hope of the future world this life, which is miserably involved in the many and great evils of this world, is happy as it is also safe. For if not yet safe, how could it be happy? And therefore the Apostle Paul, speaking not of men without prudence, temperance, fortitude, and justice, but of those whose lives were regulated by true piety, and whose virtues were therefore true, says, "For we are saved by hope: now hope which is seen is not hope; for what a man seeth, why doth he yet hope for? But if we hope for that we see not, then do we with patience wait for it."[10] As, therefore, we are saved, so we are made happy by hope. And as we do not as yet possess a present, but look for a future salvation,

[10] Rom. viii. 24.

so is it with our happiness, and this "with patience"; for we are encompassed with evils, which we ought patiently to endure, until we come to the ineffable enjoyment of unmixed good; for there shall be no longer anything to endure. Salvation, such as it shall be in the world to come, shall itself be our final happiness. And this happiness these philosophers refuse to believe in, because they do not see it, and attempt to fabricate for themselves a happiness in this life, based upon a virtue which is as deceitful as it is proud.

V

OF THE SOCIAL LIFE, WHICH, THOUGH MOST DESIRABLE, IS FREQUENTLY DISTURBED BY MANY DISTRESSES

We give a much more unlimited approval to their idea that the life of the wise man must be social. For how could the city of God (concerning which we are already writing no less than the nineteenth book of this work) either take a beginning or be developed, or attain its proper destiny, if the life of the saints were not a social life? But who can enumerate all the great grievances with which human society abounds in the misery of this mortal state? Who can weigh them? Hear how one of their comic writers makes one of his characters express the common feelings of all men in this matter: "I am married; this is one misery. Children are born to me; they are additional cares."[11] What shall I say of the miseries of love which Terence also recounts—"slights, suspicions, quarrels, war to-day, peace to-morrow?"[12] Is not human life full of such things? Do they not often occur even in honorable friendships? On all hands we experience these slights, suspicions, quarrels, war, all of which are undoubted

[11] Terent. *Adelph.* v. 4.
[12] *Eunuch,* i. I.

evils; while, on the other hand, peace is a doubtful good, because we do not know the heart of our friend, and though we did know it to-day, we should be as ignorant of what it might be to-morrow. Who ought to be, or who are more friendly than those who live in the same family? And yet who can rely even upon this friendship, seeing that secret treachery has often broken it up, and produced enmity as bitter as the amity was sweet, or seemed sweet by the most perfect dissimulation? It is on this account that the words of Cicero so move the heart of every one, and provoke a sigh: "There are no snares more dangerous than those which lurk under the guise of duty or the name of relationship. For the man who is your declared foe you can easily baffle by precaution; but this hidden, intestine, and domestic danger not merely exists, but overwhelms you before you can foresee and examine it."[13] It is also to this that allusion is made by the divine saying, "A man's foes are those of his own household"[14]—words which one cannot hear without pain; for though a man have sufficient fortitude to endure it with equanimity, and sufficient sagacity to baffle the malice of a pretended friend, yet if he himself is a good man, he cannot but be greatly pained at the discovery of the perfidy of wicked men, whether they have always been wicked and merely feigned goodness, or have fallen from a better to a malicious disposition. If, then, home, the natural refuge from the ills of life, is itself not safe, what shall we say of the city, which, as it is larger, is so much the more filled with lawsuits civil and criminal, and is never free from the fear, if sometimes from the actual outbreak, of disturbing and bloody insurrections and civil wars?

[13] *In Verrem,* ii. I. 15.
[14] Matt. x. 36.

ST. AUGUSTINE

VI

OF THE ERROR OF HUMAN JUDGMENTS WHEN THE TRUTH
IS HIDDEN

What shall I say of these judgments which men pronounce
on men, and which are necessary in communities, whatever
outward peace they enjoy? Melancholy and lamentable judgments they are, since the judges are men who cannot discern
the consciences of those at their bar, and are therefore frequently compelled to put innocent witnesses to the torture
to ascertain the truth regarding the crimes of other men.
What shall I say of torture applied to the accused himself?
He is tortured to discover whether he is guilty, so that,
though innocent, he suffers most undoubted punishment for
crime that is still doubtful, not because it is proved that he
committed it, but because it is not ascertained that he did
not commit it. Thus the ignorance of the judge frequently
involves an innocent person in suffering. And what is still
more unendurable—a thing, indeed, to be bewailed, and, if
that were possible, watered with fountains of tears—is this,
that when the judge puts the accused to the question, that
he may not unwittingly put an innocent man to death, the
result of this lamentable ignorance is that this very person,
whom he tortured that he might not condemn him if innocent, is condemned to death both tortured and innocent. For
if he has chosen, in obedience to the philosophical instruc-
tions to the wise man, to quit this life rather than endure
any longer such tortures, he declares that he has committed
the crime which in fact he has not committed. And when he
has been condemned and put to death, the judge is still
in ignorance whether he has put to death an innocent or a
guilty person, though he put the accused to the torture for
the very purpose of saving himself from condemning the
innocent; and consequently he has both tortured an innocent

186

man to discover his innocence, and has put him to death without discovering it. If such darkness shrouds social life, will a wise judge take his seat on the bench or no? Beyond question he will. For human society, which he thinks it a wickedness to abandon, constrains him and compels him to this duty. And he thinks it no wickedness that innocent witnesses are tortured regarding the crimes of which other men are accused; or that the accused are put to the torture, so that they are often overcome with anguish, and, though innocent, make false confessions regarding themselves, and are punished; or that, though they be not condemned to die, they often die during, or in consequence of, the torture; or that sometimes the accusers, who perhaps have been prompted by a desire to benefit society by bringing criminals to justice, are themselves condemned through the ignorance of the judge, because they are unable to prove the truth of their accusations though they are true, and because the witnesses lie, and the accused endures the torture without being moved to confession. These numerous and important evils he does not consider sins; for the wise judge does these things, not with any intention of doing harm, but because his ignorance compels him, and because human society claims him as a judge. But though we therefore acquit the judge of malice, we must none the less condemn human life as miserable. And if he is compelled to torture and punish the innocent because his office and his ignorance constrain him, is he a happy as well as a guiltless man? Surely it were proof of more profound considerateness and finer feeling were he to recognize the misery of these necessities, and shrink from his own implication in that misery; and had he any piety about him, he would cry to God "From my necessities deliver Thou me."[15]

[15] Ps. xxv. 17.

VII

OF THE DIVERSITY OF LANGUAGES, BY WHICH THE INTERCOURSE OF MEN IS PREVENTED; AND OF THE MISERY OF WARS, EVEN OF THOSE CALLED JUST

After the state or city comes the world, the third circle of human society—the first being the house, and the second the city. And the world, as it is larger, so it is fuller of dangers, as the greater sea is the more dangerous. And here, in the first place, man is separated from man by the difference of languages. For if two men, each ignorant of the other's language, meet, and are not compelled to pass, but, on the contrary, to remain in company, dumb animals, though of different species, would more easily hold intercourse than they, human beings though they be. For their common nature is no help to friendliness when they are prevented by diversity of language from conveying their sentiments to one another; so that a man would more readily hold intercourse with his dog than with a foreigner. But the imperial city has endeavored to impose on subject nations not only her yoke, but her language, as a bond of peace, so that interpreters, far from being scarce, are numberless. This is true; but how many great wars, how much slaughter and bloodshed, have provided this unity! And though these are past, the end of these miseries has not yet come. For though there have never been wanting, nor are yet wanting, hostile nations beyond the empire, against whom wars have been and are waged, yet, supposing there were no such nations, the very extent of the empire itself has produced wars of a more obnoxious description—social and civil wars—and with these the whole race has been agitated, either by the actual conflict or the fear of a renewed outbreak. If I attempted to give an adequate description of these manifold disasters, these stern and lasting necessities, though I am quite unequal to the task, what limit could I set? But, say they, the wise man will wage just

188

wars. As if he would not all the rather lament the necessity of just wars, if he remembers that he is a man; for if they were not just he would not wage them, and would therefore be delivered from all wars. For it is the wrong-doing of the opposing party which compels the wise man to wage just wars; and this wrong-doing, even though it gave rise to no war, would still be matter of grief to man because it is man's wrong-doing. Let every one, then, who thinks with pain on all these great evils, so horrible, so ruthless, acknowledge that this is misery. And if any one either endures or thinks of them without mental pain, this is a more miserable plight still, for he thinks himself happy because he has lost human feeling.

VIII

THAT THE FRIENDSHIP OF GOOD MEN CANNOT BE SECURELY RESTED IN, SO LONG AS THE DANGERS OF THIS LIFE FORCE US TO BE ANXIOUS

In our present wretched condition we frequently mistake a friend for an enemy, and an enemy for a friend. And if we escape this pitiable blindness, is not the unfeigned confidence and mutual love of true and good friends our one solace in human society, filled as it is with misunderstandings and calamities? And yet the more friends we have, and the more widely they are scattered, the more numerous are our fears that some portion of the vast masses of the disasters of life may light upon them. For we are not only anxious lest they suffer from famine, war, disease, captivity, or the inconceivable horrors of slavery, but we are also affected with the much more painful dread that their friendship may be changed into perfidy, malice, and injustice. And when these contingencies actually occur—as they do the more frequently the more friends we have, and the more widely they are scattered and when they come to our knowledge, who but the man who has experienced it can tell with what pangs the heart is torn? We would, in fact, prefer to hear that they were dead, although we could not without anguish hear of even this. For if their life has solaced us with the charms of friendship, can it be that their death should affect us with no sadness? He who will have none of this sadness must, if possible, have no friendly intercourse. Let him interdict or extinguish friendly affection; let him burst with ruthless insensibility the bonds of every human relationship; or let him contrive so to use them that no sweetness shall distil into his spirit. But if this is utterly impossible, how shall we contrive to feel no bitterness in the death of those whose life has been sweet to us? Hence arises that grief which affects the tender heart like a wound or a bruise, and which is healed by the application of kindly consolation. For though the cure is affected all the more easily and rapidly the better condition the soul is in, we must not on this account suppose that there is nothing at all to heal. Although, then, our present life is afflicted, sometimes in a milder, sometimes in a more painful degree, by the death of those very dear to us, and especially of useful public men, yet we would prefer to hear that such men were dead rather than to hear or perceive that they had fallen from the faith, or from virtue—in other words, that they were spiritually dead. Of this vast material for misery the earth is full, and therefore it is written, "Is not human life upon earth a trial?"[16] And with the same reference the Lord says, "Woe to the world because of offenses!"[17] and again, "Because iniquity abounded, the love of many shall wax cold."[18] And hence we enjoy some gratification when our good friends die; for though their death leaves us in sorrow, we have the con-

[16] Job vii. I.
[17] Matt. xvii. 7.
[18] Matt. xxiv. 12.

solatory assurance that they are beyond the ills by which in
this life even the best of men are broken down or corrupted,
or are in danger of both results.

IX

OF THE FRIENDSHIP OF THE HOLY ANGELS, WHICH MEN CANNOT BE SURE OF IN THIS LIFE, OWING TO THE DECEIT OF THE DEMONS WHO HOLD IN BONDAGE THE WORSHIPPERS OF A PLURALITY OF GODS

The philosophers who wished us to have the gods for our
friends rank the friendship of the holy angels in the fourth
circle of society, advancing now from the three circles of
society on earth to the universe, and embracing heaven itself.
And in this friendship we have indeed no fear that the angels
will grieve us by their death or deterioration. But as we cannot mingle with them as familiarly as with men (which itself
is one of the grievances of this life), and as Satan, as we
read,[19] sometimes transforms himself into an angel of light,
to tempt those whom it is necessary to discipline, or just to
deceive, there is great need of God's mercy to preserve us
from making friends of demons in disguise, while we fancy
we have good angels for our friends; for the astuteness and
deceitfulness of these wicked spirits is equalled by their hurt-
fulness. And is this not a great misery of human life, that we
are involved in such ignorance as, but for God's mercy,
makes us a prey to these demons? And it is very certain that
the philosophers of the godless city, who have maintained
that the gods were their friends, had fallen a prey to the
malignant demons who rule that city, and whose eternal punishment is to be shared by it. For the nature of these beings
is sufficiently evinced by the sacred or rather sacrilegious

[19] 2 Cor. xi. 14.

191

observances which form their worship, and by the filthy games in which their crimes are celebrated, and which they themselves originated and exacted from their worshippers as a fit propitiation.

X

THE REWARD PREPARED FOR THE SAINTS AFTER THEY HAVE ENDURED THE TRIAL OF THIS LIFE

But not even the saints and faithful worshippers of the one true and most high God are safe from the manifold temptations and deceits of the demons. For in this abode of weakness, and in these wicked days, this state of anxiety has also its use, stimulating us to seek with keener longing for that security where peace is complete and unassailable. There we shall enjoy the gifts of nature, that is to say, all that God the Creator of all natures has bestowed upon ours—gifts not only good, but eternal—not only of the spirit, healed now by wisdom, but also of the body renewed by the resurrection. There the virtues shall no longer be struggling against any vice or evil, but shall enjoy the reward of victory, the eternal peace which no adversary shall disturb. This is the final blessedness, this the ultimate consummation, the unending end. Here, indeed, we are said to be blessed when we have such peace as can be enjoyed in a good life; but such blessedness is mere misery compared to that final felicity. When we mortals possess such peace as this mortal life can afford, virtue, if we are living rightly, makes a right use of the advantages of this peaceful condition; and when we have it not, virtue makes a good use even of the evils a man suffers. But this is true virtue, when it refers all the advantages it makes a good use of, and all that it does in making good use of good and evil things, and itself also, to that end in which we shall enjoy the best and greatest peace possible.

XI

OF THE HAPPINESS OF THE ETERNAL PEACE, WHICH
CONSTITUTES THE END OR TRUE PERFECTION OF THE SAINTS

And thus we may say of peace, as we have said of eternal
life, that it is the end of our good; and the rather because
the Psalmist says of the city of God, the subject of this laborious work, "Praise the Lord, O Jerusalem; praise thy God,
O Zion: for He hath strengthened the bars of thy gates; He
hath blessed thy children within thee; who hath made thy
borders peace."[20] For when the bars of her gates shall be
strengthened, none shall go in or come out from her; consequently we ought to understand the peace of her borders as
that final peace we are wishing to declare. For even the
mystical name of the city itself, that is, *Jerusalem,* means,
as I have already said, "Vision of Peace." But as the word
peace is employed in connection with things in this world
in which certainly life eternal has no place, we have preferred to call the end or supreme good of this city life eternal
rather than peace. Of this end the Apostle says, "But now,
being freed from sin, and become servants to God, ye have
your fruit unto holiness, and the end life eternal."[21] But, on
the other hand, as those who are not familiar with Scripture
may suppose that the life of the wicked is eternal life, either
because of the immortality of the soul, which some of the
philosophers even have recognized, or because of the endless
punishment of the wicked, which forms a part of our faith,
and which seems impossible unless the wicked live for ever,
it may therefore be advisable, in order that every one may
readily understand what we mean, to say that the end or
supreme good of this city is either peace in eternal life, or
eternal life in peace. For peace is a good so great, that even

[20] Ps. cxlvii. 12–14.
[21] Rom. vi. 22.

in this earthly and mortal life there is no word we hear with such pleasure, nothing we desire with such zest, or find to be more thoroughly gratifying. So that if we dwell for a little longer on this subject, we shall not, in my opinion, be wearisome to our readers, who will attend both for the sake of understanding what is the end of this city of which we speak, and for the sake of the sweetness of peace which is dear to all.

XII

THAT EVEN THE FIERCENESS OF WAR AND ALL THE DISQUIETUDE OF MEN MAKE TOWARDS THIS ONE END OF PEACE, WHICH EVERY NATURE DESIRES

Whoever gives even moderate attention to human affairs and to our common nature, will recognize that if there is no man who does not wish to be joyful, neither is there any one who does not wish to have peace. For even they who make war desire nothing but victory—desire, that is to say, to attain to peace with glory. For what else is victory than the conquest of those who resist us? and when this is done there is peace. It is therefore with the desire for peace that wars are waged, even by those who take pleasure in exercising their warlike nature in command and battle. And hence it is obvious that peace is the end sought for by war. For every man seeks peace by waging war, but no man seeks war by making peace. For even they who intentionally interrupt the peace in which they are living have no hatred of peace, but only wish it changed into a peace that suits them better. They do not, therefore, wish to have no peace, but only one more to their mind. And in the case of sedition, when men have separated themselves from the community, they yet do not effect what they wish, unless they maintain some kind of peace with their fellow-conspirators. And therefore even robbers take care to maintain peace with their comrades, that

The City of God

they may with greater effect and greater safety invade the peace of other men. And if an individual happens to be of such unrivalled strength, and to be so jealous of partnership, that he trusts himself with no comrades, but makes his own plots, and commits depredations and murders on his own account, yet he maintains some shadow of peace with such persons as he is unable to kill, and from whom he wishes to conceal his deeds. In his own home, too, he makes it his aim to be at peace with his wife and children, and any other members of his household; for unquestionably their prompt obedience to his every look is a source of pleasure to him. And if this be not rendered, he is angry, he chides and punishes; and even by this storm he secures the calm peace of his own home, as occasion demands. For he sees that peace cannot be maintained unless all the members of the same domestic circle be subject to one head, such as he himself is in his own house. And therefore if a city or nation offered to submit itself to him, to serve him in the same style as he had made his household serve him, he would no longer lurk in a brigand's hiding-places, but lift his head in open day as a king, though the same covetousness and wickedness should remain in him. And thus all men desire to have peace with their own circle whom they wish to govern as suits themselves. For even those whom they make war against they wish to make their own, and impose on them the laws of their own peace.

But let us suppose a man such as poetry and mythology speak of—a man so insociable and savage as to be called rather a semi-man than a man.[22] Although, then, his kingdom was the solitude of a dreary cave, and he himself was so singularly bad-hearted that he was named Καχός, which is the Greek word for *bad;* though he had no wife to soothe him with endearing talk, no children to play with, no sons to

[22] He refers to the giant Cacus.

do his bidding, no friend to enliven him with intercourse, not even his father Vulcan (though in one respect he was happier than his father, not having begotten a monster like himself); although he gave to no man, but took as he wished whatever he could, from whomsoever he could, when he could; yet in that solitary den, the floor of which, as Virgil[23] says, was always reeking with recent slaughter, there was nothing else than peace sought, a peace in which no one should molest him, or disquiet him with any assault or alarm. With his own body he desired to be at peace, and he was satisfied only in proportion as he had this peace. For he ruled his members, and they obeyed him; and for the sake of pacifying his mortal nature, which rebelled when it needed anything, and of allaying the sedition of hunger which threatened to banish the soul from the body, he made forays, slew, and devoured, but used the ferocity and savageness he displayed in these actions only for the preservation of his own life's peace. So that, had he been willing to make with other men the same peace which he made with himself in his own cave, he would neither have been called bad, nor a monster, nor a semi-man. Or if the appearance of his body and his vomiting smoky fires frightened men from having any dealings with him, perhaps his fierce ways arose not from a desire to do mischief, but from the necessity of finding a living. But he may have had no existence, or, at least, he was not such as the poets fancifully describe him, for they had to exalt Hercules, and did so at the expense of Cacus. It is better, then, to believe that such a man or semi-man never existed, and that this, in common with many other fancies of the poets, is mere fiction. For the most savage animals (and he is said to have been almost a wild beast) encompass their own species with a ring of protecting peace. They cohabit, beget, produce, suckle, and bring up their young,

[23] *Aeneid,* viii. 195.

though very many of them are not gregarious, but solitary —not like sheep, deer, pigeons, starlings, bees, but such as lions, foxes, eagles, bats. For what tigress does not gently purr over her cubs, and lay aside her ferocity to fondle them? What kite, solitary as he is when circling over his prey, does not seek a mate, build a nest, hatch the eggs, bring up the young birds, and maintain with the mother of his family as peaceful a domestic alliance as he can? How much more powerfully do the laws of man's nature move him to hold fellowship and maintain peace with all men so far as in him lies, since even wicked men wage war to maintain the peace of their own circle, and wish that, if possible, all men belonged to them, that all men and things might serve but one head, and might, either through love or fear, yield themselves to peace with him! It is thus that pride in its perversity apes God. It abhors equality with other men under Him; but, instead of His rule, it seeks to impose a rule of its own upon its equals. It abhors, that is to say, the just peace of God, and loves its own unjust peace; but it cannot help loving peace of one kind or other. For there is no vice so clean contrary to nature that it obliterates even the faintest traces of nature.

He, then, who prefers what is right to what is wrong, and what is well-ordered to what is perverted, sees that the peace of unjust men is not worthy to be called peace in comparison with the peace of the just. And yet even what is perverted must of necessity be in harmony with, and in dependence on, and in some part of the order of things, for otherwise it would have no existence at all. Suppose a man hangs with his head downwards, this is certainly a perverted attitude of body and arrangement of its members; for that which nature requires to be above is beneath, and *vice versa*. This perversity disturbs the peace of the body, and is therefore painful. Nevertheless the spirit is at peace with its body, and labors for its preservation, and hence the suffering; but if it is banished from the body by its pains, then, so long as the bodily framework holds together, there is in the remains a kind of peace among the members, and hence the body remains suspended. And inasmuch as the earthly body tends towards the earth, and rests on the bond by which it is suspended, it tends thus to its natural peace, and the voice of its own weight demands a place for it to rest; and though now lifeless and without feeling, it does not fall from the peace that is natural to its place in creation, whether it already has it, or is tending towards it. For if you apply embalming preparations to prevent the bodily frame from mouldering and dissolving, a kind of peace still unites part to part, and keeps the whole body in a suitable place on the earth—in other words, in a place that is at peace with the body. If, on the other hand, the body receive no such care, but be left to the natural course, it is disturbed by exhalations that do not harmonize with one another, and that offend our senses; for it is this which is perceived in putrefaction until it is assimilated to the elements of the world, and particle by particle enters into peace with them. Yet throughout this process the laws of the most high Creator and Governor are strictly observed, for it is by Him the peace of the universe is administered. For although minute animals are produced from the carcass of a larger animal, all these little atoms, by the law of the same Creator, serve the animals they belong to in peace. And although the flesh of dead animals be eaten by others, no matter where it be carried, nor what it be brought into contact with, nor what it be converted and changed into, it still is ruled by the same laws which pervade all things for the conservation of every mortal race, and which bring things that fit one another into harmony.

XIII

OF THE UNIVERSAL PEACE WHICH THE LAW OF NATURE
PRESERVES THROUGH ALL DISTURBANCES, AND BY WHICH
EVERY ONE REACHES HIS DESERT IN A WAY REGULATED
BY THE JUST JUDGE

The peace of the body then consists in the duly proportioned arrangement of its parts. The peace of the irrational soul is the harmonious repose of the appetites, and that of the rational soul the harmony of knowledge and action. The peace of body and soul is the well-ordered and harmonious life and health of the living creature. Peace between man and God is the well-ordered obedience of faith to eternal law. Peace between man and man is well-ordered concord. Domestic peace is the well-ordered concord between those of the family who rule and those who obey. Civil peace is a similar concord among the citizens. The peace of the celestial city is the perfectly ordered and harmonious enjoyment of God, and of one another in God. The peace of all things is the tranquility of order. Order is the distribution which allots things equal and unequal, each to its own place. And hence, though the miserable, in so far as they are such, do certainly not enjoy peace, but are severed from that tranquillity of order in which there is no disturbance, nevertheless, inasmuch as they are deservedly and justly miserable, they are by their very misery connected with order. They are not, indeed, conjoined with the blessed, but they are disjoined from them by the law of order. And though they are disquieted, their circumstances are notwithstanding adjusted to them, and consequently they have some tranquillity of order, and therefore some peace. But they are wretched because, although not wholly miserable, they are not in that place where any mixture of misery is impossible. They would, however, be more wretched if they had not that peace which arises from being in harmony with the natural order of things. When they suffer, their peace is in so far disturbed; but their peace continues in so far as they do not suffer, and in so far as their nature continues to exist. As, then, there may be life without pain, while there cannot be pain without some kind of life, so there may be peace without war, but there cannot be war without some kind of peace, because war supposes the existence of some natures to wage it, and these natures cannot exist without peace of one kind or other.

And therefore there is a nature in which evil does not or even cannot exist; but there cannot be a nature in which there is no good. Hence not even the nature of the devil himself is evil, in so far as it is nature, but it was made evil by being perverted. Thus he did not abide in the truth,[24] but could not escape the judgment of the Truth; he did not abide in the tranquillity of order, but did not therefore escape the power of the Ordainer. The good imparted by God to his nature did not screen him from the justice of God by which order was preserved in his punishment; neither did God punish the good which He had created, but the evil which the devil had commited. God did not take back all He had imparted to his nature, but something He took and something He left, that there might remain enough to be sensible of the loss of what was taken. And this very sensibility to pain is evidence of the good which has been taken away and the good which has been left. For, were nothing good left, there could be no pain on account of the good which had been lost. For he who sins is still worse if he rejoices in his loss of righteousness. But he who is in pain, if he derives no benefit from it, mourns at least the loss of health. And as righteousness and health are both good things, and as the loss of any good thing is matter of grief, not of joy—if, at least, there is no compensation, as spiritual righteousness may compensate for the loss of bodily health—cer-

[24] John viii. 44.

tainly it is more suitable for a wicked man to grieve in punishment than to rejoice in his fault. As, then, the joy of a sinner who has abandoned what is good is evidence of a bad will, so his grief for the good he has lost when he is punished is evidence of a good nature. For he who laments the peace his nature has lost is stirred to do so by some relics of peace which make his nature friendly to itself. And it is very just that in the final punishment the wicked and godless should in anguish bewail the loss of the natural advantages they enjoyed, and should perceive that they were most justly taken from them by that God whose benign liberality they had despised. God, then, the most wise Creator and most just Ordainer of all natures, who placed the human race upon earth as its greatest ornament, imparted to men some good things adapted to this life, to wit, temporal peace, such as we can enjoy in this life from health and safety and human fellowship, and all things needful for the preservation and recovery of this peace, such as the objects which are accommodated to our outward senses, light, night, the air, and waters suitable for us, and everything the body requires to sustain, shelter, heal, or beautify it: and all under this most equitable condition, that every man who made a good use of these advantages suited to the peace of this mortal condition, should receive ampler and better blessings, namely, the peace of immortality, accompanied by glory and honor in an endless life made fit for the enjoyment of God and of one another in God; but that he who used the present blessings badly should both lose them and should not receive the others.

201

XIV

OF THE ORDER AND LAW WHICH OBTAIN IN HEAVEN AND EARTH, WHEREBY IT COMES TO PASS THAT HUMAN SOCIETY IS SERVED BY THOSE WHO RULE IT

The whole use, then, of things temporal has a reference to this result of earthly peace in the earthly community, while in the city of God it is connected with eternal peace. And therefore, if we were irrational animals, we should desire nothing beyond the proper arrangement of the parts of the body and the satisfaction of the appetites—nothing, therefore, but bodily comfort and abundance of pleasures, that the peace of the body might contribute to the peace of the soul. For if bodily peace be wanting, a bar is put to the peace even of the irrational soul, since it cannot obtain the gratification of its appetites. And these two together help out the mutual peace of soul and body, the peace of harmonious life and health. For as animals, by shunning pain, show that they love bodily peace, and, by pursuing pleasure to gratify their appetites, show that they love peace of soul, so their shrinking from death is a sufficient indication of their intense love of that peace which binds soul and body in close alliance. But, as man has a rational soul, he subordinates all this which he has in common with the beasts to the peace of his rational soul, that his intellect may have free play and may regulate his actions, and that he may thus enjoy the well-ordered harmony of knowledge and action which constitutes, as we have said, the peace of the rational soul. And for this purpose he must desire to be neither molested by pain, nor disturbed by desire, nor extinguished by death, that he may arrive at some useful knowledge by which he may regulate his life and manners. But, owing to the liability of the human mind to fall into mistakes, this very pursuit of knowledge may be a snare to him unless he has a divine Master, whom he may obey without misgiving, and who may

202

at the same time give him such help as to preserve his own freedom. And because, so long as he is in this mortal body, he is a stranger to God, he walks by faith, not by sight; and he therefore refers all peace, bodily or spiritual or both, to that peace which mortal man has with the immortal God, so that he exhibits the well-ordered obedience of faith to eternal law. But as this divine Master inculcates two precepts—the love of God and the love of our neighbor—and as in these precepts a man finds three things he has to love—God, himself, and his neighbor—and that he who loves God loves himself thereby, it follows that he must endeavor to get his neighbor to love God, since he is ordered to love his neighbor as himself. He ought to make this endeavor in behalf of his wife, his children, his household, all within his reach, even as he would wish his neighbor to do the same for him if he needed it; and consequently he will be at peace, or in well-ordered concord, with all men, as far as in him lies. And this is the order of this concord, that a man, in the first place, injure no one, and, in the second, do good to every one he can reach. Primarily, therefore, his own household are his care, for the law of nature and of society gives him readier access to them and greater opportunity of serving them. And hence the Apostle says, "Now, if any provide not for his own, and specially for those of his own house, he hath denied the faith, and is worse than an infidel."[25] This is the origin of domestic peace, or the well-ordered concord of those in the family who rule and those who obey. For they who care for the rest rule—the husband the wife, the parents the children, the masters the servants; and they who are cared for obey—the women their husbands, the children their parents, the servants their masters. But in the family of the just man who lives by faith and is as yet a pilgrim journeying on to the celestial city, even those who rule serve those whom they

[25] 1 Tim. v. 8.

seem to command; for they rule not from a love of power, but from a sense of the duty they owe to others—not because they are proud of authority, but because they love mercy.

XV

OF THE LIBERTY PROPER TO MAN'S NATURE, AND THE
SERVITUDE INTRODUCED BY SIN—A SERVITUDE IN
WHICH THE MAN WHOSE WILL IS WICKED IS
THE SLAVE OF HIS OWN LUST, THOUGH HE
IS FREE SO FAR AS REGARDS OTHER MEN

This is prescribed by the order of nature: it is thus that God has created man. For "let them," He says, "have dominion over the fish of the sea, and over the fowl of the air, and over every creeping thing which creepeth on the earth."[26] He did not intend that His rational creature, who was made in His image, should have dominion over anything but the irrational creation—not man over man, but man over the beasts. And hence the righteous men in primitive times were made shepherds of cattle rather than kings of men, God intending thus to teach us what the relative position of the creatures is, and what the desert of sin; for it is with justice, we believe, that the condition of slavery is the result of sin. And this is why we do not find the word "slave" in any part of Scripture until righteous Noah branded the sin of his son with this name. It is a name, therefore, introduced by sin and not by nature. The origin of the Latin word for slave is supposed to be found in the circumstance that those who by the law of war were liable to be killed were sometimes preserved by their victors, and were hence called servants.[c] And these circumstances could never have arisen save through sin. For even when we wage a just war, our adversaries must be sin-

[26] Gen. i. 26.
[c] This is not a (scientifically) correct etymology.—Ed.

ning; and every victory, even though gained by wicked men, is a result of the first judgment of God, who humbles the vanquished either for the sake of removing or of punishing their sins. Witness that man of God, Daniel, who, when he was in captivity, confessed to God his own sins and the sins of his people, and declared with pious grief that these were the cause of the captivity.[27] The prime cause, then of slavery is sin, which brings man under the dominion of his fellow— that which does not happen save by the judgment of God, with whom is no unrighteousness, and who knows how to award fit punishments to every variety of offence. But our Master in heaven says, "Every one who doeth sin is the servant of sin."[28] And thus there are many wicked masters who have religious men as their slaves, and who are yet themselves in bondage; "for of whom a man is overcome, of the same is he brought in bondage."[29] And beyond question it is a happier thing to be the slave of a man than of a lust; for even this very lust of ruling, to mention no others, lays waste men's hearts with the most ruthless dominion. Moreover, when men are subjected to one another in a peaceful order, the lowly position does as much good to the servant as the proud position does harm to the master. But by nature, as God first created us, no one is the slave either of man or of sin. This servitude is, however, penal, and is appointed by that law which enjoins the preservation of the natural order and forbids its disturbance; for if nothing had been done in violation of that law, there would have been nothing to restrain by penal servitude. And therefore the Apostle admonishes slaves to be subject to their masters, and to serve them heartily and with good-will, so that, if they cannot be freed by their masters, they may themselves make their slavery in some

[27] Dan. ix.
[28] John viii. 34.
[29] 2 Pet. ii. 19.

sort free, by serving not in crafty fear, but in faithful love, until all unrighteousness pass away, and all principality and every human power be brought to nothing, and God be all in all.

Paracelsus (1493?-1541)

On Man in the Cosmos

> The centre of all things is man, he is the
> middle point of heaven and earth. . . .

The whole world surrounds man as a circle surrounds one
point. From this it follows that all things are related to this
one point, no differently from an apple seed which is surrounded and preserved by the fruit, and which draws its sustenance from it. . . . Similarly, man is a seed and the world
is his apple; and just as the seed fares in the apple, so does
man fare in the world, which surrounds him. . . . Each
thing has its own origin; partly in the eternal, and partly
in the temporal. And wisdom, whether it be heavenly or
earthly, can be achieved only through the attractive force of
the centre and the circle.

Let man consider who he is and what he should and must
become. For the *compositio humana* is prodigious, and its
oneness is formed of a very great diversity. . . . Man needs
more than common intelligence to know who he is; only
he who studies himself properly and knows whence he comes
and who he is will also give profound attention to the eternal.

Everything that comes from the flesh is animal and follows an animal course; heaven has little influence on it. Only
that which comes from the stars is specifically human in us;
this is subject to their influence. But that which comes from
the spirit, the divine part of man, has been formed in us in

PARACELSUS

the likeness of God, and upon this neither earth nor heaven
has any influence.

You should look upon man as a part of nature whose end
lies in heaven. In the heavens you can see man, each part
for itself; for man is made of heaven. And the matter out
of which man was created also indicates to you the pattern
after which he was formed. . . . External nature moulds the
shape of internal nature, and if external nature vanishes,
the inner nature is also lost; for the outer is the mother of
the inner. Thus man is like the image of the four elements
in a mirror; if the four elements fall apart, man is destroyed.
If that which faces the mirror is at rest, then the image in
the mirror is at rest too. And so philosophy is nothing other
than the knowledge and discovery of that which has its
reflection in the mirror. And just as the image in the mirror
gives no one any idea about his nature, and cannot be the
object of cognition, but is only a dead image, so is man, considered in himself: nothing can be learned from him alone.
For knowledge comes only from that outside being whose
mirrored image he is.

Heaven is man, and man is heaven, and all men together
are the one heaven, and heaven is nothing but one man. You
must know this to understand why one place is this way and
the other that way, why this is new and that is old, and why
there are everywhere so many diverse things. But all this
cannot be discovered by studying the heavens. . . . All that
can be discovered is the distribution of their active influences. . . . We, men, have a heaven, and it lies in each of us
in its entire plenitude, undivided and corresponding to
each man's specificity. Thus each human life takes its own
course, thus dying, death, and disease are unequally distributed, in each case according to the action of the heavens.
For if the same heaven were in all of us, all men would have
to be equally sick and equally healthy. But this is not so;
the unity of the Great Heaven is split into our diversities by

208

the various moments at which we are born. As soon as a child is conceived, it receives its own heaven. If all children had been born at the same moment, all of them would have had the same heaven in them, and their lives would have followed the same course. Therefore, the starry vault imprints itself on the inner heaven of a man. A miracle without equal!

Just as the firmament with all its constellations forms a whole in itself, likewise man in himself is a free and mighty firmament. And just as the firmament rests in itself and is not ruled by any creature, the firmament of man is not ruled by other creatures, but stands for itself and is free of all bonds. For there are two kinds of created things: heaven and the earth are of one kind, man is of the other. . . . Everything that astronomical theory has profoundly fathomed by studying the planetary aspects and the stars . . . can also be applied to the firmament of the body.

The light of nature in man comes from the stars, and his flesh and blood belong to the material elements. Thus two influences operate in man. One is that of the firmamental light, which includes wisdom, art, reason. All these are the children of this father. . . . The second influence emanates from matter, and it includes concupiscence, eating, drinking, and everything that relates to the flesh and blood. Therefore one must not ascribe to the stars that which originates in the blood and flesh. For heaven does not endow one with concupiscence or greed. . . . From heaven come only wisdom, art, and reason.

As great as the difference in form and shape between the two bodies, the visible and the invisible, the material and the eternal, is the difference between their natures. . . . They are like a married pair, one in the flesh, but twofold in their nature. . . . And because this is so, a contradiction dwells in man. . . . Namely, the stars in him have a different disposition, a different mind, a different orientation than the lower elements; and on the other hand, these elements in turn have a different wisdom and a different disposition than the stars in man. For instance: the elemental, material body wants to live in luxury and lewdness; the stars, the ethereal body, the inner counterpart of the upper sphere, want to study, learn, pursue arts, and so forth. As a result there arises an antinomy in man himself. The visible, material body wants one thing, and the invisible, ethereal body wants another thing, they do not want the same thing. . . . Therefore there dwells in each of these bodies an urge to exceed that which is given to it, and neither wants to follow a middle course and act with measure. Both strive to exceed their bounds, and each wants to expel the other; thus enmity arises between them. For everything that exceeds its measure brings destruction in its train.

Everything that man accomplishes or does, that he teaches or wants to learn, must have its right proportion; it must follow its own line and remain within its circle, to the end that a balance be preserved, that there be no crooked thing, that nothing exceed the circle.

Blessed and thrice blessed is he who observes the right measure and needs none of the help devised by men, but follows the path that God prescribed to him.

God could surely have created man out of nothingness by merely saying: "So be it!" This he did not do, but took him from nature, placed him in nature, left him to nature, and subjected him to nature as her child. But He also subjected nature to him, indeed as a father. . . . Thus nature is subject to man, she belongs to him as to one of her blood; he is her child, her fruit, which was made of her in the body of the elements . . . and in the ethereal body.

In nature we find a light that illumines us more than the sun and the moon. For it is so ordered that we see but half of man and all the other creatures, and therefore must explore them further. . . . Nor should we become drowned in our daily work, for whosoever seeks . . . shall find. . . .

On Man in the Cosmos

And if we follow the light of nature, we learn that there exists another half of man, and that man does not consist of blood and flesh alone . . . but also of a body that cannot be discerned by our crude eyesight.

The moon emits light, yet by this light colours are not discernible; but as soon as the sun rises, all the colours can be distinguished. Similarly nature has a light that shines like the sun; and as the light of the sun exceeds the light of the moon, so the light of nature far exceeds the power of the eyes. In its light all things invisible become visible; remember always that the one light outshines the other.

Know that our world and everything we see in its compass and everything we can touch constitute only one half of the cosmos. The world we do not see is equal to ours in weight and measure, in nature and properties. From this it follows that there exists another half of man in which this invisible world operates. If we know of the two worlds, we realize that both halves are needed to constitute the whole man; for they are like two men united in one body.

The sun can shine through a glass, and fire can radiate warmth through the walls of the stove, although the sun does not pass through the glass and the fire does not go through the stove; in the same way, the human body can act at a distance while remaining at rest in one place, like the sun, which shines through the glass and yet does not pass through it. Hence nothing must be attributed to the body itself but only to the forces that flow from it—just as the smell of an animal is suffused while the animal's body may be at rest.

Nature emits a light, and by its radiance she can be known. But in man there is still another light apart from that which is innate in nature. It is the light through which man experiences, learns, and fathoms the supernatural. Those who seek in the light of nature speak from knowledge of nature; but those who seek in the light of man speak from knowledge of super-nature. For man is more than nature; he is nature, but he is also a spirit, he is also an angel, and he has the properties of all three. If he walks in nature, he serves nature; if he walks in the spirit, he serves the spirit; if he walks with the angel, he serves the angel. The first is given to the body, the others are given to the soul, and are its jewel.

The book in which the letters of the mysteries are written visibly, discernibly, tangibly, and legibly, so that everything one desires to know can best be found in this self-same book, inscribed by the finger of God; the book compared with which, if it is correctly read, all other books are nothing but dead letters—know that this book is the book of man, and should not be sought anywhere but in man alone. Man is the book in which all the mysteries are recorded; but this book is interpreted by God.

If you would gain understanding of the whole treasury that the letters enclose, possess, and encompass, you must gain it from far off, namely, from Him who taught man how to compose the letters. . . . For it is not on paper that you will find the power to understand, but in Him who put the words on paper.

Man is born of the earth, therefore he also has in him the nature of the earth. But later, in his new birth, he is of God and in this form receives divine nature. Just as man in nature is illumined by the sidereal light that he may know nature, so he is illumined by the Holy Ghost that he may know God in His essence. For no one can know God unless he is of divine nature, and no one can know nature unless he is of nature. Everyone is bound to that in which he originates and to which he must at some time return.

The light of nature is a steward of the Holy Light. What harm comes to the natural tongue because the fiery tongue has spoken? Or how does the fiery tongue offend against the natural one? It is the same as with a man and a woman, who both give birth to a child; without both this could not be.

On Man in the Cosmos

Similarly, both lights were given man, to dwell within him. How marvellously man is made and formed if one penetrates into his true nature . . . and it is a great thing—consider for once, that there is nothing in heaven or in earth that is not also in man. . . . In him is God who is also in Heaven; and all the forces of Heaven operate likewise in man. Where else can Heaven be rediscovered if not in man? Since it acts from us, it must also be in us. Therefore it knows our prayer even before we have uttered it, for it is closer to our hearts than to our words. . . . God made His Heaven in man beautiful and great, noble and good; for God is in His Heaven, i.e., in man. For He Himself says that He is in us, and that we are His temple.

Thoughts are free and are subject to no rule. On them rests the freedom of man, and they tower above the light of nature. For thoughts give birth to a creative force that is neither elemental nor sidereal. . . . Thoughts create a new heaven, a new firmament, a new source of energy, from which new arts flow. . . . When a man undertakes to create something, he establishes a new heaven, as it were, and from it the work that he desires to create flows into him. . . . For such is the immensity of man that he is greater than heaven and earth.

Friedrich Engels (1820-1895)

Ludwig Feuerbach

IDEALISM AND MATERIALISM

The great basic question of all philosophy, especially of modern philosophy, is that concerning the relation of thinking and being. From the very early times when men, still completely ignorant of the structure of their own bodies, under the stimulus of dream apparitions[1] came to believe that their thinking and sensation were not activities of their bodies, but of a distinct soul which inhabits the body and leaves it at death—from this time, men have been driven to reflect about the relation between this soul and the outside world. If in death it took leave of the body and lived on, there was no occasion to invent yet another distinct death for it. Thus arose the idea of its immortality which at that stage of development appeared not at all as a consolation but as a fate against which it was no use fighting, and often enough, as among the Greeks, as a positive misfortune. Not religious desire for consolation, but the quandary arising from the common universal ignorance of what to do with this soul (once its existence had been accepted) after the

---

[1] Among savages and lower barbarians the idea is still universal that the human forms which appear in dreams are souls which have temporarily left their bodies; the real man is therefore held responsible for acts committed by his dream apparition against the dreamer. Thus B. Imthurn found this belief current, for example, among the Indians of Guiana in 1884.

death of the body—led in a general way to the tedious notion of personal immortality. In an exactly similar manner the first gods arose through the personification of natural forces. And these gods in the further development of religions assumed more and more an extra-mundane form, until finally by a process of abstraction, I might almost say of distillation, occurring naturally in the course of man's intellectual development, out of the many more or less limited and mutually limiting gods there arose in the minds of men the idea of the one exclusive god of the monotheistic religions.

Thus the question of the relation of thinking to being, the relation of spirit to nature—the paramount question of the whole of philosophy—has, no less than all religion, its roots in the narrow-minded and ignorant notions of savagery. But this question could for the first time be put forward in its whole acuteness, could achieve its full significance, only after European society had awakened from the long hibernation of the Christian Middle Ages. The question of the position of thinking in relation to being, a question which, by the way, had played a great part also in the scholasticism of the Middle Ages, the question: which is primary, spirit or nature—that question, in relation to the Church, was sharpened into this: "Did god create the world or has the world been in existence eternally?"

The answers which the philosophers gave to this question split them into two great camps. Those who asserted the primacy of spirit to nature and, therefore, in the last instance, assumed world creation in some form or other—(and among the philosophers, Hegel, for example, this creation often becomes still more intricate and impossible than in Christianity)—comprised the camp of idealism. The others, who regarded nature as primary, belong to the various schools of materialism.

These two expressions, idealism and materialism, primarily signifying nothing more than this; and here also they are

215

not used in any other sense. What confusion arises when some other meaning is put into them will be seen below.

But the question of the relation of thinking and being has yet another side: in what relation do our thoughts about the world surrounding us stand to this world itself? Is our thinking capable of the cognition of the real world? Are we able in our ideas and notions of the real world to produce a correct reflection of reality? In philosophical language this question is called the question of the "identity of thinking and being," and the overwhelming majority of philosophers give an affirmative answer to this question. With Hegel, for example, its affirmation is self-evident; for what we perceive in the real world is precisely its thought-content—that which makes the world a gradual realisation of the absolute idea, which absolute idea has existed somewhere from eternity, independent of the world and before the world. But it is manifest without more ado that thought can know a content which is from the outset a thought-content. It is equally manifest that what is here to be proved is already tacitly contained in the presupposition. But that in no way prevents Hegel from drawing the further conclusion from his proof of the identity of thinking and being that his philosophy, because it is correct for his own thinking, is therefore the only correct one, and that the identity of thinking and being must prove its validity by mankind immediately translating his philosophy from theory into practice and transforming the whole world according to Hegelian principles. This is an illusion which he shares with well-nigh all philosophers.

In addition there is yet another set of different philosophers—those who question the possibility of any cognition (or at least of an exhaustive cognition) of the world. To them, among the moderns, belong Hume and Kant, and they have played a very important role in philosophical development. What is decisive in the refutation of this view has already been said by Hegel—in so far as this was possible

216

from an idealist standpoint. The materialistic additions made by Feuerbach are more ingenious than profound. The most telling refutation of this as of all other philosophical fancies is practice, viz., experiment and industry. If we are able to prove the correctness of our conception of a natural process by making it ourselves, bringing it into being out of its conditions and using it for our own purposes into the bargain, then there is an end of the Kantian incomprehensible "thing-in-itself." The chemical substances produced in the bodies of plants and animals remained just such "things-in-themselves" until organic chemistry began to produce them one after another, whereupon the "thing-in-itself" became a thing for us, as, for instance, alizarin, the colouring matter of the madder, which we no longer trouble to grow in the madder roots in the field, but produce much more cheaply and simply from coal tar. For three hundred years the Copernican solar system was an hypothesis with a hundred, a thousand or ten thousand chances to one in its favour, but still always an hypothesis. But when Leverrier, by means of the data provided by this system, not only deduced the necessity of the existence of an unknown planet, but also calculated the position in the heavens which this planet must necessarily occupy, and when Galle really found this planet, the Copernican system was proved. If, nevertheless, the Neo-Kantians are attempting to resurrect the Kantian conception in Germany and the agnostics that of Hume in England (where in fact it had never ceased to survive), this is—in view of their theoretical and practical refutation accomplished long ago—scientifically a regression and practically merely a shamefaced way of surreptitiously accepting materialism, while denying it before the world.

But during this long period from Descartes to Hegel and from Hobbes to Feuerbach, the philosophers were by no means impelled, as they thought they were, solely by the force of pure reason. On the contrary. What really pushed them forward was the powerful and ever more rapidly on-rushing progress of natural science and industry. Among the materialists this was plain on the surface, but the idealist systems also filled themselves more and more with a materialist content and attempted pantheistically to reconcile the antithesis between mind and matter. Thus, ultimately, the Hegelian system represents merely a materialism idealistically turned upside down in method and content.

It is, therefore, comprehensible that Starcke in his characterisation of Feuerbach first of all investigates the latter's position in regard to this fundamental question of the relation of thinking and being. After a short introduction, in which the views of the preceding philosophers, particularly since Kant, are described in unnecessarily ponderous philosophical language, and in which Hegel, by an all too formalistic adherence to certain passages of his work, gets far less than his due, there follows a detailed description of the course of development of Feuerbach's "metaphysics" itself, as this course was reconstructed out of the sequence of those writings of this philosopher which have a bearing here. This description is industriously and carefully elaborated, only, like the whole book, it is loaded with a ballast of philosophical phraseology by no means everywhere unavoidable, which is the more disturbing in its effect, the less the author keeps to the manner of expression of one and the same school, or even of Feuerbach himself, and the more he interjects expressions of very different schools—especially of the tendencies now rampant and calling themselves philosophical.

The course of evolution of Feuerbach is that of an Hegelian—a never quite orthodox Hegelian, it is true—into a materialist; an evolution which at a definite stage necessitates a complete rupture with the idealist system of his predecessor. With irresistible force Feuerbach is finally forced to the realisation that the Hegelian pre-mundane existence of the "absolute idea," the "pre-existence of the logical cate-

218

Ludwig Feuerbach

gories" before the world existed, is nothing more than the fantastic survival of the belief in the existence of an extra-mundane creator; that the material, sensuously perceptible world to which we ourselves belong is the only reality; and that our consciousness and thinking, however suprasensuous they may seem, are the product of a material, bodily organ, the brain. Matter is not a product of mind, but mind itself is merely the highest product of matter. This is, of course, pure materialism. But, having got so far, Feuerbach stops short. He cannot overcome the customary philosophical prejudice, prejudice not against the thing but against the name materialism. He says: "To me materialism is the foundation of the edifice of human essence and knowledge, but to me it is not what it is to the physiologist, to the natural scientist in the narrower sense, for example, Moleschott, and necessarily so indeed from their standpoint and profession, the building itself. Backwards I fully agree with the materialists; but not forwards."

Here Feuerbach lumps together the materialism that is a general world outlook resting upon a definite conception of the relation between matter and mind, and the special form in which this world outlook was expressed at a definite stage of historical development, viz., in the eighteenth century. More than that, he confuses it with the shallow and vulgarised form in which the materialism of the eighteenth century continues to exist today in the minds of naturalists and physicians, the form which was preached on their tours in the 'fifties by Buchner, Vogt and Moleschott. But just as idealism underwent a series of stages of development, so also did materialism. With each epoch-making discovery even in the sphere of natural science it has to change its form; and after history also was subjected to materialist treatment, here also a new avenue of development has opened.

The materialism of the last century was predominantly mechanical, because at that time, of all natural sciences,

FRIEDRICH ENGELS

mechanics and indeed only the mechanics of solid bodies—
celestial and terrestrial—in short, the mechanics of gravity,
had come to any definite close. Chemistry at that time
existed only in its infantile, phlogistic form. Biology still
lay in swaddling clothes; vegetable and animal organisms
had been only roughly examined and were explained as the
result of purely mechanical causes. As the animal was to
Descartes, so was man a machine to the materialists of the
eighteenth century. This exclusive application of the standards of mechanics to processes of a chemical and organic
nature—in which processes, it is true, the laws of mechanics
are also valid, but are pushed into the background by other
and higher laws—constitutes a specific but at that time
inevitable limitation of classical French materialism.

The second specific limitation of this materialism lay in
its inability to comprehend the universe as a process—as
matter developing in an historical process. This was in
accordance with the level of the natural science of that time,
and with the metaphysical, i.e., anti-dialectical manner of
philosophising connected with it. Nature, it was known,
was in constant motion. But according to the ideas of that
time, this motion turned eternally in a circle and therefore
never moved from the spot; it produced the same results
over and over again. This conception was at that time inevitable. The Kantian theory of the origin of the solar system
had been put forward but recently and was regarded merely
as a curiosity. The history of the development of the earth,
geology, was still totally unknown, and the conception that
the animate natural beings of today are the result of a long
sequence of development from the simple to the complex
could not at that time scientifically be put forward at all.
The unhistorical view of nature was therefore inevitable.
We have the less reason to reproach the philosophers of the
eighteenth century on this account, since the same thing is
found in Hegel. According to him, nature, as a mere "aliena-

220

Ludwig Feuerbach

tion" of the idea, is incapable of development in time—capable only of extending its manifoldness in space, so that it displays simultaneously and alongside of one another all the stages of development comprised in it, and is condemned to an eternal repetition of the same process. This absurdity of a development in space, but outside of time—the fundamental condition of all development—Hegel imposes upon nature just at the very time when geology, embryology, the physiology of plants and animals, and organic chemistry were being built up, and when everywhere on the basis of these new sciences brilliant foreshadowings of the later theory of evolution were appearing (e.g., Goethe and Lamarck). But the system demanded it; hence the method, for the sake of the system, had to become untrue to itself.

This same unhistorical conception prevailed also in the domain of history. Here the struggle against the remnants of the Middle Ages blurred the view. The Middle Ages were regarded as a mere interruption of history by a thousand years of universal barbarism. The great progress made in the Middle Ages—the extension of the area of European culture, the bringing into existence there of great nations, capable of survival, and finally the enormous technical progress of the fourteenth and fifteenth centuries—all this was not seen. Consequently a rational insight into the great historical inter-connections was made impossible, and history served at best as a collection of examples and illustrations for the use of philosophers.

The vulgarising pedlars who in Germany in the 'fifties busied themselves with materialism by no means overcame the limitations of their teachers. All the advances of natural science which had been made in the meantime served them only as new proofs against the existence of a creator of the world; and, in truth, it was quite outside their scope to develop the theory any further. Though idealism was at the end of its tether and was dealt a death blow by the Revolu-

221

tion of 1848, it had the satisfaction of seeing that materialism had for the moment fallen lower still. Feuerbach was
unquestionably right when he refused to take responsibility
for this materialism; only he should not have confounded
the doctrines of these hedge-preachers with materialism in
general. . . .

DIALECTICAL MATERIALISM

Strauss, Bauer, Stirner, Feuerbach—these were the off-
shoots of Hegelian philosophy, in so far as they did not abandon the field of philosophy. Strauss, after his *Life of Jesus* and
Dogmatics, produced only literary studies in philosophy and
ecclesiastical history after the fashion of Renan. Bauer only
achieved something in the field of the history of the origin
of Christianity, though what he did here was important.
Stirner remained a curiosity, even after Bakunin blended
him with Proudhon and labelled the blend "anarchism."
Feuerbach alone was of significance as a philosopher. But `
not only did philosophy—claimed to soar above all sciences
and to be the all comprehensive science of sciences—remain
for him an impassable barrier, an unassailable holy thing,
but as a philosopher, too, he stopped half way; the lower half
of him was materialist, the upper half idealist. He was incapable of disposing of Hegel through criticism; he simply
threw him aside as useless, while he himself, compared with
the encyclopedic wealth of the Hegelian system, achieved
nothing positive beyond a grandiloquent religion of love
and a meagre, impotent system of morals.

Out of the dissolution of the Hegelian school, however,
there developed still another tendency, the only one which
has borne real fruit. And this tendency is essentially connected with the name of Marx.[2]

[2] Here I may be permitted to make a personal explanation. Lately
repeated reference has been made to my share in this theory, and so I

Ludwig Feuerbach

The separation from the Hegelian school was here also the result of a return to the materialist standpoint. That means it was resolved to comprehend the real world—nature and history—just as it presents itself to everyone who approaches it free from pre-conceived idealist fancies. It was decided relentlessly to sacrifice every idealist fancy which could not be brought into harmony with the facts conceived in their own and not in a fantastic connection. And materialism means nothing more than this. But here the materialistic world outlook was taken really seriously for the first time and was carried through consistently—at least in its basic features—in all domains of knowledge concerned.

Hegel was not simply put aside. On the contrary, one started out from his revolutionary side described above, from the dialectical method. But in its Hegelian form this method was unusable. According to Hegel, dialectics is the self-development of the concept. The absolute concept does not only exist—where unknown—from eternity, it is also the actual living soul of the whole existing world. It develops into itself through all the preliminary stages which are treated at length in the *Logic* and which are all included in it. Then it "alienates" itself by changing into nature, where, without consciousness of itself, disguised as the necessity of

can hardly avoid saying a few words here to settle this particular point. I cannot deny that both before and during my forty years' collaboration with Marx I had a certain independent share in laying the formulations, and more particularly in elaborating the theory. But the greater part of its leading basic principles, particularly in the realm of economics and history, and, above all, its final, clear formulation, belong to Marx. What I contributed—at any rate with the exception of a few special studies—Marx could very well have done without me. What Marx accomplished I would not have achieved. Marx stood higher, saw farther, and took a wider and quicker view than all the rest of us. Marx was a genius; we others were at best talented. Without him the theory would not be what it is today. It therefore rightly bears his name.

nature, it goes through a new development and finally comes again to self-consciousness in man. This self-consciousness then elaborates itself again in history from the crude form until finally the absolute concept again comes to itself completely in the Hegelian philosophy. According to Hegel, therefore, the dialectical development apparent in nature and history, i.e., the causal inter-connection of the progressive movement from the lower to the higher, which asserts itself through all zigzag movements and temporary setbacks, is only a miserable copy of the self-movement of the concept going on from eternity, no one knows where, but at all events independently of any thinking human brain. This ideological reversal had to be done away with. We comprehended the concepts in our heads once more materialistically —as images of real things instead of regarding the real things as images of this or that stage of development of the absolute concept. Thus dialectics reduced itself to the science of the general laws of motion—both of the external world and of human thought—two sets of laws which are identical in substance, but differ in their expression in so far as the human mind can apply them consciously, while in nature and also up to now for the most part in human history, these laws assert themselves unconsciously in the form of external necessity in the midst of an endless series of seeming accidents. Thereby the dialectic of the concept itself became merely the conscious reflex of the dialectical motion of the real world and the dialectic of Hegel was placed upon its head; or rather, turned off its head, on which it was standing before, and placed upon its feet again. And this materialist dialectic which for years has been our best working tool and our sharpest weapon was, remarkably enough, discovered not only by us, but also independently of us and even of Hegel by a German worker, Joseph Dietzgen.

In this way, however, the revolutionary side of Hegelian philosophy was again taken up and at the same time freed

Ludwig Feuerbach

from the idealist trammels which in Hegel's hands had prevented its consistent execution. The great basic thought that the world is not to be comprehended as a complex of ready-made *things,* but as a complex of *processes,* in which the things apparently stable no less than their mind-images in our heads, the concepts, go through an uninterrupted change of coming into being and passing away, in which, in spite of all seeming accidents and of all temporary retrogression, a progressive development asserts itself in the end—this great fundamental thought has, especially since the time of Hegel, so thoroughly permeated ordinary consciousness that in this generality it is scarcely ever contradicted. But to acknowledge this fundamental thought in words and to apply it in reality in detail to each domain of investigation are two different things. If, however, investigation always proceeds from this standpoint, the demand for final solutions and eternal truths ceases once for all; one is always conscious of the necessary limitation of all acquired knowledge, of the fact that it is conditioned by the circumstances in which it was acquired. On the other hand, one no longer permits oneself to be imposed upon by the antitheses, insuperable for the still common old metaphysics, between true and false, good and bad, identical and different, necessary and accidental. One knows that these antitheses have only a relative validity; that which is recognised now as true has also its latent false side which will later manifest itself, just as that which is now regarded as false has also its true side by virtue of which it could previously have been regarded as true. One knows that what is maintained to be necessary is composed of sheer accidents and that the so-called accidental is the form behind which necessity hides itself—and so on.

The old method of investigation and thought which Hegel calls "metaphysical," which preferred to investigate *things* as given, as fixed and stable, a method the relics of which still strongly haunt people's minds, had a good deal of his-

225

torical justification in its day. It was necessary first to examine things before it was possible to examine processes. One had first to know what a particular thing was before one could observe the changes going on in connection with it. And such was the case with natural science. The old metaphysics which accepted things as finished objects arose from a natural science which investigated dead and living things as finished objects. But when this investigation had progressed so far that it became possible to take the decisive step forward of transition to the systematic investigation of the changes which these things undergo in nature itself, then the last hour of the old metaphysics sounded in the realm of philosophy also. And in fact, while natural science up to the end of the last century was predominantly a *collecting* science, a science of finished things, in our century it is essentially a *classifying* science, a science of the processes, of the origin and development of these things and of the interconnection which binds all these natural processes into one great whole. Physiology, which investigates the processes occurring in plant and animal organisms; embryology, which deals with the development of individual organisms from germ to maturity; geology, which investigates the gradual formation of the earth's surface—all these are the offspring of our century.

But, above all, there are three great discoveries which had enabled our knowledge of the inter-connection of natural processes to advance by leaps and bounds: first, the discovery of the cell as the unit from whose multiplication and differentiation the whole plant and animal body develops—so that not only is the development and growth of all higher organisms recognized to proceed according to a single general law, but also, in the capacity of the cell to change, the way is pointed out by which organisms can change their species and thus go through a more than individual development. Second, the transformation of energy, which had

Ludwig Feuerbach

demonstrated that all the so-called forces operative in the first instance in inorganic nature—mechanical force and its complement, so-called potential energy, heat, radiation (light or radiant heat), electricity, magnetism and chemical energy —are different forms of manifestation of universal motion, which pass into one another in definite proportions so that in place of a certain quantity of another makes its appearance and thus the whole motion of nature is reduced to this incessant process of transformation from one form into another. Finally, the proof which Darwin first developed in connected form that the stock of organic products of nature surrounding us today, including mankind, is the result of a long process of evolution from a few original unicellular germs, and that these again have arisen from protoplasm or albumen which came into existence by chemical means.

Thanks to these three great discoveries and the other immense advances in natural science, we have now arrived at the point where we can demonstrate as a whole the inter-connection between the processes in nature not only in particular spheres but also in the inter-connection of these particular spheres themselves, and so can present in an approximately systematic form a comprehensive view of the inter-connection in nature by means of the facts provided by empirical natural science itself. To furnish this comprehensive view was formerly the task of so-called natural philosophy. It could do this only by putting in place of the real but as yet unknown inter-connections ideal and imaginary ones, filling out the missing facts by figments of the mind and bridging the actual gaps merely in imagination. In the course of this procedure it conceived many brilliant ideas and foreshadowed many later discoveries, but it also produced a considerable amount of nonsense, which indeed could not have been otherwise. Today, when one needs to comprehend the results of natural scientific investigation only dialectically, that is, in the sense of their own inter-

connections, in order to arrive at a "system of nature" sufficient for our time; when the dialectical character of this
inter-connection is forcing itself against their will even into
the metaphysically-trained minds of the natural scientists,
today this natural philosophy is finally disposed of. Every
attempt at resurrecting it would be not only superfluous but
a step backwards . . . .

Friedrich Engels (1820-1895)

Anti-Dühring

Morality and Law; Eternal Truths

. . . Is human thought sovereign? Before we can answer
yes or no we must first enquire: what is human thought? Is
it the thought of the individual man? No. But it exists only
as the individual thought of many billions of past, present
and future men. If, then, I say that the total thought of all
these human beings, including future ones, which is em-
braced in my idea, is *sovereign,* able to know the world as
it exists, if only mankind lasts long enough and in so far as
no limits are imposed on its knowledge by its perceptive
organs or the objects to be known, then I am saying something
which is pretty banal and, in addition, pretty barren. For the
most valuable result from it would be that it should make
us extremely distrustful of our present knowledge, inasmuch
as in all probability we are but little beyond the beginning
of human history, and the generations which will put *us*
right are likely to be far more numerous than those whose
knowledge we—often enough with a considerable degree of
contempt—are in a position to correct.

Herr Dühring himself declares that consciousness, and
therefore also thought and knowledge, of necessity can only
become manifest in a series of individual beings. We can
only ascribe sovereignty to the thought of each of these individuals in so far as we are not aware of any power which
would be able to impose any idea forcibly on him, when he

is of sound mind and wide awake. But as for the sovereign validity of the knowledge in each individual's mind, we all know that there can be no talk of such a thing, and that all previous experience shows that without exception such knowledge always contains much more that is capable of being improved upon than that which cannot be improved upon or is correct.

In other words, the sovereignty of thought is realised in a series of extremely unsovereignly-thinking human beings; the knowledge which has an unconditional claim to truth is realised in a series of relative errors; neither the one nor the other can be fully realised except through an endless eternity of human existence.

Here once again we find the same contradiction as we found above, between the character of human thought, necessarily conceived as absolute, and its reality in individual human beings with their extremely limited thought. This is a contradiction which can only be solved in the infinite progression, or what is for us, at least from a practical standpoint, the endless succession, of generations of mankind. In this sense human thought is just as much sovereign, and its capacity for knowledge just as much unlimited as limited. It is sovereign and unlimited in its disposition, its vocation, its possibilities and its historical purpose; it is not sovereign and it is limited in its individual expression and in its realisation at each particular moment.

It is just the same with eternal truths. If mankind ever reached the stage at which it could only work with eternal truths, with conclusions which possess sovereign validity and have an unconditional claim to truth, it would then have reached the point where the infinity of the intellectual world both in its actuality and in its potentiality had been exhausted, and this would mean that the famous miracle of the infinite series which has been counted would have been performed.

But in spite of all this, are there any truths which are so securely based that any doubt of them seems to us to amount to insanity? That twice two makes four, that the three angles of a triangle are equal to two right angles, that Paris is in France, that a man who gets no food dies of hunger, and so forth? Are there then nevertheless *eternal* truths, final and ultimate truths?

Certainly there are. We can divide the whole realm of knowledge in the traditional way into three great departments. The first includes all sciences which are concerned with inanimate nature and are to a greater or less degree susceptible of mathematical treatment: mathematics, astronomy, mechanics, physics, chemistry. If it gives anyone any pleasure to use mighty words for very simple things, it can be asserted that *certain* results obtained by these sciences are eternal truths, final and ultimate truths; for which reason these sciences are also known as the *exact* sciences. But very far from all their results have this validity. With the introduction of variable magnitudes and the extension of their variability to the infinitely small and infinitely large, mathematics, in other respects so strictly moral, fell from grace; it ate of the tree of knowledge, which opened up to it a career of most colossal achievements, but at the same time a path of error. The virgin state of absolute validity and irrefutable certainty of everything mathematical was gone for ever; mathematics entered the realm of controversy, and we have reached the point where most people differentiate and integrate not because they understand what they are doing but from pure faith, because up to now it has always come out right. Things are even worse with astronomy and mechanics, and in physics and chemistry we are surrounded by hypotheses as by a swarm of bees. And it must of necessity be so. In physics we are dealing with the motion of molecules, in chemistry with the formation of molecules out of atoms, and if the interference of light waves is not a myth, we have absolutely no prospect of ever seeing these interesting objects with our own eyes. As time goes on, final and ultimate truths become remarkably rare in this field.

We are even worse off for them in geology, which by its nature has to deal chiefly with events which took place not only in our absence but in the absence of any human being whatever. The winning of final and absolute truths on this field is therefore a very troublesome business, and the crop is extremely small.

The second department of science is the one which covers the investigation of living organisms. In this fluid there is such a multitude of inter-relationships and causalities that not only does the solution of each question give rise to a host of other questions, but each separate problem can only be solved piecemeal, through a series of investigations which often requires centuries to complete; and even then the need for a systematic presentation of all their inter-relations makes it necessary once more to surround the final and ultimate truths with a luxuriant growth of hypotheses. What a long series of intermediaries from Galen to Malpighi was necessary for correctly establishing such a simple matter as the circulation of the blood in mammals, how slight is our knowledge of the origin of blood corpuscles, and how numerous are the missing links even today, for example, in our attempts to bring the symptoms of a disease into some rational relationship with its causes! And often enough discoveries, such as that of the cell, are made which compel us to revise completely all formerly established final and ultimate truths in the realm of biology, and to put whole piles of them on the scrap heap once and for all. Anyone who wants to establish really pure and immutable truths in this science will therefore have to be content with such platitudes as: all men are mortal, all female mammals have lacteal glands, and the like; he will not even be able to assert that the higher mammals digest with their stomach and intestines and not with their heads, for the nervous activity which is centralised in the head is indispensable to digestion.

But eternal truths are in an even worse plight in the third, the historical group of sciences. The subjects investigated by these in their historical sequence and in their present forms are the conditions of human life, social relationships, forms of law and government, with their ideal superstructure, of philosophy, religion, art, etc. In organic nature we are at least dealing with a succession of phenomena which, so far as our immediate observation is concerned, are recurring with fair regularity between very wide limits. Organic species have on the whole remained unchanged since the time of Aristotle. In social history, however, the repetition of conditions is the exception and not the rule, once we pass beyond the primitive stage of man, the so-called Stone Age; and when such repetitions occur, they never arise under exactly similar conditions—as for example the existence of an original common ownership of the land among all civilised peoples, and the way in which this came to an end. In the sphere of human history our knowledge is therefore even more backward than in the realm of biology. Furthermore, when by way of exception the inner connection between the social and political forms in an epoch come to be recognised, this as a rule only occurs when these forms are already out of date and are nearing extinction. Therefore, knowledge is here essentially relative, inasmuch as it is limited to the perception of relationships and consequences of certain social and state forms which exist only at a particular epoch and among particular people and are of their very nature transitory. Anyone therefore who sets out on this field to hunt down final and ultimate truths, truths which are pure or absolutely immutable, will bring home but little, apart from platitudes and commonplaces of the sorriest kind—for example, that generally speaking man cannot live except by labour; that up to the present mankind for the most part has been divided into rulers and ruled; that Napoleon died on May 5, 1821, and others of like kind.

Now it is a remarkable thing that it is precisely in this sphere that we most frequently encounter truths which claim to be eternal, final and ultimate and all the rest of it. That twice two make four, that birds have beaks, and similar statements, are proclaimed as eternal truths only by those who aim at deducing, from the existence of eternal truths in general, the conclusion that there are also eternal truths in the sphere of human history—eternal morality, eternal justice, and so on—which claim a validity and scope equal to those of the truths and deductions of mathematics. And then we can confidently rely on this same friend of humanity taking the first opportunity to assure us that all previous fabricators of eternal truths have been to a greater or lesser degree asses and charlatans, that they have all fallen into error and made mistakes; but that *their* error and *their* fallibility has been in accordance with natural law, and prove the existence of truth and accuracy in *his* case; and that he, the prophet who has now arisen, has in his bag, all ready made, final and ultimate truth, eternal morality and eternal justice. This has all happened so many hundreds and thousands of times that we can only feel astonished that there should still be people credulous enough to believe this, not of others, but of themselves . . .

We might have made mention above of the sciences which investigate the laws of human thought, i.e., logic and dialectics. In these, however, we do not fare any better as regards eternal truths. Herr Dühring declares that dialectics proper is pure nonsense, and the many books which have been and in the future will be written on logic provide on the other hand abundant proof that in this science too final and ultimate truths are much more sparsely sown than is commonly believed.

For that matter, there is absolutely no need to be alarmed

at the fact that the stage of knowledge which we have now reached is as little final as all that have preceded it. It already embraces a vast mass of facts and requires very great specialisation of study on the part of anyone who wants to become an expert in any particular science. But a man who applies the measure of pure, immutable, final and ultimate truth to knowledge which, by the very nature of its object, must either remain relative for long successions of generations and be completed only step by step, or which, as in cosmogony, geology and the history of man, must always remain defective and incomplete because of the faultiness of historical material—such a man only proves thereby his own ignorance and perversity, even if the real background to his pretensions is not, as it is in this case, his claim to personal infallibility. Truth and error, like all concepts which are expressed in polar opposites, have absolute validity only in an extremely limited field, as we have just seen, and as even Herr Dühring would realise if he had any acquaintance with the first elements of dialectics, which deal precisely with the inadequacy of all polar opposites. As soon as we apply the antithesis between truth and error outside of that narrow field which has been referred to above it becomes relative and therefore unserviceable for exact scientific modes of expression; and if we attempt to apply it as absolutely valid outside that field we then really find ourselves beaten: both poles of the antithesis change into their opposites, truth becomes error and error truth. Let us take as an example the well-known Boyle's law, by which, if the temperature remains constant, the volume of gases varies inversely with the pressure to which they are subjected. Regnault found that this law does not hold good in certain cases. Had he been a philosopher of reality he would have had to say: Boyle's law is mutable, and is therefore not a pure truth, therefore it is not a truth at all, therefore it is an error. But had he done this he would have committed an error far

FRIEDRICH ENGELS

greater than the one that was contained in Boyle's law; his grain of truth would have been lost sight of in a sandhill of error; he would have distorted his originally correct conclusion into an error compared with which Boyle's law, along with the little particle of error that clings to it, would have seemed like truth. But Regnault, being a man of science, did not indulge in such childishness, but continued his investigations and discovered that Boyle's law is in general only approximately correct, and in particular loses its validity in the case of gases which can be liquefied by pressure, as soon as the pressure approaches the point at which liquefaction begins. Boyle's law therefore was proved to be correct only within definite limits. But is it absolutely and finally true even within those limits? No physicist would assert that this was so. He would say that it holds good within certain limits of pressure and temperature and for certain gases; and even within these more restricted limits he would not exclude the possibility of a still narrower limitation or altered formulation as the result of future investigations. This is how things stand with final and ultimate truths in physics for example. Really scientific works therefore as a rule avoid such dogmatic and moral expressions as error and truth, while these expressions meet us everywhere in works such as the philosophy of reality, in which empty phrase-mongering attempts to impose on us as the sovereign result of sovereign thought. . . .

If we have not made much progress with truth and error, we can make even less with good and bad. This antithesis belongs exclusively to the domain of morals, that is, a domain drawn from the history of mankind, and it is precisely in this field that final and ultimate truths are most sparsely sown. The conceptions of good and bad have varied so much from nation to nation and from age to age that they have been in direct contradiction to each other. But all the same, someone may object, good is not bad and bad is not good; if good is confused with bad there is an end to all

morality, and everyone can do and leave undone whatever
he cares. This is also, stripped of his oracular phrases, Herr
Dühring's opinion. But the matter cannot be so simply disposed of. If it was such an easy business there would certainly be no dispute at all over good and bad; everyone
would know what was good and what was bad. But how do
things stand to-day? What morality is preached to us to-day?
There is first Christian-feudal morality, inherited from past
centuries of faith; and this again has two main subdivisions,
Catholic and Protestant moralities, each of which in turn has
no lack of further subdivisions from the Jesuit-Catholic and
Orthodox-Protestant to loose "advanced" moralities. Alongside of these we find the modern bourgeois morality and with
it too the proletarian morality of the future, so that in the
most advanced European countries alone the past, present
and future provide three great groups of moral theories
which are in force simultaneously and alongside of each
other. Which is then the true one? Not one of them, in the
sense of having absolute validity; but certainly that morality
which contains the maximum of durable elements is the one
which, in the present, represents the overthrow of the present,
represents the future: that is, the proletarian.

But when we see that the three classes of modern society,
the feudal aristocracy, the bourgeoisie and the proletariat,
each have their special morality, we can only draw the one
conclusion, that men, consciously or unconsciously, derive
their moral ideas in the last resort from the practical relations on which their class position is based—from the economic relations in which they carry on production and
exchange.

But nevertheless there is much that is common to the three
moral theories mentioned above—is this not at least a portion
of a morality which is externally fixed? These moral theories
represent three different stages of the same historical development, and have therefore a common historical background,

and for that reason alone they necessarily have much in common. Even more, in similar or approximately similar stages of economic development moral theories must of necessity be more or less in agreement. From the moment when private property in movable objects developed, in all societies in which this private property existed there must be the moral law in common: Thou shalt not steal. Does this law thereby become an eternal moral law? By no means. In a society in which the motive for stealing has been done away with, in which therefore at the very most only lunatics would ever steal, how the teacher of morals would be laughed at who tried solemnly to proclaim the eternal truth: Thou shalt not steal!

We therefore reject every attempt to impose on us any moral dogma whatsoever as an eternal, ultimate and for ever immutable moral law on the pretext that the moral world too has its permanent principles which transcend history and the differences between nations. We maintain on the contrary that all former moral theories are the product, in the last analysis, of the economic stage which society had reached at that particular epoch. And as society has hitherto moved in class antagonisms, morality was always a class morality; it has either justified the domination and the interests of the ruling class, or, as soon as the oppressed class has become powerful enough, it has represented the revolt against this domination and the future interests of the oppressed. That in this process there has on the whole been progress in morality, as in all other branches of human knowledge, cannot be doubted. But we have not yet passed beyond class morality. A really human morality which transcends class antagonisms and their legacies in thought becomes possible only at a stage of society which has not only overcome class contradictions but has even forgotten them in practical life. . . .

José Ortega y Gasset (1883-   )

The Revolt of the Masses

"The Self-Satisfied Age"

To resume; the new social fact here analysed is this: European history reveals itself, for the first time, as handed over to the decisions of the ordinary man as such. Or to turn it into the active voice: the ordinary man, hitherto guided by others, has resolved to govern the world himself. This decision to advance to the social foreground has been brought about in him automatically, when the new type of man he represents had barely arrived at maturity. If from the viewpoint of what concerns public life, the psychological structure of this new type of mass-man be studied, what we find is as follows: (1) An inborn, root-impression that life is easy, plentiful, without any grave limitations; consequently, each average man finds within himself a sensation of power and triumph which, (2) invites him to stand up for himself as he is, to look upon his moral and intellectual endowment as excellent, complete. This contentment with himself leads him to shut himself off from any external court of appeal; not to listen, not to submit his opinions to judgment, not to consider others' existence. His intimate feeling of power urges him always to exercise predominance. He will act then as if he and his like were the only beings existing in the world; and, consequently, (3) will intervene in all matters, imposing his own vulgar views without respect or regard for others, without limit or reserve, that is to say, in accordance with a system of "direct action."

It was this series of aspects which made us think of certain defective types of humanity, such as the spoiled child, and the primitive in revolt, that is, the barbarian. (The normal primitive, on the other hand, is the most submissive to external authority every known, be it religion, taboo, social tradition, or customs.) There is no need to be surprised at my heaping up hard names against this type of human being. This present essay is nothing more than a preliminary skirmish against this triumphant man, and the announcement that a certain number of Europeans are about to turn energetically against his attempt to tyrannise. For the moment it is only a first skirmish, the frontal attack will come later, perhaps very soon, and in a very different form from that adopted by this essay. The frontal attack must come in such a way that the mass-man cannot take precautions against it; he will see it before him and will not suspect that it precisely is the frontal attack.

This type which at present is to be found everywhere, and everywhere imposes his own spiritual barbarism, is, in fact, the spoiled child of human history. The spoiled child is the heir who behaves exclusively as a mere heir. In this case the inheritance is civilisation—with its conveniences, its security; in a word, with all its advantages. As we have seen, it is only in circumstances of easy existence such as our civilisation has produced, that a type can arise, marked by such a collection of features, inspired by such a character. It is one of a number of deformities produced by luxury in human material. There might be a deceptive tendency to believe that a life born into a world of plenty would be better, more really a life than one which consists in a struggle against scarcity. Such is not the case, for reasons of the strictest and most fundamental nature, which this is not the place to enlarge upon. For the present, instead of those reasons, it is sufficient to recall the ever-recurrent fact which constitutes the tragedy of every hereditary aristocracy. The aristocrat inherits, that is to say, he finds attributed to his person, conditions of life which he has not created, and which, therefore, are not produced in organic union with his personal, individual existence. At birth he finds himself installed, suddenly and without knowing how, in the midst of his riches and his prerogatives. In his own self, he has nothing to do with them, because they do not come from him. They are the giant armour of some other person, some other human being, his ancestor. And he has to live as an heir, that is to say, he has to wear the trappings of another existence. What does this bring us to? What life is the "aristocrat" by inheritance going to lead, his own or that of his first noble ancestor? Neither one nor the other. He is condemned to *represent* the other man, consequently to *be* neither that other nor himself. Inevitably his life loses all authenticity, and is transformed into pure representation or fiction of another life. The abundance of resources that he is obliged to make use of gives him no chance to live out his own personal destiny, his life is atrophied. *All life is the struggle, the effort to be itself.* The difficulties which I meet with in order to realise my existence are precisely what awakens and mobilises my activities, my capacities. If my body was not a weight to me, I should not be able to walk. If the atmosphere did not press on me, I should feel my body as something vague, flabby, unsubstantial. So in the "aristocratic" heir his whole individuality grows vague, for lack of use and vital effort. The result is that specific stupidity of "our old nobility" which is unlike anything else—a stupidity which, strictly speaking, has never yet been described in its intimate tragic mechanism—that tragic mechanism which leads all hereditary aristocracy to irremediable degeneration.

So much merely to counteract our ingenuous tendency to believe that a superabundance of resources favours existence.

JOSÉ ORTEGA Y GASSET

Quite the contrary. A world superbundant[1] in possibilities automatically produces deformities, vicious types of human life, which may be brought under the general class, the "heir-man," of which the "aristocrat" is only one particular case, the spoiled child another, and the mass-man of our time, more fully, more radically, a third. (It would, moreover, be possible to make more detailed use of this last allusion to the "aristocrat," by showing how many of his characteristic traits, in all times and among all peoples, germinate in the mass-man. For example: his propensity to make out of games and sports the central occupation of his life; the cult of the body—hygienic regime and attention to dress; lack of romance in his dealings with woman; his amusing himself with the "intellectual," while at bottom despising him and at times ordering his flunkeys or his bravoes to chastise him; his preference for living under an absolute authority rather than under a regime of free-discussion,[2] etc.)

[1] The increase, and even the abundance, of resources are not to be confused with the excess. In the XIXth Century the facilities of life increase, and this produces the amazing growth—quantitative and qualitative—of life that I have noted above. But a moment has come when the civilised world, in relation to the capacity of the average man, has taken on an appearance of superabundance, of excess of riches, of superfluity. A single example of this: the security seemingly offered by progress (i.e. the ever-growing increase of vital advantages) demoralises the average man, inspiring him with a confidence which is false, vicious, and atrophying.

[2] In this, as in other matters, the English aristocracy seems to be an exception to what we have said. But though the case is an admirable one, it would suffice to indicate in outline the history of England in order to show that this exception proves the rule. Contrary to what is usually said, the English nobility has been the least "superabundant" of Europe, and has lived in more constant danger than any other. And because it has always lived in danger, it has succeeded in winning respect for itself—which implies that it has ceaselessly remained in the breach. The fundamental fact is forgotten that England was until well

The Revolt of the Masses

I persist then, at the risk of boring the reader, in making the point that this man full of uncivilised tendencies, this newest of the barbarians, is an automatic product of modern civilisation, especially of the form taken by this civilisation in the XIXth Century. He has not burst in on the civilised world from outside like the "great white barbarians" of the Vth Century; neither has he been produced within it by spontaneous, mysterious generation, as Aristotle says of the tadpoles in the pond; he is its natural fruit. One may formulate, as follows, a law confirmed by palaeontology and bio-geography: human life has arisen and progressed only when the resources it could count on were balanced by the problems it met with. This is true, as much in the spiritual order as in the physical. Thus, to refer to a very concrete aspect of corporal existence, I may recall that the human species has flourished in zones of our planet where the hot season is compensated by a season of intense cold. In the tropics the animal-man degenerates, and vice versa, inferior races—the pygmies, for example—have been pushed back towards the tropics by races born after them and superior in the scale of evolution.[3]

The civilisation of the XIXth Century is, then, of such a character that it allows the average man to take his place in a world of superabundance, of which he perceives only the lavishness of the means at his disposal, nothing of the pains involved. He finds himself surrounded by marvellous instruments, healing medicines, watchful governments, comfortable privileges. On the other hand, he is ignorant how diffi-

into the XVIIIth Century the poorest country in Western Europe. It was this fact that saved the nobility. Not being abundant in resources, it had very early to enter into commercial and industrial occupations— considered ignoble on the Continent—that is to say, it decided very soon to lead an economic existence creative in character, and not to depend solely on its privileges.

[3] See Olbricht, *Klima und Entwicklung*, 1923.

cult it is to invent those medicines and those instruments and to assure their production in the future; he does not realise how unstable is the organisation of the State and is scarcely conscious to himself of any obligations. This lack of balance falsifies his nature, vitiates it in its very roots, causing him to lose contact with the very substance of life, which is made up of absolute danger, is radically problematic. The form most contradictory to human life that can appear among the human species is the "self-satisfied man." Consequently, when he becomes the predominant type, it is time to raise the alarm and to announce that humanity is threatened with degeneration, that is, with relative death. On this view, the vital level represented by Europe at the present day is superior to the whole of the human past, but if we look to the future, we are made to fear that it will neither preserve the level reached nor attain to a higher one, but rather will recede and fall back upon lower heights.

This, I think, brings out with sufficient clearness the superlative abnormality represented by the "self-satisfied man." He is a man who has entered upon life to do "what he jolly well likes." This, in fact, is the illusion suffered by the *fils de famille*. We know the reason why: in the family circle, everything, even the greatest faults, are in the long run left unpunished. The family circle is relatively artificial, and tolerates many acts which in society, in the world outside, would automatically involve disastrous consequences for their author. But the man of this type thinks that he can behave outside just as he does at home; believes that nothing is fatal, irremediable, irrevocable. That is why he thinks that he can do what he likes.[4] An almighty mistake!

[4] What the home is in relation to society, such on a larger scale is one nation before the assemblage of nations. One of the manifestations, at once most evident and overwhelming, of the ruling "self-satisfaction" is, as we shall see, the determination taken by some nations to "do what they jolly well please" in the consortium of nations. This, in their

The Revolt of the Masses

"You will go where you are taken to," as the parrot is told in the Portuguese story. It is not that one *ought* not to do just what one pleases; it is simply that one cannot do other than what each of us *has* to do, *has* to be. The only way out is to refuse to do what has to be done, but this does not set us free to do something else just because it pleases us. In this matter we only possess a negative freedom of will, a *noluntas*. We can quite well turn away from our true destiny, but only to fall a prisoner in the deeper dungeons of our destiny. I cannot make this clear to each of my readers in what concerns his individual destiny as such, because I do not know each of my readers; but it is possible to make it clear in those portions, those facets, of his destiny which are identical with those of others. For example, every present-day European knows, with a certainty much more forcible than that of all his expressed "ideas" and "opinions," that the European of to-day *must* be a liberal. Let us not discuss whether it is this or the other form of liberalism which must be his. I am referring to the fact that the most reactionary of Europeans knows, in the depths of his conscience, that the effort made by Europe in the last century, under the name of liberalism, is, in the last resort, something inevitable, inexorable; something that Western man to-day *is*, whether he likes it or not.

Even though it be proved, with full and incontrovertible evidence, that there is falsity and fatality in all the concrete shapes under which the attempt has been made to realise the categorical imperative of political liberty inscribed on the destiny of Europe, the final evidence that in the last century it was right *in substance* still holds good. This final evidence is present equally in the European Communist as in the

ingenuousness, they call "nationalism." I, who detest all false submission to internationalism, find absurd, on the other hand, this passing phase of self-conceit on the part of the least developed of the nations.

Fascist, whatever attitudes they may adopt to convince themselves to the contrary. All "know" that beyond all the just
criticisms launched against the manifestations of liberalism
there remains its unassailable truth, a truth not theoretic,
scientific, intellectual, but of an order radically different and
more decisive, namely, a truth of destiny. Theoretic truths
not only are disputable, but their whole meaning and force
lie in their being disputed, they spring from discussion.
They live as long as they are discussed, and they are made
exclusively for discussion. But destiny—what from a vital
point of view one has to be or has not to be—is not discussed,
it is either accepted or rejected. If we accept it, we are genuine; if not, we are the negation, the falsification of ourselves.[5]
Destiny does not consist in what we feel we should like to
do; rather it is recognised in its clear features in the consciousness that we *must* do what we do not feel like doing.

Well, then, the "satisfied man" is characterised by his
"knowing" that certain things cannot be, and nevertheless,
for that very reason, pretending in act and word to be convinced of the opposite. The Fascist will take his stand against
political liberty, precisely because he knows that in the long
run this can never fail, but is inevitably a part of the very
substance of European life, and will be returned to when its
presence is truly required, in the hour of grave crisis. For
the tonic that keeps the mass-man in form is insincerity,
"the joke." All his actions are devoid of the note of inevitability, they are done as the *fils de famille* carries out his
escapades. All that haste, in every order of life, to adopt

---

[5] Abasement, degradation is simply the manner of life of the man who
has refused to be what it is his duty to be. This, his genuine being, none
the less does not die; rather is changed into an accusing shadow, a
phantom which constantly makes him feel the inferiority of the life he
lives compared with the one he ought to live. The debased man survives
his self-inflicted death.

tragic, conclusive, final attitudes is mere appearance. Men play at tragedy because they do not believe in the reality of the tragedy which is actually being staged in the civilised world.

It would be a nice matter if we were forced to accept as the genuine self of an individual, whatever he tried to make us accept as such. If anyone persists in maintaining that he believes two and two make five, and there is no reason for supposing him to be insane, we may be certain that he does not believe it, however much he may shout it out, or even if he allows himself to be killed for maintaining it. A hurricane of farsicality, everywhere and in every form, is at present raging over the lands of Europe. Almost all the positions taken up and proclaimed are false ones. The only efforts that are being made are to escape from our real destiny, to blind ourselves to its evidence, to be deaf to its deep appeal, to avoid facing up to *what has to be*. We are living in comic fashion, all the more comic the more apparently tragic is the mask adopted. The comic exists wherever life has no basis of inevitableness on which a stand is taken without reserves. The mass-man will not plant his foot on the immovably firm ground of his destiny, he prefers a fictitious existence suspended in air. Hence, never as now have we had these lives without substance or root—*déracinés* from their own destiny—which let themselves float on the lightest current. This is the epoch of "currents" and of "letting things slide." Hardly anyone offers any resistance to the superficial whirlwinds that arise in art, in ideas, in politics, or in social usages. Consequently, rhetoric flourishes more than ever. The surrealist thinks he has outstripped the whole of literary history when he has written (here a word that there is no need to write) where others have written "jasmines, swans and fauns." But what he has really done has been simply to bring to light another form of rhetoric which hitherto lay hidden in the latrines.

The present situation is made more clear by noting what, in spite of its peculiar features, it has in common with past periods. Thus, hardly does Mediterranean civilisation reach its highest point—towards the IIIrd Century B.C.—when the cynic makes his appearance. Diogenes, in his mud-covered sandals, tramps over the carpets of Aristippus. The cynic pullulated at every corner, and in the highest places. This cynic did nothing but *saboter* the civilisation of the time. He was the nihilist of Hellenism. He created nothing, he made nothing. His role was to undo—or rather to attempt to undo, for he did not succeed in his purpose. The cynic, a parasite of civilisation, lives by denying it, for the very reason that he is convinced that it will not fail. What would become of the cynic among a savage people where everyone, naturally and quite seriously, fulfils what the cynic farcically considers to be his personal role? What is your Fascist if he does not speak ill of liberty, or your surrealist if he does not blaspheme against art?

None other could be the conduct of this type of man born into a too well-organised world, of which he perceives only the advantages and not the dangers. His surroundings spoil him, because they are "civilisation," that is, a home, and the *fils de famille* feels nothing that impels him to abandon his mood of caprice, nothing which urges him to listen to outside counsels from those superior to himself. Still less anything which obliges him to make contact with the inexorable depths of his own destiny.

SUGGESTIONS FOR FURTHER READING

Hannah Arendt, *The Human Condition.*
Hilaire Belloc, *The Servile State.*
Ruth Benedict, *Patterns of Culture.*
Thomas Hobbes, *Leviathan.*

The Revolt of the Masses

Karl Jaspers, *Man in the Modern Age.*
John Locke, *Second Treatise on Civil Government.*
Benjamin Nelson, *Man in Contemporary Society.*
F. C. S. Northrop, *Philosophical Anthropology and Practical Politics.*
Max Picard, *The World of Silence.*
Plato, *The Republic.*
David Riesman and others, *The Lonely Crowd.*
Jean-Jacques Rousseau, *The Social Contract.*
William L. Shirer, *The Rise and Fall of the Third Reich.*
Henry David Thoreau, *Civil Disobedience.*
Thorstein Veblen, *The Theory of the Leisure Class.*
Norbert Wiener, *The Human Use of Human Beings: Cybernetics and Society.*

PART THREE
Man as Creature

Introduction

The great religions of Semitic origin are united at least in their belief in one God and in the possibility of his communicating with men. The idea of such a communication is by no means an unproblematic one as far as philosophers are concerned, for when the intellect comes up against the actual claim that a hidden God has revealed what it could not establish under its own power, it must either turn away or somehow contrive to accommodate the visible and the invisible in a single consciousness. At any rate, for centuries it has been part of Western man's life to find himself confronted by that claim and vexed by the tensions it creates. Aware of this, most if not all major philosophers, believers and nonbelievers alike, have had something to say about religion.

Among Christian thinkers who struggled with the idea of revelation and its bearing on man's self-understanding, Blaise Pascal is one of the towering figures in the centuries that followed the medieval period. A mathematical genius, he was also knowledgeable in the modern sciences that had begun to flower about a hundred years prior to his birth in 1623. He celebrated, as much as any thinker, the powers latent in human reason but warned just as fervently against their misdirection. Properly used, he felt, those powers can guide man to self-knowledge and ultimately to salvation, but what exactly is their proper use? The readings from

Pascal's *Pensées* reveal his effort to come to grips with this question.

With the understanding that something in the world claims to be a communication from God, we may now look more closely at the possibility of such a thing. In "A Project of Thought" Kierkegaard looks into the peculiar and complex character of this possibility. With the individual in the role of Learner and God in the role of Teacher, the author sketches out his drama in categories clearly borrowed from Christianity. The narrative can be understood readily enough, but at the same time the key ideas embodied in it resist being understood or made transparent if they are taken as standing for something real. One such idea is that of the Deity becoming a human teacher, bringing "the Truth" to men alienated from it, and then vanishing. For all its impenetrability, this is as much a claim about the nature of man as any theory proposed by philosophers, yet so different from theirs that toward the end Kierkegaard steps back from his project and wonders whether it really falls within the scope of human invention. If there exists a scheme of thought beyond man's devising—which in fact no man will confess to having invented—then the individual who hears of it is thrown back upon himself at the strangeness of it and compelled to notice what it proposes concerning himself. Hot or cold, his response to it, seriously examined, offers material for a fuller understanding of himself.

"A Project of Thought" was conceived as exploring the concept of a divine communication in abstraction from any historical claim that such a thing is real. Howard A. Johnson's essay "The Deity in Time" is an analysis, and virtually a summary also, of Kierkegaard's religious philosophizing. In the works cited by Dr. Johnson, Kierkegaard describes the collisions between Christian and secular conceptions of the

Introduction

nature of man, collisions brought about by the claim that the eternal has put in an appearance at a certain historical moment.

The possibility of a divine communication has its opponents as well. In this camp Friedrich Nietzsche has been a powerful influence since his death in 1900. No more slashing talent has ever directed itself against the Christian conception of man. Our selection from *The Joyful Wisdom* exhibits such characteristically Nietzschean themes as the death of God, the denial of man's creaturehood, psychogenetic explanations of morality and religion, and the inescapable animality of humankind. No single judgment can do justice to the breadth and intensity of Nietzsche's thought. Without pretending to offer summary judgment, however, his reader can put questions to the texts. Does the author perhaps pretend here and there to know things which humans as such are in no position to find out? Are his representations of "faith" and other Christian conceptions accurate? Is it possible for one human to "see through" the moral and religious decisions of others?

Jacques Maritain's analysis of contemporary atheism distinguishes several types of disbelief in God, but concentrates on the positive, absolute atheism we encounter in Nietzsche, in the dialectical materialism of official Marxist philosophy, and more recently in Jean-Paul Sartre. As Maritain sees it, the outright "No" of atheism concerning the God of the Testaments is not a reasoned position but an act of freedom, of revolt. How, then, does it differ from a resentful balk at the idea of being a mere creature? This attitude is evident in Nietzsche's famous confession: "If there were gods, how could I bear not to be a god?" If human nature contains the possibility of being told something by a Deity, it also includes the possibility of man's rankling at the disclosure of his own creaturehood.

Blaise Pascal (1623-1662)

Pensées

Fragments

72*

Man's disproportion.

[This is where our innate knowledge leads us. If it be not true, there is no truth in man; and if it be true, he finds therein great cause for humiliation, being compelled to abase himself in one way or another. And since he cannot exist without this knowledge, I wish that, before entering on deeper researches into nature, he would consider her both seriously and at leisure, that he would reflect upon himself also, and knowing what proportion there is . . .] Let man then contemplate the whole of nature in her full and grand majesty, and turn his vision from the low objects which surround him. Let him gaze on that brilliant light, set like an eternal lamp to illumine the universe; let the earth appear to him a point in comparison with the vast circle described by the sun; and let him wonder at the fact that this vast circle is itself but a very fine point in comparison with that described by the stars in their revolution round the firmament. But if our view be arrested there, let our imagination pass beyond; it will sooner exhaust the power of conception

---

* Section numbers are based on *Pensées de Blaise Pascal*, Leon Brunschwieg, ed. (Paris: Hachette, 1904), the standard edition.

than nature that of supplying material for conception. The whole visible world is only an imperceptible atom in the ample bosom of nature. No idea approaches it. We may enlarge our conceptions beyond all imaginable space; we only produce atoms in comparison with the reality of things. It is an infinite sphere, the centre of which is everywhere, the circumference nowhere. In short it is the greatest sensible mark of the almighty power of God, that imagination loses itself in that thought.

Returning to himself, let man consider what he is in comparison with all existence; let him regard himself as lost in this remote corner of nature; and from the little cell in which he finds himself lodged, I mean the universe, let him estimate at their true value the earth, kingdoms, cities, and himself. What is a man in the Infinite?

But to show him another prodigy equally astonishing, let him examine the most delicate things he knows. Let a mite be given him, with its minute body and parts incomparably more minute, limbs with their joints, veins in the limbs, blood in the veins, humours in the blood, drops in the humours, vapours in the drops. Dividing these last things again, let him exhaust his powers of conception, and let the last object at which he can arrive be now that of our discourse. Perhaps he will think that here is the smallest point in nature. I will let him see therein a new abyss. I will paint for him not only the visible universe, but all that he can conceive of nature's immensity in the womb of this abridged atom. Let him see therein an infinity of universes, each of which has its firmament, its planets, its earth, in the same proportion as in the visible world; in each earth animals, and in the last mites, in which he will find again all that the first had, finding still in these others the same thing without end and without cessation. Let him lose himself in wonders as amazing in their littleness as the others in their vastness. For who will not be astounded at the fact that our body, which a little while ago was imperceptible in the universe, itself imperceptible in the bosom of the whole, is now a colossus, a world, or rather a whole, in respect of the nothingness which we cannot reach? He who regards himself in this light will be afraid of himself, and observing himself sustained in the body given him by nature between those two abysses of the Infinite and Nothing, will tremble at the sight of these marvels; and I think that, as his curiosity changes into admiration, he will be more disposed to contemplate them in silence than to examine them with presumption.

For in fact what is man in nature? A Nothing in comparison with the Infinite, an All in comparison with the Nothing, a mean between nothing and everything. Since he is infinitely removed from comprehending the extremes, the end of things and their beginning are hopelessly hidden from him in an impenetrable secret; he is equally incapable of seeing the Nothing from which he was made, and the Infinite in which he is swallowed up.

What will he do then, but perceive the appearance of the middle of things, in an eternal despair of knowing either their beginning or their end. All things proceed from the Nothing, and are borne towards the Infinite. Who will follow these marvellous processes? The Author of these wonders understands them. None other can do so.

Through failure to contemplate these Infinites, men have rashly rushed into the examination of nature, as though they bore some proportion to her. It is strange that they have wished to understand the beginnings of things, and hence to arrive at the knowledge of the whole, with a presumption as infinite as their object. For surely this design cannot be formed without presumption or without a capacity infinite like nature.

If we are well informed, we understand that, as nature has graven her image and that of her Author on all things, they almost all partake of her double infinity. Thus we see that all the sciences are infinite in the extent of their researches. For who doubts that geometry, for instance, has an infinite infinity of problems to solve? They are also infinite in the multitude and fineness of their premises; for it is clear that those which are put forward as ultimate are not self-supporting, but are based on others, which, again having others for their support, do not permit of finality. But we represent some as ultimate for reason, in the same way as in regard to material objects we call that an indivisible point beyond which our senses can no longer perceive anything, although by its nature it is infinitely divisible.

Of these two Infinites of science, that of greatness is the most palpable, and hence a few persons have pretended to know all things. "I will speak of the whole," said Democritus.

But the infinitely little is the least obvious. Philosphers have much oftener claimed to have reached it, and it is here they have all stumbled. This has given rise to such common titles as *First Principles, Principles of Philosophy,* and the like as ostentatious in fact, though not in appearance, as that one which blinds us, *De omni scibili.*

We naturally believe ourselves far more capable of reaching the centre of things than of embracing their circumference. The visible extent of the world visibly exceeds us; but as we exceed little things, we think ourselves more capable of knowing them. And yet we need no less capacity for attaining the Nothing than the All. Infinite capacity is required for both, and it seems to me that whoever shall have understood the ultimate principles of being might also attain to the knowledge of the Infinite. The one depends on the other, and one leads to the other. These extremes meet and reunite by force of distance, and find each other in God, and in God alone.

Let us then take our compass; we are something, and we are not everything. The nature of our existence hides from us the knowledge of first beginnings which are born of the

Pensées

Nothing; and the littleness of our being conceals from us
the sight of the Infinite.
Our intellect holds the same position in the world of
thought as our body occupies in the expanse of nature.
Limited as we are in every way, this state which holds the
mean between two extremes is present in all our impotence.
Our senses perceive no extreme. Too much sound deafens us;
too much light dazzles us; too great distance or proximity
hinders our view. Too great length and too great brevity of
discourse tend to obscurity; too much truth is paralysing (I
know some who cannot understand that to take four from
nothing leaves nothing). First principles are too self-evident
for us; too much pleasure disagrees with us. Too many con-
cords are annoying in music; too many benefits irritate us;
we wish to have the wherewithal to over-pay our debts.
*Beneficia eo usque laeta sunt dum videntur exsolvi posse;
ubi multum antevenere, pro gratia odium redditur.* We
feel neither extreme heat nor extreme cold. Excessive qualities are prejudicial to us and not perceptible by the senses;
we do not feel but suffer them. Extreme youth and extreme
age hinder the mind, as also too much and too little education. In short, extremes are for us as though they were not,
and we are not within their notice. They escape us, or we
them.
This is our true state; this is what makes us incapable of
certain knowledge and of absolute ignorance. We sail within
a vast sphere, ever drifting in uncertainty, driven from end
to end. When we think to attach ourselves to any point and
to fasten to it, it wavers and leaves us; and if we follow it,
it eludes our grasp, slips past us, and vanishes for ever. Nothing stays for us. This is our natural condition, and yet most
contrary to our inclination; we burn with desire to find solid
ground and an ultimate sure foundation whereon to build
a tower reaching to the Infinite. But our whole groundwork
cracks, and the earth opens to abysses.

Let us therefore not look for certainty and stability. Our reason is always deceived by fickle shadows; nothing can fix the finite between the two Infinites, which both enclose and fly from it.

If this be well understood, I think that we shall remain at rest, each in the state wherein nature has placed him. As this sphere which has fallen to us as our lot is always distant from either extreme, what matters it that man should have a little more knowledge of the universe? If he has it, he but gets a little higher. Is he not always infinitely removed from the end, and is not the duration of our life equally removed from eternity, even if it lasts ten years longer?

In comparison with these Infinites all finites are equal, and I see no reason for fixing our imagination on one more than on another. The only comparison which we make of ourselves to the finite is painful to us.

If man made himself the first object of study, he would see how incapable he is of going further. How can a part know the whole? But he may perhaps aspire to know at least the parts to which he bears some proportion. But the parts of the world are all so related and linked to one another, that I believe it impossible to know one without the other and without the whole.

Man, for instance, is related to all he knows. He needs a place wherein to abide, time through which to live, motion in order to live, elements to compose him, warmth and food to nourish him, air to breathe. He sees light; he feels bodies; in short, he is in a dependent alliance with everything. To know man, then, it is necessary to know how it happens that he needs air to live, and, to know the air, we must know how it is thus related to the life of man, etc. Flame cannot exist without air; therefore to understand the one, we must understand the other.

Since everything then is cause and effect, dependent and supporting, mediate and immediate, and all is held together by a natural though imperceptible chain, which binds together things most distant and most different, I hold it equally impossible to know the parts without knowing the whole, and to know the whole without knowing the parts in detail.

[The eternity of things in itself or in God must also astonish our brief duration. The fixed and constant immobility of nature, in comparison with the continual change which goes on within us, must have the same effect.]

And what completes our incapability of knowing things is the fact that they are simple, and that we are composed of two opposite natures, different in kind, soul and body. For it is impossible that our rational part should be other than spiritual; and if any one maintain that we are simply corporeal, this would far more exclude us from the knowledge of things, there being nothing so inconceivable as to say that matter knows itself. It is impossible to imagine how it should know itself.

So if we are simply material, we can know nothing at all; and if we are composed of mind and matter, we cannot know perfectly things which are simple, whether spiritual or corporeal. Hence it comes that almost all philosophers have confused ideas of things, and speak of material things in spiritual terms, and of spiritual things in material terms. For they say boldly that bodies have a tendency to fall, that they seek after their centre, that they fly from destruction, that they fear the void, that they have inclinations, sympathies, antipathies, all of which attributes pertain only to mind. And in speaking of minds, they consider them as in a place, and attribute to them movement from one place to another; and these are qualities which belong only to bodies.

Instead of receiving the ideas of these things in their purity, we colour them with our own qualities, and stamp with our composite being all the simple things which we contemplate.

Who would not think, seeing us compose all things of

mind and body, but that this mixture would be quite intelligible to us? Yet it is the very thing we least understand. Man is to himself the most wonderful object in nature; for he cannot conceive what the body is, still less what the mind is, and least of all how a body should be united to a mind. This is the consummation of his difficulties, and yet it is his very being. *Modus quo corporibus adhaerent spiritus comprehendi ab hominibus non potest, et hoc tamen homo est.* Finally, to complete the proof of our weakness, I shall conclude with these two considerations. . . .

73

[But perhaps this subject goes beyond the capacity of reason. Let us therefore examine her solutions to problems within her powers. If there be anything to which her own interest must have made her apply herself most seriously, it is the inquiry into her own sovereign good. Let us see, then, wherein these strong and clear-sighted souls have placed it, and whether they agree.

One says that the sovereign good consists in virtue, another in the knowledge of nature, another in truth, *Felix qui potuit rerum cognoscere causas,* another in total ignorance, another in indolence, others in disregarding appearances, another in wondering at nothing, *nihil admirari prope res una quae possit facere et servare beatum,* and the true sceptics in their indifference, doubt, and perpetual suspense, and others, wiser, think to find a better definition. We are well satisfied.

To transpose after the laws to the following title.

We must see if this fine philosophy has gained nothing certain from so long and so intent study; perhaps at least the soul will know itself. Let us hear the rulers of the world on this subject. What have they thought of her substance?

264

Have they been more fortunate in locating her? What have they found out about her origin, duration, and departure?
Is then the soul too noble a subject for their feeble lights? Let us then abase her to matter and see if she knows whereof is made the very body which she animates, and those others which she contemplates and moves at her will. What have those great dogmatists, who are ignorant of nothing, known of this matter? *Harum sententiarum.*
This would doubtless suffice, if reason were reasonable. She is reasonable enough to admit that she has been unable to end anything durable, but she does not yet despair of reaching it; she is as ardent as ever in this search, and is confident she has within her the necessary powers for this conquest. We must therefore conclude, and, after having examined her powers in their effects, observe them in themselves, and see if she has a nature and a grasp capable of laying hold of the truth.]

81

It is natural for the mind to believe, and for the will to love; so that, for want of true objects, they must attach themselves to false.

82

Imagination.

It is that deceitful part in man, that mistress of error and falsity, the more deceptive that she is not always so; for she would be an infallible rule of truth, if she were an infallible rule of falsehood. But being most generally false, she gives no sign of her nature, impressing the same character on the true and the false.

I do not speak of fools, I speak of the wisest men; and it is among them that the imagination has the great gift of

BLAISE PASCAL

persuasion. Reason protests in vain; it cannot set a true value on things.

This arrogant power, the enemy of reason, who likes to rule and dominate it, has established in man a second nature to show how all-powerful she is. She makes men happy and sad, healthy and sick, rich and poor; she compels reason to believe, doubt, and deny; she blunts the senses, or quickens them; she has her fools and sages; and nothing vexes us more than to see that she fills her devotees with a satisfaction far more full and entire than does reason. Those who have a lively imagination are a great deal more pleased with themselves than the wise can reasonably be. They look down upon men with haughtiness; they argue with boldness and confidence, others with fear and diffidence; and this gaiety of countenance often gives them the advantage in the opinion of the hearers, such favour have the imaginary wise in the eyes of judges of like nature. Imagination cannot make fools wise; but she can make them happy, to the envy of reason which can only make its friends miserable; the one covers them with glory, the other with shame.

What but this faculty of imagination dispenses reputation, awards respect and vereration to persons, works, laws, and the great? How insufficient are all the riches of the earth without her consent!

Would you not say that this magistrate, whose venerable age commands the respect of a whole people, is governed by pure and lofty reason, and that he judges causes according to their true nature without considering those mere trifles which only affect the imagination of the weak? See him go to sermon, full of devout zeal, strengthening his reason with the ardour of his love. He is ready to listen with exemplary respect. Let the preacher appear, and let nature have given him a hoarse voice or a comical cast of countenance, or let his barber have given him a bad shave, or let by chance his dress be more dirtied than usual, then however great the

266

truths he announces, I wager our senator loses his gravity.

If the greatest philosopher in the world find himself upon a plank wider than actually necessary, but hanging over a precipice, his imagination will prevail, though his reason convince him of his safety. Many cannot bear the thought without a cold sweat. I will not state all its effects.

Every one knows that the sight of cats or rats, the crushing of a coal, etc., may unhinge the reason. The tone of voice affects the wisest, and changes the force of a discourse or a poem.

Love or hate alters the aspect of justice. How much greater confidence has an advocate, retained with a large fee, in the justice of his cause! How much better does his bold manner make his case appear to the judges, deceived as they are by appearances! How ludicrous is reason, blown with a breath in every direction!

I should have to enumerate almost every action of men who scarce waver save under her assaults. For reason has been obliged to yield, and the wisest reason takes as her own principles those which the imagination of man has everywhere rashly introduced. [He who would follow reason only would be deemed foolish by the generality of men. We must judge by the opinion of the majority of mankind. Because it has pleased them, we must work all day for pleasures seen to be imaginary; and after sleep has refreshed our tired reason, we must forthwith start up and rush after phantoms, and suffer the impressions of this mistress of the world. This is one of the sources of error, but it is not the only one.]

Our magistrates have known well this mystery. Their red robes, the ermine in which they wrap themselves like furry cats, the courts in which they administer justice, the *fleurs-de-lis,* and all such august apparel were necessary; if the physicians had not their cassocks and their mules, if the doctors had not their square caps and their robes four times too wide, they would never have duped the world, which cannot resist so original an appearance. If magistrates had true justice, and if physicians had the true art of healing, they would have no occasion for square caps; the majesty of these sciences would of itself be venerable enough. But having only imaginary knowledge, they must employ those silly tools that strike the imagination with which they have to deal; and thereby in fact they inspire respect. Soldiers alone are not disguised in this manner, because indeed their part is the most essential; they establish themselves by force, the others by show.

Therefore our kings seek out no disguises. They do not mask themselves in extraordinary costumes to appear such; but they are accompanied by guards and halberdiers. Those armed and red-faced puppets who have hands and power for them alone, those trumpets and drums which go before them, and those legions round about them, make the stoutest tremble. They have not dress only, they have might. A very refined reason is required to regard as an ordinary man the Grand Turk, in his superb seraglio, surrounded by forty thousand janissaries.

We cannot even see an advocate in his robe and with his cap on his head, without a favourable opinion of his ability. The imagination disposes of everything; it makes beauty, justice, and happiness, which is everything in the world. I should much like to see an Italian work, of which I only know the title, which alone is worth many books, *Della opinione regina del mondo*. I approve of the book without knowing it, save the evil in it, if any. These are pretty much the effects of that deceptive faculty, which seems to have been expressly given us to lead us into necessary error. We have, however, many other sources of error.

Not only are old impressions capable of misleading us; the charms of novelty have the same power. Hence arise all the disputes of men, who taunt each other either with following the false impressions of childhood or with running rashly after the new. Who keeps the due mean? Let him appear and prove it. There is no principle, however natural to us from infancy, which may not be made to pass for a false impression either of education or of sense.

"Because," say some, "you have believed from childhood that a box was empty when you saw nothing in it, you have believed in the possibility of a vacuum. This is an illusion of your senses, strengthened by custom, which science must correct." "Because," say others, "you have been taught at school that there is no vacuum, you have perverted your common sense which clearly comprehended it, and you must correct this by returning to your first state." Which has deceived you, your senses or your education?

We have another source of error in diseases. They spoil the judgment and the senses; and if the more serious produce a sensible change, I do not doubt that slighter ills produce a proportionate impression.

Our own interest is again a marvellous instrument for nicely putting out our eyes. The justest man in the world is not allowed to be judge in his own cause; I know some who, in order not to fall into this self-love, have been perfectly unjust out of opposition. The sure way of losing a just cause has been to get it recommended to these men by their near relatives.

Justice and truth are two such subtle points, that our tools are too blunt to touch them accurately. If they reach the point, they either crush it, or lean all round, more on the false than on the true.

[Man is so happily formed that he has no . . . good of the true, and several excellent of the false. Let us now see how much. . . . But the most powerful cause of error is the war existing between the senses and reason.]

100

Self-love.

The nature of self-love and of this human Ego is to love self only and consider self only. But what will man do? He cannot prevent this object that he loves from being full of faults and wants. He wants to be great, and he sees himself small. He wants to be happy, and he sees himself miserable. He wants to be perfect, and he sees himself full of imperfections. He wants to be the object of love and esteem among men and he sees that his faults merit only their hatred and contempt. This embarrassment in which he finds himself produces in him the most unrighteous and criminal passion that can be imagined; for he conceives a mortal enmity against that truth which reproves him, and which convinces him of his faults. He would annihilate it, but, unable to destroy it in its essence, he destroys it as far as possible in his own knowledge and in that of others; that is to say, he devotes all his attention to hiding his faults both from others and from himself, and he cannot endure either that others should point them out to him, or that they should see them.

Truly it is an evil to be full of faults; but it is a still greater evil to be full of them, and to be unwilling to recognise them, since that is to add the further fault of a voluntary illusion. We do not like others to deceive us; we do not think it fair that they should be held in higher esteem by us than they deserve; it is not then fair that we should deceive them, and should wish them to esteem us more highly than we deserve.

Thus, when they discover only the imperfections and vices which we really have, it is plain they do us no wrong, since it is not they who cause them; they rather do us good, since they help us to free ourselves from an evil, namely, the ignorance of these imperfections. We ought not to be angry at their knowing our faults and despising us; it is but right that they should know us for what we are, and should despise us, if we are contemptible.

Such are the feelings that would arise in a heart full of equity and justice. What must we say then of our own heart, when we see in it a wholly different disposition? For is it not true that we hate truth and those who tell it us, and that we like them to be deceived in our favour, and prefer to be esteemed by them as being other than what we are in fact? One proof of this makes me shudder. The Catholic religion does not bind us to confess our sins indiscriminately to everybody; it allows them to remain hidden from all other men save one, to whom she bids us reveal the innermost recesses of our heart, and show ourselves as we are. There is only this one man in the world whom she orders us to undeceive, and she binds him to an inviolable secrecy, which makes this knowledge to him as if it were not. Can we imagine anything more charitable and pleasant? And yet the corruption of man is such that he finds even this law harsh; and it is one of the main reasons which has caused a great part of Europe to rebel against the Church.

How unjust and unreasonable is the heart of man, which feels it disagreeable to be obliged to do in regard to one man what in some measure it were right to do to all men! For is it right that we should deceive men?

There are different degrees in this aversion to truth; but all may perhaps be said to have it in some degree, because it is inseparable from self-love. It is this false delicacy which makes those who are under the necessity of reproving others choose so many windings and middle courses to avoid offence. They must lessen our faults, appear to excuse them, intersperse praises and evidence of love and esteem. Despite all this, the medicine does not cease to be bitter to self-love. It takes as little as it can, always with disgust, and often with a secret spite against those who administer it.

Hence it happens that if any have some interest in being loved by us, they are averse to render us a service which they know to be disagreeable. They treat us as we wish to be treated. We hate the truth, and they hide it from us. We desire flattery, and they flatter us. We like to be deceived, and they deceive us.

So each degree of good fortune which raises us in the world removes us farther from truth, because we are most afraid of wounding those whose affection is most useful and whose dislike is most dangerous. A prince may be the by-word of all Europe, and he alone will know nothing of it. I am not astonished. To tell the truth is useful to those to whom it is spoken, but disadvantageous to those who tell it, because it makes them disliked. Now those who live with princes love their own interests more than that of the prince whom they serve; and so they take care not to confer on him a benefit so as to injure themselves.

This evil is no doubt greater and more common among the higher classes; but the lower are not exempt from it, since there is always some advantage in making men love us. human life is thus only a perpetual illusion; men deceive and flatter each other. No one speaks of us in our presence as he does of us in our absence. Human society is founded on mutual deceit; few friendships would endure if each knew what his friend said of him in his absence, although he then spoke in sincerity and without passion.

Man is then only disguise, falsehood, and hypocrisy, both in himself and in regard to others. He does not wish any one to tell him the truth; he avoids telling it to others, and all these dispositions, so removed from justice and reason, have a natural root in his heart.

101

I set it down as a fact that if all men knew what each said of the other, there would not be four friends in the world. This is apparent from the quarrels which arise from the indiscreet tales told from time to time. [I say, further, all men would be . . .]

102

Some vices only lay hold of us by means of others, and these, like branches, fall on removal of the trunk.

103

The example of Alexander's chastity has not made so many continent as that of his drunkenness has made intemperate. It is not shameful not to be as virtuous as he, and it seems excusable to be no more vicious. We do not believe ourselves to be exactly sharing in the vices of the vulgar, when we see that we are sharing in those of great men; and yet we do not observe that in these matters they are ordinary men. We hold on to them by the same end by which they hold on to the rabble; for, however exalted they are, they are still united at some point to the lowest of men. They are not suspended in the air, quite removed from our society. No, no; if they are greater than we, it is because their heads are higher; but their feet are as low as ours. They are all on the same level, and rest on the same earth; and by that extremity they are as low as we are, as the meanest folk, as infants, and as the beasts.

104

When our passion leads us to do something, we forget our duty; for example, we like a book and read it, when we ought to be doing something else. Now, to remind ourselves of our duty, we must set ourselves a task we dislike; we then plead that we have something else to do, and by this means remember our duty.

105

How difficult it is to submit anything to the judgment of another, without prejudicing his judgment by the manner

BLAISE PASCAL

in which we submit it! If we say, "I think it beautiful," "I think it obscure," or the like, we either entice the imagination into that view, or irritate it to the contrary. It is better to say nothing; and then the other judges according to what really is, that is to say, according as it then is, and according as the other circumstances, not of our making, have placed it. But we at least shall have added nothing, unless it be that silence also produces an effect, according to the turn and the interpretation which the other will be disposed to give it, or as he will guess it from gestures or countenance, or from the tone of the voice, if he is a physiognomist. So difficult is it not to upset a judgment from its natural place, or, rather, so rarely is it firm and stable!

143

Diversion.

Men are entrusted from infancy with the care of their honour, their property, their friends, and even with the property and the honour of their friends. They are overwhelmed with business, with the study of languages, and with physical exercise; and they are made to understand that they cannot be happy unless their health, their honour, their fortune and that of their friends be in good condition, and that a single thing wanting will make them unhappy. Thus they are given cares and business which make them bustle about from break of day.—It is, you will exclaim, a strange way to make them happy! What more could be done to make them miserable? —Indeed! what could be done? We should only have to relieve them from all these cares; for then they would see themselves: they would reflect on what they are, whence they came, whither they go, and thus we cannot employ and divert them too much. And this is why, after having given them so much business, we advise them, if they have some time for

274

relaxation, to employ it in amusement, in play, and to be always fully occupied.

How hollow and full of ribaldry is the heart of man!

144

I spent a long time in the study of the abstract sciences, and was disheartened by the small number of fellow-students in them. When I commenced the study of man, I saw that these abstract sciences are not suited to man, and that I was wandering farther from my own state in examining them, than others in not knowing them. I pardoned their little knowledge; but I thought at least to find many companions in the study of man, and that it was the true study which is suited to him. I have been deceived; still fewer study it than geometry. It is only from the want of knowing how to study this that we seek the other studies. But is it not that even here is not the knowledge which man should have, and that for the purpose of happiness it is better for him not to know himself?

145

[One thought alone occupies us; we cannot think of two things at the same time. This is lucky for us according to the world, not according to God.]

146

Man is obviously made to think. It is his whole dignity and his whole merit; and his whole duty is to think as he ought. Now, the order of thought is to begin with self, and with its Author and its end.

Now, of what does the world think? Never of this, but of dancing, playing the lute, singing, making verses, running at the ring, etc., fighting, making oneself king, without thinking what it is to be a king and what to be a man.

147

We do not content ourselves with the life we have in ourselves and in our own being; we desire to live an imaginary life in the mind of others, and for this purpose we endeavour to shine. We labour unceasingly to adorn and preserve this imaginary existence, and neglect the real. And if we possess calmness, or generosity, or truthfulness, we are eager to make it known, so as to attach these virtues to that imaginary existence. We would rather separate them from ourselves to join them to it; and we would willingly be cowards in order to acquire the reputation of being brave. A great proof of the nothingness of our being, not to be satisfied with the one without the other, and to renounce the one for the other! For he would be infamous who would not die to preserve his honour.

148

We are so presumptuous that we would wish to be known by all the world, even by people who shall come after, when we shall be no more; and we are so vain that the esteem of five or six neighbours delights and contents us.

430

For Port Royal.

The Beginning, after having explained the incomprehensibility.—The greatness and the wretchedness of man are so evident that the true religion must necessarily teach us both that there is in man some great source of greatness, and a

great source of wretchedness. It must then give us a reason
for these astonishing contradictions.

In order to make man happy, it must prove to him that
there is a God; that we ought to love Him; that our true
happiness is to be in Him, and our sole evil to be separated
from Him; it must recognise that we are full of darkness
which hinders us from knowing and loving Him; and that
thus, as our duties compel us to love God, and our lusts turn
us away from Him, we are full of unrighteousness. It must
give us an explanation of our opposition to God and to our
own good. It must teach us the remedies for these infirmities,
and the means of obtaining these remedies. Let us therefore
examine all the religions of the world, and see if there be
any other than the Christian which is sufficient for this
purpose.

Shall it be that of the philosophers, who put forward as
the chief good, the good which is in ourselves? Is this the
true good? Have they found the remedy for our ills? Is man's
pride cured by placing him on an equality with God? Have
those who have made us equal to the brutes, or the Moham-
medans who have offered us earthly pleasures as the chief
good even in eternity, produced the remedy for our lusts?
What religion, then, will teach us to cure pride and lust?
What religion will in fact teach us our good, our duties,
the weakness which turns us from them, the cause of this
weakness, the remedies which can cure it, and the means of
obtaining these remedies?

All other religions have not been able to do so. Let us
see what the wisdom of God will do.

"Expect neither truth," she says, "nor consolation from
men. I am she who formed you, and who alone can teach
you what you are. But you are now no longer in the state in
which I formed you. I created man holy, innocent, perfect.
I filled him with light and intelligence. I communicated to
him my glory and my wonders. The eye of man saw then

the majesty of God. He was not then in the darkness which blinds him, nor subject to mortality and the woes which afflict him. But he has not been able to sustain so great glory without falling into pride. He wanted to make himself his own centre, and independent of my help. He withdrew himself from my rule; and, on his making himself equal to me by the desire of finding his happiness in himself, I abandoned him to himself. And setting in revolt the creatures that were subject to him, I made them his enemies; so that man is now become like the brutes, and so estranged from me that there scarce remains to him a dim vision of his Author. So far has all his knowledge been extinguished or disturbed! The senses, independent of reason, and often the masters of reason, have led him into pursuit of pleasure. All creatures either torment or tempt him, and domineer over him, either subduing him by their strength, or fascinating him by their charms, a tyranny more awful and more imperious.

"Such is the state in which men now are. There remains to them some feeble instinct of the happiness of their former state; and they are plunged in the evils of their blindness and their lust, which have become their second nature.

"From this principle which I disclose to you, you can recognise the cause of those contradictions which have astonished all men, and have divided them into parties holding so different views. Observe, now, all the feelings of greatness and glory which the experience of so many woes cannot stifle, and see if the cause of them must not be in another nature."

For Port-Royal to-morrow (Prospopaea).

"It is in vain, O men, that you seek within yourselves the remedy for your ills. All your light can only reach the knowledge that not in yourselves will you find truth or good. The philosophers have promised you that, and have been unable to do it. They neither know what is your true good, nor what is your true state. How could they have given reme-

278

dies for your ills, when they did not even know them? Your
chief maladies are pride, which takes you away from God,
and lust, which binds you to earth; and they have done nothing else but cherish one or other of these diseases. If they
gave you God as an end, it was only to administer to your
pride; they made you think that you are by nature like Him,
and conformed to Him. And those who saw the absurdity of
this claim put you on another precipice, by making you
understand that your nature was like that of the brutes, and
led you to seek your good in the lusts which are shared by
the animals. This is not the way to cure you of your unrighteousness, which these wise men never knew. I alone can
make you understand who you are. . . ."

Adam, Jesus Christ.

If you are united to God, it is by grace, not by nature. If
you are humbled, it is by penitence, not by nature.

Thus this double capacity. . . .

You are not in the state of your creation.

As these two states are open, it is impossible for you not
to recognise them. Follow your own feelings, observe yourselves, and see if you do not find the lively characteristics of
these two natures. Could so many contradictions be found
in a simple subject?

—Incomprehensible.—Not all that is incomprehensible
ceases to exist. Infinite number. An infinite space equal to
a finite.

—Incredible that God should unite Himself to us.—This
consideration is drawn only from the sight of our vileness.
But if you are quite sincere over it, follow it as far as I have
done, and recognise that we are indeed so vile that we are
incapable in ourselves of knowing if His mercy cannot make
us capable of Him. For I would know how this animal,
who knows himself to be so weak, has the right to measure
the mercy of God, and set limits to it, suggested by his own
fancy. He has so little knowledge of what God is, that he

does not know what he himself is, and, completely disturbed at the sight of his own state, dares to say that God cannot make him capable of communion with Him.

But I would ask him if God demands anything else from him than the knowledge and love of Him, and why, since his nature is capable of love and knowledge, he believes that God cannot make Himself known and loved by him. Doubtless he knows at least that he exists, and that he loves something. Therefore, if he sees anything in the darkness wherein he is, and if he finds some object of his love among the things on earth, why, if God impart to him some ray of His essence, will he not be capable of knowing and of loving Him in the manner in which it shall please Him to communicate Himself to us? There must then be certainly an intolerable presumption in arguments of this sort, although they seem founded on an apparent humility, which is neither sincere nor reasonable, if it does not make us admit that, not knowing of ourselves what we are, we can only learn it from God.

"I do not mean that you should submit your belief to me without reason, and I do not aspire to overcome you by tyranny. In fact, I do not claim to give you a reason for everything. And to reconcile these contradictions, I intend to make you see clearly, by convincing proofs, those divine signs in me, which may convince you of what I am, and may gain authority for me by wonders and proofs which you cannot reject; so that you may then believe without . . . the things which I teach you, since you will find no other ground for rejecting them, except that you cannot know of yourselves if they are true or not.

"God has willed to redeem men, and to open salvation to those who seek it. But men render themselves so unworthy of it, that it is right that God should refuse to some, because of their obduracy, what He grants to others from a compassion which is not due to them. If he had willed to overcome the obstinacy of the most hardened, He could have done so by revealing Himself so manifestly to them that they could not have doubted of the truth of His essence; as it will appear at the last day, with such thunders, and such a convulsion of nature, that the dead will rise again, and the blindest will see Him.

"It is not in this manner that He has willed to appear in His advent of mercy, because, as so many make themselves unworthy of His mercy, He has willed to leave them in the loss of the good which they do not want. It was not then right that He should appear in a manner manifestly divine, and completely capable of convincing all men; but it was also not right that He should come in so hidden a manner that He could not be known by those who should sincerely seek Him. He has willed to make Himself quite recognisable by those; and thus, willing to appear openly to those who seek Him with all their heart, and to be hidden from those who flee from Him with all their heart, He so regulates the knowledge of Himself that He has given signs of Himself, visible to those who seek Him, and not to those who seek Him not. There is enough light for those who only desire to see, and enough obscurity for those who have a contrary disposition."

Søren Kierkegaard

Philosophical Fragments
A Project of Thought

A

How far does the Truth admit of being learned? With this question let us begin. It was a Socratic question, or became such in consequence of the parallel Socratic question with respect to virtue, since virtue was again determined as insight. (*Protagoras, Gorgias, Meno, Euthydemus.*) In so far as the Truth is conceived as something to be learned, its non-existence is evidently presupposed, so that in proposing to learn it one makes it the object of an inquiry. Here we are confronted with the difficulty to which Socrates calls attention in the *Meno* (80, near the end), and there characterizes as a "pugnacious proposition"; one cannot seek for what he knows, and it seems equally impossible for him to seek for what he does not know. For what a man knows he cannot seek, since he knows it; and what he does not know he cannot seek, since he does not even know for what to seek. Socrates thinks the difficulty through in the doctrine of Recollection, by which all learning and inquiry is interpreted as a kind of remembering; one who is ignorant needs only a reminder to help him come to himself in the consciousness of what he knows. Thus the Truth is not introduced into the individual from without, but was within him. This thought receives further development at the hands of Socrates, and it ultimately becomes the point of concen-

282

tration for the pathos of the Greek consciousness, since it serves as a proof for the immortality of the soul; but with a backward reference, it is important to note, and hence as proof for the soul's preexistence.[1]

In the light of this idea it becomes apparent with what wonderful consistency Socrates remained true to himself, through his manner of life giving artistic expression to what he had understood. He entered into the role of midwife and sustained it throughout; not because his thought "had no positive content,"[2] but because he perceived that this relation is the highest that one human being can sustain to another. And in this surely Socrates was everlastingly right; for even if a divine point of departure is ever given, between man and man this is the true relationship, provided we reflect

[1] Taking the thought in its naked absoluteness, not reflecting upon possible variations in the soul's preexistent state, we find this Greek conception recurring in both an older and more recent speculation: an eternal creation; an eternal procession from the Father; an eternal coming into being of the Deity; an eternal self-sacrifice; a past resurrection; a past judgment. All these thoughts are essentially the Greek doctrine of Recollection, only that this is not always perceived, since they have been arrived at by way of an advance. If we split the thought up into a reckoning of the different states ascribed to the soul in its preexistence, the everlasting *prae*'s of such an approximating mode of thought are like the everlasting *post*'s of the corresponding forward approximations. The contradictions of existence are explained by positing a *prae* as needed (because of an earlier state the individual has come into his present otherwise inexplicable situation); or by positing a *post* as needed (on another planet the individual is to be placed in a more favorable situation, in view of which his present state is not inexplicable).

[2] Such is the criticism commonly passed upon Socrates in our age, which boasts of its positivity much as if a polytheist were to speak with scorn of the negativity of a monotheist; for the polytheist has many gods, the monotheist only one. So our philosophers have many thoughts, all valid to a certain extent; Socrates had only one, which was absolute.

upon the absolute and refuse to dally with the accidental, from the heart renouncing the understanding of the half-truths which seem the delight of men and the secret of the System. Socrates was a midwife subjected to examination by the God; his work was in fulfilment of a divine mission (Plato's *Apology*), though he seemed to men in general a most singular creature (*Theaetetus,* 149); it was in accordance with a divine principle, as Socrates also understood it, that he was by the God forbidden to beget (*Theaetetus,* 150); for between man and man the maieutic relationship is the highest, and begetting belongs to the God alone.

From the standpoint of the Socratic thought every point of departure in time is *eo ipso* accidental, an occasion, a vanishing moment. The teacher himself is no more than this; and if he offers himself and his instruction on any other basis, he does not give but takes away, and is not even the other's friend, much less his teacher. Herein lies the profundity of the Socratic thought, and the noble humanity he so thoroughly expressed, which refused to enter into a false and vain fellowship with clever heads, but felt an equal kinship with a tanner; whence he soon "came to the conclusion that the study of Physics was not man's proper business, and therefore began to philosophize about moral matters in the workshops and in the market-place" (Diogenes Laertius, II, v, 21), but philosophized with equal absoluteness everywhere. With slipshod thoughts, with higgling and haggling, maintaining a little here and conceding a little there, as if the individual might to a certain extent owe something to another, but then again to a certain extent not; with loose words that explain everything except what this "to a certain extent" means—with such makeshifts it is not possible to advance beyond Socrates, nor will one reach the concept of a Revelation, but merely remain within the sphere of idle chatter. In the Socratic view each individual is his own center, and the entire world centers in him, because his self-

284

knowledge is a knowledge of God. It was thus Socrates understood himself, and thus he thought that everyone must understand himself, in the light of this understanding interpreting his relationship to each individual, with equal humility and with equal pride. He had the courage and self-possession to be sufficient unto himself, but also in his relations to his fellowmen to be merely an occasion, even when dealing with the meanest capacity. How rare is such magnanimity! How rare in a time like ours, when the parson is something more than the clerk, when almost every second person is an authority, while all these distinctions and all these many authorities are mediated in a common madness, a *commune naufragium*. For while no human being was ever truly an authority for another, or ever helped anyone by posing as such, or was ever able to take his client with him in truth, there is another sort of success that may by such methods be won; for it has never yet been known to fail that one fool, when he goes astray, takes several others with him.

With this understanding of what it means to learn the Truth, the fact that I have been instructed by Socrates or by Prodicus or by a servant-girl, can concern me only historically; or in so far as I am a Plato in sentimental enthusiasm, It may concern me poetically. But this enthusiasm, beautiful as it is, and such that I could wish both for myself and all others a share of this "disposition to passion," which only a Stoic could frown upon; and though I may be lacking in the Socratic magnanimity and the Socratic self-denial to think its nothingness—this enthusiasm, so Socrates would say, is only an illusion, a want of clarity in a mind where earthly inequalities seethe almost voluptuously. Nor can it interest me otherwise than historically that Socrates' or Prodicus' doctrine was this or that; for the Truth in which I rest was within me, and came to light through myself, and not even Socrates could have given it to me, as little as the driver can pull the load for the horses, though he may help them by applying the lash.[3] My relation to Socrates or Prodicus cannot concern me with respect to my eternal happiness, for this is given me retrogressively through my possession of the Truth, which I had from the beginning without knowing it. If I imagine myself meeting Socrates or Prodicus or the servant-girl in another life, then here again neither of them could be more to me than an occasion, which Socrates fearlessly expressed by saying that even in the lower world he proposed merely to ask questions; for the underlying principle of all questioning is that the one who is asked must have the Truth in himself, and be able to acquire it by himself. The temporal point of departure is nothing; for as soon as I discover that I have known the Truth from eternity without being aware of it, the same instant this moment of occasion is hidden in the Eternal, and so incorporated with it that I cannot even find it so to speak, even if I sought it; because in my eternal consciousness there is neither here nor there, but only an *ubique et nusquam*.

B

Now if things are to be otherwise, the Moment in time must have a decisive significance, so that I will never be able to forget it either in time or eternity; because the Eternal, which hitherto did not exist, came into existence in this moment. Under this presupposition let us now proceed to

[3] There is a passage in the *Clitophon*, which I cite only as the testimony of a third party, since this dialogue is not believed to be genuine. Clitophon complains that the discourses of Socrates about virtue are merely inspirational, and that as soon as he has sufficiently recommended virtue in general he leaves each one to himself. Clitophon thinks that this must find its explanation either in the fact that Socrates does not know more, or else that he is unwilling to communicate more.

consider the consequences for the problem of how far it is possible to acquire a knowledge of the Truth.

THE ANTECEDENT STATE

We begin with the Socratic difficulty about seeking the Truth, which seems equally impossible whether we have it or do not have it. The Socratic thought really abolishes this disjunction, since it appears that at bottom every human being is in possession of the Truth. This was Socrates' explanation; we have seen what follows from it with respect to the moment. Now if the latter is to have decisive significance, the seeker must be destitute of the Truth up to the very moment of his learning it; he cannot even have possessed it in the form of ignorance, for in that case the moment becomes merely occasional. What is more, he cannot even be described as a seeker; for such is the expression we must give to the difficulty if we do not wish to explain it Socratically. He must therefore be characterized as beyond the pale of the Truth, not approaching it like a proselyte, but departing from it; or as being in Error. He is then in a state of Error. But how is he now to be reminded, or what will it profit him to be reminded of what he has not known, and consequently cannot recall?

THE TEACHER

If the Teacher serves as an occasion by means of which the learner is reminded, he cannot help the learner to recall that he really knows the Truth; for the learner is in a state of Error. What the Teacher can give him occasion to remember is, that he is in Error. But in this consciousness the learner is excluded from the Truth even more decisively than before, when he lived in ignorance of his Error. In this manner the Teacher trusts the learner away from him, pre-

287

cisely by serving as a reminder; only that the learner, in thus being thrust back upon himself, does not discover that he knew the Truth already, but discovers his Error; with respect to which act of consciousness the Socratic principle holds, that the Teacher is merely an occasion whoever he may be, even if he is a God. For my own Error is something I can discover only by myself, since it is only when I have discovered it that it is discovered, even if the whole world knew of it before. (Under the presupposition we have adopted concerning the moment, this remains the only analogy to the Socratic order of things.)

Now if the learner is to acquire the Truth, the Teacher must bring it to him; and not only so, but he must also give him the condition necessary for understanding it. For if the learner were in his own person the condition for understanding the Truth, he need only recall it. The condition for understanding the Truth is like the capacity to inquire for it: the condition contains the conditioned, and the question implies the answer. (Unless this is so, the moment must be understood in the Socratic sense.)

But one who gives the learner not only the Truth, but also the condition for understanding it, is more than teacher. All instruction depends upon the presence, in the last analysis, of the requisite condition; if this is lacking, no teacher can do anything. For otherwise he would find it necessary not only to transform the learner, but to re-create him before beginning to teach him. But this is something that no human being can do; if it is to be done, it must be done by the God himself.

In so far as the learner exists he is already created, and hence God must have endowed him with the condition for understanding the Truth. For otherwise his earlier existence must have been merely brutish, and the Teacher who gave him the Truth and with it the condition was the original creator of his human nature. But in so far as the moment

288

is to have decisive significance (and unless we assume this we remain at the Socratic standpoint) the learner is destitute of this condition, and must therefore have been deprived of it. This deprivation cannot have been due to an act of the God (which would be a contradiction), nor to an accident (for it would be a contradiction to assume that the lower could overcome the higher); it must therefore be due to himself. If he could have lost the condition in such a way that the loss was not due to himself, and if he could remain in the state of deprivation without his own responsibility, it would follow that his earlier possession of the condition was accidental merely. But this is a contradiction, since the condition for understanding the Truth is an essential condition. Error is then not only outside the Truth, but polemic in its attitude toward it; which is expressed by saying that the learner has himself forfeited the condition, and is engaged in forfeiting it.

The Teacher is then the God himself, who in acting as an occasion prompts the learner to recall that he is in Error, and that by reason of his own guilt. But this state, the being in Error by reason of one's own guilt, what shall we call it? Let us call it *Sin*.

The Teacher, then, is the God, and he gives the learner the requisite condition and the Truth. What shall we call such a Teacher?—for we are surely agreed that we have already far transcended the ordinary functions of a teacher. In so far as the learner is in Error, but in consequence of his own act (and in no other way can he possibly be in this state, as we have shown above), he might seem to be free; for to be what one is by one's own act is freedom. And yet he is in reality unfree and bound and exiled; for to be free from the Truth is to be exiled from the Truth, and to be exiled by one's own self is to be bound. But since he is bound by himself, may he not loose his bonds and set himself free? For whatever binds me, the same should be able to set me free

289

when it wills; and since this power is here his own self, he should be able to liberate himself. But first at any rate he must will it. Suppose him now to be so profoundly impressed by what the Teacher gave him occasion to remember (and this must not be omitted from the reckoning); suppose that he wills his freedom. In that case, i.e., if by willing to be free he could by himself become free, the fact that he had been bound would become a state of the past, tracelessly vanishing in the moment of liberation; the moment would not be charged with decisive significance. He was not aware that he had bound himself, and now he had freed himself.[4] Thus

[4] Let us take plenty of time to consider the point, since there is no pressing need for haste. By proceeding slowly one may sometimes fail to reach the goal, but by indulging in undue haste one may sometimes be carried past it. Let us talk about this a little in the Greek manner. Suppose a child had been presented with a little sum of money, and could buy with it either a good book, for example, or a toy, both at the same price. If he buys the toy, can he then buy the book for the same money? Surely not, since the money is already spent. But perhaps he may go to the bookseller and ask him to make an exchange, letting him have the book in return for the toy. Will not the bookseller say: My dear child, your toy is not worth anything; it is true that when you still had the money you could have bought the book instead of the toy, but a toy is a peculiar kind of thing, for once it is bought it loses all value. Would not the child think that this was very strange? And so there was also a time when man could have bought either freedom or bondage at the same price, this price being the soul's free choice and commitment in the choice. He chose bondage; but if he now comes forward with a proposal for an exchange, would not the God reply: Undoubtedly there was a time when you could have bought whichever you pleased, but bondage is a very strange sort of thing; when it is bought it has absolutely no value, although the price paid for it was originally the same. Would not such an individual think this very strange? Again, suppose two opposing armies drawn up in the field, and that a knight arrives whom both armies invite to fight on their side; he makes his choice, is vanquished and taken prisoner. As prisoner

interpreted the moment receives no decisive significance, and yet this was the hypothesis we proposed to ourselves in the beginning. By the terms of our hypothesis, therefore, he will not be able to set himself free. And so it is in very truth; for he forges the chains of his bondage with the strength of his freedom, since he exists in it without compulsion; and thus his bonds grow strong, and all his powers unite to make him the slave of sin. What now shall we call such a Teacher, one who restores the lost condition and gives the learner the Truth? Let us call him *Saviour,* for he saves the learner from his bondage and from himself; let us call him *Redeemer,* for he redeems the learner from the captivity into which he had plunged himself, and no captivity is so terrible and so impossible to break, as that in which the individual keeps himself. And still we have not said all that is necessary; for by his self-imposed bondage the learner has brought upon himself a burden of guilt, and when the Teacher gives him the condi-

he is brought before the victor, to whom he foolishly presumes to offer his services on the same terms as were extended to him before the battle. Would not the victor say to him: My friend, you are now my prisoner; there was indeed a time when you could have chosen differently, but now everything is changed. Was this not strange enough? Yet if it were not so, if the moment had no decisive significance, the child must at bottom have bought the book, merely imagining in his ignorance and misunderstanding that he had bought the toy; the captive knight must really have fought on the other side, the facts having been obscured by the fog, so that at bottom he had fought on the side of the leader whose prisoner he now imagined himself to be. "The vicious and the virtuous have not indeed power over their moral actions; but at first they had the power to become either the one or the other, just as one who throws a stone has power over it until he has thrown it, but not afterwards" (Aristotle). Otherwise throwing would be an illusion; the thrower would keep the stone in his hand in spite of all his throwing; it would be like the "flying arrow" of the sceptics, which did not fly.

tion and the Truth he constitutes himself an *Atonement,* taking away the wrath impending upon that of which the learner has made himself guilty.

Such a Teacher the learner will never be able to forget. For the moment he forgets him he sinks back again into himself, just as one who while in original possession of the condition forgot that God exists, and thereby sank into bondage. If they should happen to meet in another life, the Teacher would again be able to give the condition to anyone who had not yet received it; but to one who had once received the condition he would stand in a different relation. The condition was a trust, for which the recipient would always be required to render an account. But what shall we call such a Teacher? A teacher may determine whether the pupil makes progress or not, but he cannot judge him; for he ought to have Socratic insight enough to perceive that he cannot give him what is essential. This Teacher is thus not so much teacher as *Judge.* Even when the learner has most completely appropriated the condition, and most profoundly apprehended the Truth, he cannot forget this Teacher, or let him vanish Socratically, although this is far more profound than illusory sentimentality or untimely pettiness of spirit. It is indeed the highest, unless that other be the Truth.

And now the moment. Such a moment has a peculiar character. It is brief and temporal indeed, like every moment; it is transient as all moments are; it is past, like every moment in the next moment. And yet it is decisive, and filled with the Eternal. Such a moment ought to have a distinctive name; let us call it the *Fullness of Time.*

THE DISCIPLE

When the disciple is in a state of Error (and otherwise we return to Socrates) but is none the less a human being, and now receives the condition and the Truth, he does not become a human being for the first time, since he was a man already. But he becomes another man; not in the frivolous sense of becoming another individual of the same quality as before, but in the sense of becoming a man of a different quality, or as we may call him: *a new creature.*

In so far as he was in Error he was constantly in the act of departing from the Truth. In consequence of receiving the condition in the moment the course of his life has been given an opposite direction, so that he is now turned about. Let us call this change *Conversion,* even though this word be one not hitherto used; but that is precisely a reason for choosing it, in order namely to avoid confusion, for it is as if expressly coined for the change we have in mind.

In so far as the learner was in Error by reason of his own guilt, this conversion cannot take place without being taken up in his consciousness, or without his becoming aware that his former state was a consequence of his guilt. With this consciousness he will then take leave of his former state. But what leave-taking is without a sense of sadness? The sadness in this case, however, is on account of his having so long remained in his former state. Let us call such grief *Repentance;* for what is repentance but a kind of leave-taking, looking backward indeed, but yet in such a way as precisely to quicken the steps toward that which lies before?

In so far as the learner was in Error, and now receives the Truth and with it the condition for understanding it, a change takes place within him like the change from non-being to being. But this transition from non-being to being is the transition we call birth. Now one who exists cannot be born; nevertheless, the disciple is born. Let us call this transition the *New Birth,* in consequence of which the disciple enters the world quite as at the first birth, an individual human being knowing nothing as yet about the world into which he is born, whether it is inhabited, whether there are other human beings in it besides himself; for while it is

293

indeed possible to be baptized *en masse,* it is not possible to be born anew *en masse.* Just as one who has begotten himself by the aid of the Socratic midwifery now forgets everything else in the world, and in a deeper sense owes no man anything, so the disciple who is born anew owes nothing to any man, but everything to his divine Teacher. And just as the former forgets the world in his discovery of himself, so the latter forgets himself in the discovery of his Teacher.

Hence if the *Moment* is to have decisive significance—and if not we speak Socratically whatever we may say, even if through not even understanding ourselves we imagine that we have advanced far beyond that simple man of wisdom who divided judgment incorruptibly between the God and man and himself, a judge more just than Minos, Aeacus and Rhadamanthus—if the Moment has decisive significance the breach is made, and man cannot return. He will take no pleasure in remembering what Recollection brings to his mind; still less will he be able in his own strength to bring the God anew over to his side.

But is the hypothesis here expounded thinkable? Let us not be in haste to reply; for not only one whose deliberation is unduly prolonged may fail to produce an answer, but also one who while he exhibits a marvelous promptitude in replying, does not show the desirable degree of slowness in considering the difficulty before explaining it. Before we reply, let us ask ourselves from whom we may expect an answer to our question. The being born, is this fact thinkable? Certainly, why not? But for whom is it thinkable, for one who is born, or for one who is not born? This latter supposition is an absurdity which could never have entered anyone's head; for one who is born could scarcely have conceived the notion. When one who has experienced birth thinks of himself as born, he conceives this transition from non-being to being. The same principle must also hold in the case of the new birth. Or is the difficulty increased by the fact that the non-being which precedes the new birth contains more being than the non-being which preceded the first birth? But who then may be expected to think the new birth? Surely the man who has himself been born anew, since it would of course be absurd to imagine that one not so born should think it. Would it not be the height of the ridiculous for such an individual to entertain this notion?

If a human being is originally in possession of the condition for understanding the Truth, he thinks that God exists in and with his own existence. But if he is in Error he must comprehend this fact in his thinking, and Recollection will not be able to help him further than to think just this. Whether he is to advance beyond this point the *Moment* must decide (although it was already active in giving him an insight into his Error). If he does not understand this we must refer him to Socrates, though through being obsessed with the idea that he has advanced far beyond this wise man he may cause him many a vexation, like those who were so incensed with Socrates for taking away from them one or another stupid notion that they actually wanted to bite him (*Theaetetus*, 151). In the *Moment* man becomes conscious that he is born; for his antecedent state, to which he may not cling, was one of non-being. In the *Moment* man also becomes conscious of the new birth, for his antecedent state was one of non-being. Had his preceding state in either instance been one of being, the moment would not have received decisive significance for him, as has been shown above. While then the pathos of the Greek consciousness concentrates itself upon Recollection, the pathos of our project is concentrated upon the Moment. And what wonder, for is it not a most pathetic thing to come into existence from non-being?

There you have my project. But I think I hear someone say: "This is the most ridiculous of all projects; or rather, you are of all projectors of hypotheses the most ridiculous. For even when a man propounds something nonsensical, it may still remain true that it is he who has propounded it; but you behave like a lazzarone who takes money for exhibiting premises open to everybody's inspection; you are like the man who collected a fee for exhibiting a ram in the afternoon, which in the forenoon could be seen *gratis,* grazing in the open field."—"Perhaps it is so; I hide my head in shame. But assuming that I am as ridiculous as you say, let me try to make amends by proposing a new hypothesis. Everybody knows that gunpowder was invented centuries ago, and in so far it would be ridiculous of me to pretend to be the inventor; but would it be equally ridiculous of me to assume that somebody was the inventor? Now I am going to be so polite as to assume that you are the author of my project; greater politeness than this you can scarcely ask. Or if you deny this, will you also deny that someone is the author, that is to say, some human being? In that case I am as near to being the author as any other human being. So that your anger is not vented upon me because I appropriated something that belongs to another human being, but because I appropriated something of which no human being is the rightful owner; and hence your anger is by no means appeased when I deceitfully ascribe the authorship to you. Is it not strange that there should be something such in existence, in relation to which everyone who knows it knows also that he has not invented it, and that this 'pass-me-by' neither stops nor can be stopped even if we ask all men in turn? This strange fact deeply impresses me, and casts over me a spell; for it constitutes a test of the hypothesis, and proves its truth. It would certainly be absurd to expect of a man that he should of his own accord discover that he did not exist. But this is precisely the transition of the new birth, from non-being to being. That he may come to understand it afterwards can make no difference; for because a man knows how to use gunpowder and can resolve it into its constituent elements, it does not follow that he has invented it. Be then angry with me and with whoever else pretends to the authorship of this thought; but that is no reason why you should be angry with the thought itself."

Howard Albert Johnson

On Kierkegaard *

There was a man in Denmark one hundred years ago, named Søren Kierkegaard, who felt terror at the age which was then coming to birth. It was the age in which man decided to build the Kingdom of God on earth.

This was everywhere hailed as a pious project, and was encouraged even by the Christian Church. But to Kierkegaard the undertaking was a sacrilege, based on the illusion of self-redemption.

What made the illusion difficult to dispel was the curious duplexity of the phenomenon itself. It had a sparing dose of Christianity in it. It was, in part, an expression of man's genuine longing for redemption, and the doctrine of progress itself had a Christian root. But Kierkegaard detected that, for all its calling upon God, it was a new and very subtle assertion of man's sovereignty against God. In place of the old trilogy, "Nature, Man, and God," life was more and more being thought of as the interplay between *two* entities, Nature and Mankind. Nothing more was needed than a greater exercise of the intelligence by which man would be able to alter and master the natural world. Thus, Utopia was assured. Kierkegaard could not shake off his impression that little by little God was being spirited away. In the churches God was accorded the deference due to a Rector Emeritus; meanwhile,

* Howard A. Johnson, *The Deity in Time*. Used by permission of the author.

a more vigorous administration held committee meetings to settle on policy. The policies discussed began on earth and ended on earth.

From its preachers, the age demanded a testimony (Goetheo-Hegelian) that man was well on the way of becoming holy and that the Kingdom of God was a simple human possibility. Naturally, it required considerable virtuosity on the part of exegesis to get the New Testament to say this, but it was accomplished, ingeniously enough, by dropping out original sin at the beginning and eschatology at the ending. If perhaps the ideal requirements seemed a little beyond man's reach, they were cunningly explained as having been made purposely hard—just as clocks are set forward in order to get us places on time! If this bore but scant resemblance to traditional Christianity, it seemed to trouble no one . . . except Kierkegaard, for where, in such an order of things, is there any need for a *saviour?* ". . . If the requirement is no greater, then a saviour, a redeemer, grace &c, become fantastic luxuries. . . . What Christianity presupposes—namely, the tortures of a contrite conscience, the need of grace, the deeply felt need, all these frightful inward conflicts and sufferings—what Christianity presupposes in order to introduce and supply grace, salvation, the hope of eternal blessedness, all this is not to be found, or is to be found only in burlesque abridgement. . . ."[1]

The "burlesque abridgement" has received classic formulation, one hundred years later, in Richard Niebuhr's fine satiric sentence: "A God without wrath brought men without sin into a kingdom without judgment through the ministrations of a Christ without a cross."[2] It is Christianity with the bass register left out. The ancient and orthodox notion

[1] *For Self-Examination* and *Judge for Yourselves!*, Oxford, 1941, p. 209.
[2] *The Kingdom of God in America,* Willet, Clark & Company, 1937, p. 193.

that between God and man there is an infinite difference of quality has here been abolished by the simple expedient of domesticating the Eternal and eternalizing the domestic. This is the definition of culture-religion, and S.K. branded "Christendom" as such. He saw it as a profane messianism, in which man himself was scheduled to be the messiah, and the goal—chiliasm à la bourgeois. He foresaw that the age, like Jeshurun of old, would wax fat . . . and then forsake God. When Jeshurun had become sleek, he "lightly esteemed the Rock of his salvation" and bowed himself down to "new gods that came up of late." The name of these? Progress, Science, Education, Humanity. These things gave us the Century of Progress, a century of progressive concern with the creature rather than the Creator. Kierkegaard knew that upon these things the wrath of God would fall. For God is love. And God will not tolerate idols because idols are not good for man.

When he warned that the skies were about to fall, his contemporaries dubbed him a misanthropic Chicken Little. In our day, however, the tragic consequences of finite self-sufficiency have become apparent. The idol's clay feet are breaking. Like the prophets of Israel, S.K. is read and heard only after the event. His apprehension at the beginning of the age is ours at its end. The warnings with which he tried to save us from our fate now help us to interpret our fate. Kierkegaard in the nineteenth century was trying to do what God in our century is doing by means of two world wars and the threat of a third.

The contemporary novelist Jacob Wassermann, for example (in *The World's Illusion*), has understood in retrospect what Kierkegaard understood in prospect:

> Humanity to-day has lost its faith. Faith has leaked out like water from a cracked glass. Our age is tyrannised by machinery: it is a mob rule without parallel. Who will save us from machinery and from business? The golden calf has gone mad.

On Kierkegaard

The spirit of man kowtows to a warehouse. Our watchword is to be up and doing. We manufacture Christianity, a renaissance, culture, et cetera. If it's not quite the real thing, yet it will serve. Everything tends toward the external— toward expression, line, arabesque, gesture, mask. Everything is stuck on a boarding and lit by electric lamps. Everything is the very latest, until something still later begins to function. Thus the soul flees, goodness ceases, the form breaks, and reverence dies. Do you feel no horror at the generation that is growing up? The air is like that before the flood.

Having depicted S.K. as a prophet, I must at once remark that he did not wear a hairy mantle. Nor was he a grim and sour critic of human culture. In his own life he exemplified the maxim he asserted, that by the religious the aesthetic is not abolished but merely dethroned. He liked wine and good cigars and good company and the opera and long carriage rides into the country where he could enjoy the beauties of nature. The "aesthetic works," which were an important part of his literary production, demonstrate, as he meant them to do, his appreciation of the highest attainments of culture. These he opposed only when they cried, "Peace, peace; no evil shall come upon you."

Those who on the ground of his psychological peculiarities would dispense themselves from the necessity of heeding S.K. must at least recognize that he saw deeper into the human mind than more normal men have been able to see; and even the summary exposition of his thought which I essay to give here surely suffices to show that he was a cogent, consistent, and profound thinker, from whom one can escape, if at all, only by thinking more profoundly.

EXISTENTIAL THINKING

When Kierkegaard read the Hegelian philosophy, that vast system embracing all celestial and terrestrial knowledge, he had the impression that the whole world had been gained

301

and the individual human soul lost. Compendious though this globe-girdling system was, it contained no ethic, no word of advice to an existing human being as to how he should live. It proudly deserted existence and left an ethical individual in the lurch.

Death was talked about with immense erudition . . . by men who spoke as if they themselves were somehow exempt from this dread experience. Immortality was everywhere learnedly discussed, yet faith in immortality (i.e. a belief in immortality that has retroactive power to transform one's mode of existence) everywhere declined. Christianity, too, came in for studious attention, not however as a demand upon men for experience and personal appropriation, but as a phenomenon whose historicity was first to be verified by unwearying philological research and whose place in the world-historical process was then to be assigned, so as to exhibit wherein it had been adumbrated in paganism and Judaism and to what extent it accorded with the eternal truths of pure reason. And of course not even God could escape the indignity of an explanation! He too had to pass before Reason's reviewing stand and report for inspection. His existence was more and more asserted . . . by proofs; less and less proved . . . by worship.

The old age sought to justify man before God and ended with faith in God alone. Our age sought to justify God to man and ended with faith in Man alone. Theodicy replaced theology.

Whenever you find men idly tinkering with the idea of God, you may be sure that they have no very clear conception of what they themselves are. In a voluptuous metaphysical dream, philosophers fumble after a conception of God without feeling any terror thereat. On the contrary, they plume themselves upon their gnostic proclivities. The whole procedure is a degenerate cleverness, an immoral *divertissement,* in which ethics is given the run-around. An exasper-

302

ated Kierkegaard exclaims: "So rather let us sin, sin out and out, seduce maidens, murder men, commit highway robbery —after all, that can be repented of, and upon such a criminal God can still get a grip. But this proud superiority which has risen to such a height scarcely can be repented of, it has a semblance of profundity which deceives. So rather let us mock God out and out, as has been done before in the world—this is always preferable to the disparaging air of importance with which one would prove God's existence."[3]

Reflective thought, according to Kierkegaard, arrives only at the idea of God. Argument, at best, may make it probable that a God exists; but this Idea of God is only an x, itself unexplained, explaining nothing. Not one of the arguments for the existence of God can protect itself against the intrusion of dialectics. The ontological argument, for example, is a "deceptive movement of thought," an evasion of the real difficulty which is "to introduce God's ideal essence dialectically into the sphere of factual existence." The cosmological and teleological arguments are also beset with difficulties. "I contemplate the order of nature in the hope of finding God, and I see omnipotence and wisdom; but I also see much else that disturbs my mind and excites anxiety. The sum of all this is an objective uncertainty."[4]

After a naked dialectical analysis of the traditional proofs, Kierkegaard was forced to the conclusion that the "proofs" cannot give incontestable certainty. By a continued quantita-

---

[3] *Concluding Unscientific Postscript*, Princeton, 1941, p. 485.

[4] *Postscript*, p. 182. There is in the *Postscript* at p. 298 a masterly analysis of the ontological argument. This is also dealt with, along with the physico-teleological proof, in Chapter III of the *Philosophical Fragments* (Princeton, 1936). Cf. the discourse, "What It Means to Seek God," in *Thoughts on Crucial Situations in Human Life* (Augsburg, 1941), and the discourse, "God Greater than Our Heart," in *Christian Discourses* (Oxford, 1939).

tive progression no new quality is produced; there can be no smooth and easy transition to faith. It is impossible, by successive logical steps, which involve no break in quality, to reason in the following manner: it is probable that there is a God, very probable, highly probable, exceedingly probable, *ergo:* God. Similarly, with regard to Christology, we cannot start with Jesus as a man who is so good, so very good, so excellently good, so preëminently good that *therefore* He is God. "God" is something qualitatively different; our logic is guilty of a fallacy, a discontinuity, a μετάβασις εἰς ἄλλο γένος. *God* can be reached only by an act of faith, a leap.[5]

When for every *pro,* reflection can suggest an equally cogent *contra,* so that the thinker is run to a standstill and all he possesses is an objective uncertainty, here, if he is willing to take the risk of committing himself to an error, precisely here he can leap. The leap of faith is a passionate decision to believe in spite of the uncertainty. Were a man capable of proving God's existence objectively, he would not have to have *faith* that God is; he would *know.* Precisely because he cannot know, he must believe or else suspend decision. To believe in God is not to give intellectual assent to a proposition but to confide one's life to Him. Faith is a venture which chooses an objective uncertainty with infinite passion, counting every delay a deadly peril.

[5] The "leap" (*Springet*) is a favorite subject for parody on the part of people who have made up their minds beforehand not to like S.K. It will be well, then, to let Dr. Walter Lowrie explain it. "It is by this metaphor that S.K. expresses his passionate repudiation of the smooth transition Hegel sought to effect by means of mediation. S.K. protests that there is no real movement in logic, no genuine *becoming,* and that in existence every movement which effects a real change is a "leap," an act of freedom. This applies especially to faith, which is not attained by continuous and gradual approximation but by a resolution of the will, in 'the Instant' " (*Kierkegaard,* Oxford, 1938, p. 628).

On Kierkegaard

Take a picture. A wader feels his way with his foot lest he get beyond his depth. Shrewd and prudent, he wants probability, proof, demonstration that the water will support him. He insists on keeping at least one toe on the bottom. Well, he can wade from now till doomsday, but so long as he wades, he will never understand what swimming is. As a spectator standing knee-deep, he can see others swimming and perhaps describe this phenomenon with complete scientific accuracy. But as for himself? Does *he* know what swimming is like? This he can never know so long as he has not the faith to entrust himself to the water. It is impossible to swim if you will not put your life in jeopardy of drowning. You must launch out into the deep. Without risk there is no faith. Faith is swimming with seventy thousand fathoms beneath you.

WHERE DO WE STAND?

Thus does Kierkegaard make us aware of where we stand. We stand at the jumping-off place, for not by any logical construction can we span the gap. The question is, will we jump? Not to jump is despair. To jump is faith.

This needs to be explained.

Let us first of all agree to be human beings. Let us start from our actual human situation and go in search of God. Mindful of our creatureliness, we shall eschew the pretension involved in trying to stand outside existence to look at things, including God, *sub specie aeterni*. We shall abandon the role of world-historic genius and *extraordinarius* admitted to fraternize with God in the royal box as spectator of universal history, and stand quite humbly where, in fact, we do stand: as finite, existing human beings, facing the future in all its uncertainty, compelled to act in order to live. He who begins to tell us right off what God is in His own essence, what God was doing before the creation of the

305

world, etc., we shall quite summarily accuse of an attempt *à la* Munchausen.

Natural science and so also history can tell us something about the ground on which we stand. An archaeologist, returning from an expedition in the Near East, had this report to make. "We dug and dug until, at a depth of sixty feet, we uncovered the remains of a civilization 6000 years old. It had begun somehow, flourished for a while, and then had withered and died. It lay buried in its own dust. Immediately on top of that burial ground were the relics of another civilization, and so on. As I climbed out of that pit sixty feet deep, with each of my sixty steps I traversed one century of blood, sweat, and tears. There—layer upon layer— was a cross section of human history, 6000 years of it. And when, at the end of the day, I reached the top, look as I might in every direction, I could see nothing but vast, empty, barren, desert waste. And I said, Vanity of vanities. All is vanity."

We do not like this. We do not like it one bit. With the entire passion of our being we are opposed. We hunger to be freed from this futility that waits to engulf us. And do not give us the old song and dance that it is pride that makes us long for immortality. Not pride. At least, not pride alone. It is terror at the thought of extinction. It is protest against the insanity and injustice of a miserable merry-go-round that finally breaks down. We will not have it that our life is a "tale told by an idiot, full of sound and fury, signifying nothing."

But the evidence seems to be against us. A man is born, grows up, marries, begets children, becomes an alderman, takes sick, and dies—behold! these are his memoirs. Life is dog eat dog, and death takes not only the hindmost. Death takes us all.

This is man's situation. This is our predicament. Worse,

it is *my* predicament. What then? Why then, three rival ways beckon to me: the aesthetic, the ethical, and the religious.[6]

THREE "STAGES" ON LIFE'S WAY

If I want to I can sit myself down at an epicure's table to eat, drink, and be merry. But, as William James saw, no matter how merry the feasting, the skull will look in and grin at the banquet. Life lived in aesthetic categories may have an illusory brilliance, but it is nevertheless concealed despair, a desperate and unsuccessful fight against *ennui* and *angst*.[7] There is no way to break this despair except by a leap. By an act of my own free choice, I can make the jump from aesthetic eudemonism to an ethical standpoint. If so, I brace myself stoically against my coming end; in the meantime, I grit my teeth and fight for personal integrity and the civic virtues. I take up the position proposed by Sénancour: "Man is perishable. That may be; but let us perish resisting, and if it is nothingness that awaits us, do not let us so act that it shall be a just fate." Yet this again is despair, and few men are capable of living ethically, in heroic defiance of what Bertrand Russell has strikingly called "the trampling march of unconscious power." At best, ethical endeavor is back-

---

[6] There is, of course, a fourth possibility: world-and-life-negating mysticism. Here life is understood in terms of the σωμα-σημα pun. Release from the tragedy of life is sought by a retreat into eternity via recollection. For S.K., however, this is not a possibility; for the back door route to eternity by way of contemplation is barred by the fact of sin. Cf. *Fragments*, Ch. I; *Either/Or*, Vol. II, pp. 202 ff.

[7] *Angst:* anguished dread present in all human beings as the conscious or semiconscious realization of the unsupported character of all existence. Our existence rests upon an abyss of nothingness. Hence, a dread of the future.

breaking labor. But here it is like polishing the brass of a sinking vessel. For all our exertion we do not budge from the place where destruction is. The real difficulty with "unyielding despair" is that, in most cases, finally it yields. In Kierkegaard's judgment, a purely humanistic ethic cannot maintain itself for long. It loses heart. It gets stifled by the tragic sense of life.

Atheistic ethical humanism, the position here described, belongs still to what Kierkegaard calls the aesthetic (or secular) sphere. It is, he says, "an ethical form of the aesthetic" and is part of "the perilous transition from the aesthetic to the [true] ethical"; but then, if the transition be not effected, it must be stigmatized as "a degenerate form of the ethical."

If the despair inherent in atheistic ethical humanism is to be broken, says Kierkegaard, it can be broken only by leaping again. This time to an ethico-religious sphere. As Kierkegaard uses words, the authentic "ethical" means the standpoint of *theistic* ethical humanism. In certain respects, legalistic Judaism could be subsumed under this heading. So also Unitarianism. So also extremely liberal and moralistic versions of Christianity. So also, for example, Kantian ethical idealism. And so forth. Nearly every culture affords examples. By "ethical" Kierkegaard means any world-and-life-affirming ethic which rests on a theistic basis, with sanctions in an after-life.

Here we are conscious of ourselves as responsible beings, who are accountable to a Divine Law. "Thus and thus shalt thou do and thou shalt live." This is God's own truth. There is an eternal life in which wrongs will be redressed and justice done, a new world in which war shall be no more, neither tears nor sorrow nor death. Rejoice in it! Here is your absolute good, here is your *telos*. Now strive for it!

These words arouse my whole passion. I can be made free from sin and death! And this is what I want—mind, body, and soul. The bowels yearn for it. I feel a desperate need for it in the very marrow of my bones.

This is what Kierkegaard calls an existential problem. It concerns my existence both here and hereafter. It is, thus, a pathetic-dialectic problem. Pathetic, in that it involves all my passion, all my earnestness. Dialectic, in that it brings into play all my powers of thinking, attracting me and yet repelling me because it seems contrary to the evidence. Can I be indubitably sure that there really *is* such a good? No. Could it be proved incontestably? No. And yet I must venture absolutely everything for its sake? Yes. But is that not risky? Yes; this is *either/or*. *Either* despair/*or* the leap. Will you risk it? Then jump.

If I jump, venturing everything, I do not find myself transported to the seventh heaven or to any promised land or to a bed of roses. I find myself standing exactly where I stood before, but now I have a task. And that task is to relate myself to this conception of an eternal blessedness in such a way that it involves the reconstruction of my entire mode of existence. It must take hold of me in the very core of my being so as to bring the whole man into conformity with it. I give my life an absolute direction towards the absolute *telos*. And this is expressed in action through the transformation of my existence. All finite satisfactions are voluntarily relegated to the status of what may have to be renounced in favor of the eternal blessedness. The ethical task, accordingly, is simultaneously to sustain an absolute relationship to the absolute *telos* and a relative relationship to relative ends.[8]

The task is set. Now begin it. . . . Aye, *just try!* On paper the task looks easy enough. Who is not a mighty man on paper? But in real life, as soon as I set out to relate myself absolutely to the absolute *telos* and relatively to the relative ends, I discover, to my dismay, that I am in the opposite

[8] Cf. *Postscript,* pp. 347–385.

situation: I am absolutely committed to relative ends! I am stuck fast in immediacy. Something is so wrong with me that I am not yet ready to essay the ideal task but must first of all do something else before the ideal task can even be begun. I must first begin by exercising myself in the far humbler task of renunciation. The relativities have got to be dethroned. But this is hard. It hurts to give up my many goods in order to strive absolutely for the absolute good. This is like being called upon to cut off the offending hand and pluck out the offending eye. Renunciation cuts to the quick. The one God summons me to a policy of iconoclasm, and alas! I am Icon No. 1. Self-annihilation is a fearful thing. And the truth of the matter is that I never quite succeed; the first annihilation is not thorough enough; I never get beyond the possibility of falling back; self-assertion returns in multiple ways; the danger does not diminish. I shall have to keep at the task of renunciation and mortification as long as I live, and this means the persistence of inward suffering my whole life long.[9]

Thus things go backward. The task is presented to me in existence, and just as I am ready at once to cut a fine figure and want to begin, it is discovered that a new beginning is necessary, the beginning upon the immense detour of dying from immediacy; and just when the beginning is about to be made at this point, it is discovered that there, *since time has meanwhile been passing,* an ill beginning is made, and that the actual beginning must be made by acknowledging that I am guilty. I awaken, not at birth, but as one who has already been alive—for a long time. All the while I was deliberating I was ethically responsible for my use of time. Even at the instant when the task was clearly set there has been some waste, for meanwhile time has passed, and the beginning was not made at once. I am a man with a history, a man with a bad past.

[9] Cf. *Postscript,* pp. 386–468.

On Kierkegaard

The consciousness of guilt is a man's first deep plunge into existence. Now the exister is in thorough distress, i.e. now he is truly in the medium of real life. It isn't that he sometimes fails. Essentially he always fails. If a man says he finds nothing to repent of, it is because he judges himself by human standards alone. He who justifies himself, denounces himself as one who no longer stands related to the ideal standard.

"If a man would have an essential understanding of his guilt, he must understand it through being alone, just he alone, alone with the Holy One who knows all. . . . The more profound the sorrow is, the more a man feels himself to be nothing, less than nothing, and this diminishing self-esteem is the sign that the sorrowful is the seeker who is beginning to be conscious of God."[10]

Here he will discover that "confession is not merely an enumeration of particular sins, but is an understanding before God, of the continuity of sin in itself."[11] From his mistakes, his slips, he comes to understand the deeper malady: that sin is an unfathomable continuity, a *qualitative* determination. His peccadillos, though they do not exactly shatter the world, bring the deeper malady to light. The little symptomatic mistakes exhibit his distance from God, so that now he understands himself under the total determinant: guilt. This is the decisive expression for existential pathos in relation to God.

Slowly—imperceptibly, almost—Kierkegaard has led us from theistic ethical humanism to that which is, in fact, its opposite.

It was the happy presupposition of the ethicist that the personality is essentially sound. Basically man is all right. It was assumed that once the individual had accepted the moral task he could *of course* perform it. All he had to do was develop his own innate moral potentialities. The nec-

[10] *Crucial Situations,* p. 24 and p. 27.
[11] *Crucial Situations,* p. 30. Cf. *Postscript,* pp. 468–493.

311

essary strength, it was thought, lay immanent within the self. By individual self-discipline and determined self-effort, victory was assured.

It follows that, were the ethical ideal capable of realization, no scope would be found for the religious life in any deeper sense. To be sure, the ethicist has a religious vocabulary. He *speaks* of God and of immortality. But he does not enter into any personal relationship with God. God is *there,* simply as the background for the ethical life. He is there as Creator and as Lawgiver. He is there to provide ultimate sanctions for morality. He is there as a God of justice and righteousness to undergird the universe and the ethical enterprise. And *after* this life, God will mete out appropriate rewards and punishments. But during *this* life, the ethicist has not in any decisive sense, a personal relationship with God. He merely accepts his duty from Him. Ethics, then, means action, and the mood of the ethicist is victory.

But, in Kierkegaard's own experience, this mood of victory cannot endure for long if one takes the ethical requirements seriously. Actually, its requirement is so infinite that the individual always goes bankrupt.

In trying to conform his life to the ideal requirements, the ethicist begins to discover that there is something wrong with him. The more deeply this discovery is made, the more profound the sense of guilt and the sense of need. What does it profit us that an eternal blessedness is promised the righteous when the Law makes it terrifyingly evident that we ourselves are *un*righteous?

Thus, Kierkegaard has brought us—step by step—to what he calls *Religiousness A*. In formal content, Religiousness A is the same as the Kierkegaardian ethical stage, but psychologically and experientially the *mood* is different. *Religiousness A* arises when a man at last reaches the agonizing awareness of *incommensurability;* i.e., he sees with despair that he cannot measure up. Alas! he does not have what it takes.

On Kierkegaard

After hearing the Commandments in all their severity, all he can do is confess his guilt and turn to the Lord with the cry: *Kyrie eleison!*

This is *Religiousness A,* where self-esteem, self-trust, and the illusion of self-redemption are in process of destruction. It is a stage of ethical endeavor and failure, of redoubled exertion and renewed defeat, then of frantic striving and, finally, of despair. *Angst* in a new formation now seizes a man. The dreadful thing is no longer death and the encounter with nothingness; the dreadful thing is death and the encounter with God.

The ethical sphere, then, was only a transitional sphere. Its purpose was to develop a receptivity for religion. Its function was to develop within man a sense of need for God. Its highest expression is repentance as a negative action.

Who Can Be Saved?

Already the Old Testament understands that there are not many righteous, and the Apocrypha is beginning to wonder if there are any righteous enough to deserve salvation; then along comes Jesus of Nazareth who says, "With men it is impossible."

Now we are back again to that very precipice from which we tried to escape *via* ethical endeavor. We stand at the edge of the same abyss. Every ethical teaching of Jesus serves to point to this abyss, to remind us of the abyss, to show us how unbridgeable it is. Understand the Ten Commandments as Our Lord unveils them in the Sermon on the Mount, as referring not only to overt acts but to inward motive as well. Will we then be able to justify ourselves? Will we then be able to congratulate ourselves on being law-abiders? Or will we not rather find ourselves joining in the agonizing apostolic cry, "Who then *can* be saved?" This is the end of ethics as a way for men to go to God. *Religiousness A,* con-

313

sisting in all those efforts, however various, by which a man tries to transform his existence to make it pleasing to God, ends in failure.

Like Paul, Kierkegaard sees it clearly. The Law is against us. He sees that we stand condemned, trapped, indefensible. The prisoner has been boxed. There is no escape. The verdict is *guilty.* The penalty, DEATH.

But now, something very curious happens. Does Paul, does S.K. hate the Law? No. They say, "The Law, although it slays us, is good. The Law is a schoolmaster to bring us to Christ." Is this not a curious *non sequitur?* What can they mean? They mean that *Religiousness A* is the necessary propaedeutic for *Religiousness B.* The Law is the "existential training school" in ethics which, by destroying self-trust and teaching the impossibility of self-justification, drives them out in search of a *saviour.* They no longer inquire, "What good thing shall *I* do to inherit life?" Now, prompted by utter need for help from beyond the self, they cry *de profundis, "Who* shall deliver me from this death?" The Law, by telling them the bad news about themselves, has made them attentive, for the first time, to the Good News about Jesus Christ.[12]

To put this Good News as simply as possible, it is that God has done something in history on the basis of which sins are forgiven, redemption is received, the sharpness of death overcome, and the kingdom of heaven opened to all believers. The Deity has appeared in time "for us men and

---

[12] Cf. *Postscript,* pp. 493–498; cf. *The Concept of Dread* (Princeton, 1944), pp. 13 ff.: "Ethics points to ideality as a task and assumes that man is in possession of the condition requisite for performing it. Thereby ethics develops a contradiction, precisely for the fact that it makes the difficulty and the impossibility clear. What is said of the Law applies to ethics, that it is a severe schoolmaster, which in making a demand, by its demand only condemns, does not give birth to life."

for our salvation." Since man could not go to God, God has come to man. The abyss has been closed from the divine side. Because He stood where we stood—in the dock—we no longer have to stand there. *Nostra assumsit, ut conferret nobis sua.* This is *Religiousness B.* It is the Absolute Paradox. It is the *Miracle.*[13]

Here we must supply, as Kierkegaard does, the whole Apostles' Creed, for it tells us how with God all things—even that most incredible of things, man's salvation—*is* pos-

---

[13] *The Word became flesh.* "That that which in accordance with its nature is eternal, comes into existence in time, is born, grows up, and dies—this is the breach with all thinking" (*Postscript,* p. 513). This is Christianity's Absolute Paradox. Divinely, eternally theocentrically it may be no paradox, but no existing human being is able to look at it divinely, eternally, theocentrically. To him it is and remains a paradox. This is the sphere of faith. It can be believed altogether—against the understanding. If anyone imagines that he understands it, he can be sure he misunderstands it, having confounded Christianity with one or another pagan analogy. (Cf. *Postscript,* pp. 498–515.)

From the paradoxical character of the Miracle follow two important consequences:

(1) The paradox is related essentially to man as man, and qualitatively related to every man severally, whether he has much or little understanding. This is not esoteric *gnosis.* The simplest man can grasp the central fact, and the wisest man will never be able to exhaust it.

(2) Because the historical fact in question is not a simple fact, immediate contemporaneity is of no avail. Nor can learned historical inquiry help to annul the paradox so as to eliminate the risk it involves. There is no simple and direct transition from the reliability of an historical account to an eternal blessedness. In relation to the paradox we all stand equally close, equally distant. Whatever the century in which we live, whatever our varying intellectual endowments, these accidental circumstances have no power to differentiate our fortunes with respect to it. For it is a gamble, a risk, a leap. (Cf. *Fragments.* Ch. IV, Interlude, and Ch. V; cp. *Training in Christianity,* Oxford, 1941, pp. 66 ff.)

sible. Kierkegaard prefers to explain this Divine Possibility in the form of a parable.[14]

THE DIVINE INCOGNITO

There was a king who loved a humble maiden. No power on earth could stand in his way of accomplishing his purpose to marry her. But an anxious thought awoke in the heart of the king. Would she be happy in the life at his side? Would she be able to summon confidence enough never to remember what the king wished only to forget—that he was king and she, nothing but a peasant?

The king mentioned this anxiety to no one; for if he had, each courtier would have said, "Your Majesty is about to confer a favor upon the maiden, for which she can never be sufficiently grateful her whole life long." But the king did not wish to have the maiden grovel before him in abject gratitude all her life; he wanted her to be his equal, his wife, one with him in love.

It occurred to him that the union might be brought about by an *elevation* of the maiden. Make her a fine lady, give her a title and estates. The king could have done this secretly, and the maiden need never know how it was that her fortune was made. And the maiden might be greatly inclined to prize this. Intoxicated by her remarkable change of station, she might forget the old peasant days. Then could the king woo her. But the king, being a just man, perceived that such a method was deceitful. Not by deception can their love be made happy, except perhaps in appearance, for it would rest upon a falsification of the facts.

Another possibility occurred to the king. He might array himself in gorgeous robes of state and, coming suddenly to the maiden's cottage, overawe her with pomp of his power.

[14] As quoted, it is abridged, paraphrased, and mutilated, from Chapter II of the *Fragments*. S.K. asks us to bear in mind that no analogy perfectly accords with the unique evangelic fact.

316

Seeing the regal apparition, she would have bowed down and quite forgotten herself in worshipful adoration. Alas! this might have satisfied the maiden, to give glory to the king, but it could not satisfy the king, because he desired not his own glorification but hers.

Here, then, is the king's dilemma: if he does not show himself to the maiden, his love for her would die, since it could have no chance to express itself; but if he shows himself to her in all his splendor, then the maiden will die—for she cannot be a wife who is totally prostrated with fear and awe.

There once lived a people who had a profound understanding of the divine. This people thought that no one could see God and live. Who grasps this contradiction of sorrow? Not to reveal oneself is the death of love, to reveal oneself is the death of the beloved!

Outwardly, this has been the story of a king who loved a maiden. Inwardly, it is the story of God's love for men. Moved by love, God is eternally resolved to reveal Himself, to communicate His own divine life to us. It may seem a small matter for God to make Himself understood to us, but this is not so easy of accomplishment as we may think. For God is God, and we are men and sinful men. The inequality between the king and the maiden is only a poor human symbol of the inequality between God and us men. Here there is an endless qualitative difference. And the nobility of the king in not wishing to deceive the maiden or strip her of free choice in the matter is but a meagre token of the nobility of God in not wishing to deceive us and strip us of our freedom.

We have seen how the king's love of the maiden was doomed to defeat if the king deceived her by enriching her with titles and estates. Even so, God might conceivably elevate sinful man, take him up into Himself, transfigure him, fill his cup with millennial joys, and let the sinner forget himself in tumultuous ecstacy. And the sinner might call this happiness, but it would not be the real happiness that God longs to give man: full personal communion.

We have seen how the king thought of appearing to the maiden in monarchical pomp, so that the maiden might

317

forget herself in reverent admiration. Even so, God might reveal Himself to us in all His effulgent majesty; and, at the sight of Him, we would prostrate ourselves and worship Him. And that would satisfy us, but it could not satisfy God. For God does not desire His glorification but ours. God will do anything to win us to His love—anything but coerce us.

Therefore, the union must be brought about in some other way. Since we found that it could not be brought about by an elevation of the maiden (or the sinner, let us say now), it must be attempted by a *descent* on the part of the king (or let us say God now). Let the sinner be called *x*. In this *x* we must include the lowliest man on earth. For God does not make a distinction here; all have sinned and come short of the glory of God. In order that the union may be brought about, God must therefore descend to become the equal of such a one, and so He will appear in the likeness of the humblest. But the humblest in our world is one who must serve others, and God will therefore appear in the form of a *servant*. But this servant form is no mere outer garment, like the beggar-cloak in which the king thought to disguise himself. For when the king descended to the maiden masqueraded in peasant attire, this was after all a kind of deceit. But when God assumed the form of a servant, it was His true form and figure. The true God became true Man.

Behold where he stands—God! There; do you not see him? He is God. Which one? Surely not the one girt with a towel who is washing feet? Why, that man was born in a stable; there was no room for him at the inn, nor has there ever been any room for him in the world: he simply cannot be fitted in to our way of doing things. And tomorrow he is to be put out of the way once and for all. He is a blasphemer, you know; he is a sinner, for he takes his meals with publicans, he converses with harlots, he touches lepers. And you say *he* is God! Pah!—do not mock me! I have better sense than that! Say rather he is a megalomaniac or someone terribly deceived or a scoundrel or a demon (who knows?—perhaps it is by Beelzebub, the prince of demons, that he casts out demons). What an outrageous claim you make for him. It offends me to the quick!

You see, the servant-form was no mere outer garment; and therefore, God must suffer all things, endure all things, make experience of all things. He must suffer hunger in the desert, he must thirst in the time of his agony, he must be forsaken in death, absolutely like the humblest—behold the man!

His is a passion-story from birth until death. His suffering consists in bearing the burden that mankind may misunderstand his love and take offense at him. This God-Man, this Suffering Servant, who hath no form nor comeliness, who hath not beauty that we should desire him, anxiously says to each man: "Behold, I stand at the door of your humble cottage and knock; if you will open unto me, I shall come in and sit down and sup with you."

It is less terrible to fall to the ground when the mountains tremble at the Voice of God than it is to sit at table with him as an equal; and yet it is God's concern precisely to have it so.

What kind of talk is this? Gods do not besmirch themselves by going through the messiness of human birth. Gods do not get themselves crucified. A theophany, that I could understand. A Docetic appearance, even that, perhaps, I could accept. But if you tell me that ultimate Deity has appeared in time in flesh and blood, I will tell you that you are talking nonsense. This is more than paradoxical. This is absurd.

To this the Christian assents. Indeed it is absurd, and yet "the foolishness of God is wiser than men." For the Christian has a sort of double-vision: as thinker, he knows all the dialectical contradictions; as believer, he embraces them as Gospel truth. To the Jew in me this is a scandal—that one so lowly (stable-born) should give himself out to be so high and mighty; or that one so lofty (the Son of God) should permit himself to be so deeply abased; it is a paradox either way[15]. To the Greek in me this is folly—for the eternal *logos* is timeless, disembodied, dwelling above in the realm

---

[15] Cf. *Training in Christianity*, Part II.

of pure form; but here I am confronted, with rude direct-
ness, by a carpenter, who says that *he* is the *logos*, embodied,
incarnate, and that no one can come to the *logos* but by
him.[16]

As Jew, I had expected a Messiah who would vindicate
me and crown my endeavours with good things and length
of days. Instead I get a Messiah who accuses me not only of
habitual sinning but of active, positive hostility towards
God. He says that all my evolution, all my progress, all my
self-made righteousness ends in . . . crucifixion.

As Greek, I had assumed that I was my own Christ, that
in spite of all my imperfection I nevertheless possessed intact
a divine something (*nous, pneuma,* spark) which gave me
access to the eternal *logos*. By going deep into my own soul,
I could mount to the heights. The maximum of my need I
imagined to be a teacher who, by questioning me, would
awaken in me that self-activity which would enable me to
take myself into eternity by way of recollection. It matters
not at what moment or at whose instigation I begin to
remember that I am eternal; the historical is a matter of
indifference. But here is a teacher who says, "Without me
ye can do nothing. Your proposed retreat to eternity *via*
recollection is barred by the fact of sin. Because of sin, there
is no longer any immanent fundamental kinship between
you and the eternal."[17]

Thus does Christianity begin by profoundly humiliating a
man. It strips him of every intellectual and moral pretension.
It drives him naked and trembling to the throne of God.
And here, if a man will but confess that God's judgment
upon him is just and will sue for mercy, here precisely is
the miracle of acquittal, of forgiveness, of reconciliation. He
has Christ for his clothing when he confesses himself naked,

[16] Cf. *Fragments,* Ch. I.
[17] Cf. *Postscript,* pp. 184 ff., 505–508, 516–518.

Christ for his resurrection when he acknowledges himself dead.

"Becoming a Christian is then the most fearful decision of a man's life, a struggle through to attain faith against despair and offense, the twin Cerberuses that guard the entrance to a Christian life."[18]

Faith is the most disputable of things while in process of approximation; but when reflection is called to a halt by a resolution of the will (the leap), doubt is excluded and "the peace of God which passeth understanding" becomes the supreme reality of his life.

Now we are in a position to understand Kierkegaard's succinct statement of the problem: "The eternal blessedness of the individual is decided in time through the relationship to something historical, which is furthermore of such a character as to include in its composition that which by virtue of its essence cannot become historical, and must therefore become such by virtue of the Absurd."[19]

The perfection of Christianity is not a doctrine or a code or a law or a philosophy. It is a Person. Christianity is the fact that God has existed as a particular man. It rests its whole claim on Jesus as the point where eternity has intersected time. The object of faith is the reality of this God-Man, that He really exists. The answer of faith is therefore unconditionally yes or no. For it does not concern a doctrine, as to whether the doctrine is true or not; it is the answer to a question concerning a fact: "Do you or do you not suppose that He has really existed?" And the answer, be it noted, is with infinite passion. The dialectical difficulties react upon passion to intensify it and enflame it, like oil upon fire. One's eternal blessedness is at stake—but is it not a painful contradiction to base one's blessedness upon something historical?

[18] *Postscript*, p. 333.
[19] *Postscript*, p. 345.

HOWARD ALBERT JOHNSON

Is it not madness to require the greatest possible subjective passion, to the point of hating father and mother, and then to put this together with an historical knowledge, which at its maximum is only a sketchy approximation?

Here is something historical, the story of Jesus Christ.

But now is the historical fact quite certain? To this one must answer: even though it were the most certain of all historical facts it would be of no help, there cannot be any *direct* transition from an historical fact to the foundation upon it of an eternal blessedness. That is something qualitatively new.

"How then do we proceed? Thus. A man says to himself . . .: here is an historical fact which teaches me that in regard to my eternal blessedness I must have recourse to Jesus Christ. I must certainly preserve myself from taking the wrong turning into scientific inquiry and research, as to whether it is quite certainly historical; for it is historical right enough: and if it were ten times as certain in all its details it would still be no help: for *directly* I cannot be helped.[20]

[20] *Historismus* leads at most to the perception, historically motivated, that Christianity has certain advantages over paganism, Judaism, etc. Meanwhile, *historismus* is in danger of falling into a "philological occupation-complex" in which decision for Christ, personal commitment to Him, is forever postponed. We all await the publication of the latest commentary, the unearthing of a new codex, by which the remaining obscurities, it is hoped, will be cleared up. Thinking to eliminate the risk, we become stuck in a "learned parenthesis." Let the scholar labor ever so assiduously, he will not in this way become a Christian—he only becomes erudite. (Cf. *Postscript,* Book I, and *Training in Christianity,* pp. 26–39.) In the *Fragments,* p. 87, S.K. puts it like this: "If the contemporary generation had left nothing behind them but these words: 'We have believed that in such and such a year God appeared among us in the humble figure of a servant, that he lived and taught in our community, and finally died,' it would be more than enough. The con-

On Kierkegaard

"And so I say to myself: I choose; that historical fact means so much to me that I decide to stake my whole life upon that *if*. Then he lives; entirely full of the idea, risking his life for it: and his life is the proof that he believes. He did not have a few proofs, and so believed and then began to live. No, the very reverse.

"That is called risking; and without risk faith is an impossibility. . . ."[21]

The salvation that is offered is free, and yet, after all, it is bought *à tout prix*, for it involves nothing less than the total surrender of the self. "Lord, I believe; help thou mine unbelief!"

temporary generation would have done all that was necessary; for this little advertisement, this *nota bene* on a page of universal history, would be sufficient to afford an occasion for a successor, and the most voluminous account can in all eternity do nothing more." With good reason, the Kierkegaardian pseudonym, Johannes Climacus, is here putting the case as emphatically and as extremely as is possible, and I believe that, if worst comes to worst, he is right. At the same time, however, I agree with Kierkegaard who believes, personally, that we have—and must have—something more concrete to go on than the naked declaration, lacking specific content, that "the Word became flesh." But for this S.K. assigns a reason we were perhaps unprepared for. Something of what the Word made flesh actually *did* in the flesh is required—in order that the Incarnate Lord may not only constitute a specific revelation of God but also may appear before us in definite lineaments as the pattern, the paradigm, the model whom we are required to follow. (Cf. e.g. *Papirer*, X^5 A-45.) It is evident that, for Kierkegaard, Christ as Example, as embodiment of the Will of God, plays the same role as is played, for St. Paul and Luther, by the Law. The function of the Law or of Christ, as full-length portrait of the Law carried out in flesh and blood, is to crack human pride and to drive men to Christ as Redeemer.

[21] *Journals*, Oxford, 1938, ʃ1044.

CHRISTIANITY AS ADORATION AND IMITATION

What, then, will life be like if one takes this risk?

The Christian relates himself to the God-Man as one whom he adores and seeks to imitate. The first and foremost thing is adoration, and it is only through adoration of so gracious a Redeemer that there can be any question of being like Him. Christ Himself must help the one who is to imitate Him. And in one respect no one can be like Him, nor even think of wishing to imitate Him, *in so far as He is our saviour and atoner.*

When we compare ourselves to Christ, we discover that we never succeed in being like Him. Not even in what we call our best moments. Christ, as the Example, is He who makes endless demands upon us, and we feel terribly the unlikeness. Then we flee *to* the Example, and He has mercy upon us. Thus, the Example is He who most sternly and endlessly condemns us—and at the same time it is He who, as Redeemer, has mercy upon us. Kierkegaard expresses this dialectic in a noble prayer:

"Help us all and everyone, Thou who art both willing and able to help, Thou who art both the Pattern and the Redeemer, and again both the Redeemer and the Pattern, so that when the striver sinks under the Pattern, then the Redeemer raises him up again, but at the same instant Thou art the Pattern, to keep him continually striving. Thou, our Redeemer, by Thy blessed suffering and death, hast made satisfaction for all and for everything; no eternal happiness can be or shall be earned by desert—it has been deserved. Yet Thou didst leave behind Thee the traces of Thy footsteps, Thou the Holy pattern of the human race and of each individual in it, so that, saved by Thy redemption, they might every instant have confidence and boldness to will to strive to follow Thee."[22]

[22] *Judge for Yourselves!,* p. 161. Cp. the Collect for Easter II.

On Kierkegaard

Thus does ethics have a paradoxical reinstatement—an ethics on the far side of conversion, on the basis of grace.[23] Grace is Christianity's first, last, and always—but not in such a way as to abrogate ethics. Justification by grace through faith means not antinomianism but a new relation to the Law. Works are done not in the frantic exertion of saving our lives but in glad gratitude to Him who *has* saved our lives. This is obedience to a living Lord, not to an impersonal Law. The love of God, made manifest in Christ, constrains us, impels us to move out toward neighbor and the world in works of love. Nor do we do this task unaided. Through prayer and sacrament the Risen and Ascended Christ empowers us for the task by communicating to us the power of His own deathless life.[24] Thus, good works

[23] Cf. especially S.K.'s profound remarks about "the second ethics" in *The Concept of Dread,* pp. 16 ff. A pity there is no time to explore the fact that there is also, for Kierkegaard, a second aesthetics—a proper appreciation of beauty, of the arts, of food and wine—also on the basis of grace. This is part of what S.K. means by the concept "repetition." "Everything comes back—transfigured," he says. In faith, by virtue of the absurd, the man who has infinitely renounced everything now makes the second movement of infinity by which everything renounced is received a second time, cleansed and restored, raised to the second power, and employed and enjoyed eucharistically.

[24] While it is true that S.K. died in the midst of a violent attack on the Church, only the most perverse will fail to understand that what he was attacking was not *ecclesia* as such but the empirical Church of Denmark, the Establishment, as he knew it in his day, when to be a Dane was tantamount to being a Christian—i.e. one was born that way. Although it would be folly to maintain that S.K. had a proper appreciation of the Church, if we accept the New Testament conception as definitive, it would also be foolish to suppose that he was utterly lacking ecclesiologically. So far was he from doing away with the Church, he simply *presupposed* it. Of course there would be the assembly of the brethren for prayer and praise, sermon and sacrament. To convince ourselves of this, we have only to read his moving "Discourses on the

appear as the fruit of fellowship. The ethical task, although
it may involve painful collision with the world, is joyously
undertaken under the guidance and inspiration of the Holy
Ghost.

Perhaps now we can welcome Kierkegaard's brilliant distillation: "An unlimited humiliation, the boundless grace
of God, and a striving born of gratitude: these three things
constitute Christianity."[25]

This too, Kierkegaard explains in a parable for Pentecost:[26]

Once upon a time there was a rich man who ordered from
abroad at a high price a pair of entirely faultless and high-
bred horses which he desired to have for his own pleasure
and for the pleasure of driving them himself. Then about a
year or two elapsed. Anyone who previously had known these
horses would not have been able to recognize them again.
Their eyes had become dull and drowsy, their gait lacked
style and decision, they couldn't endure anything, they
couldn't hold out, they hardly could be driven four miles
without having to stop on the way, sometimes, they came to
a standstill as he sat for all he was worth attempting to drive
them, besides they had acquired all sorts of vices and bad
habits, and in spite of the fact that they of course got fodder
in over-abundance, they were falling off in flesh day by day.
Then he had the King's coachman call. He drove them for a
month—in the whole region there was not a pair of horses
that held their heads so proudly, whose glance was so fiery,
whose gait was so handsome, no other pair of horses that
could hold out so long, though it were to trot for more than
a score of miles at a stretch without stopping. How came this
about? It is easy to see. The owner, who without being a

Communion for Fridays." And, as I have shown elsewhere, when S.K.
stresses the *individual*, it is not the individual against *ecclesia* he stresses
but the individual against the *masses*, against *das Man* of Heidegger,
the de-personalized convention-ridden collectivism of our time.

[25] *Papirer*, X[3] A 734.
[26] *For Self-Examination*, pp. 104 ff.

coachman pretended to be such, drove them in accordance with the horses' understanding of what it is to drive; the royal coachman drove them in accordance with the coachman's understanding of what it is to drive.

So it is with us men. Oh, when I think of myself and of the countless men I have learned to know, I have often said to myself despondently, "Here are talents and powers and capacities enough—but the coachman is lacking." Through a long period of time, we men, from generation to generation, have been, if I may so say, driven (to stick to the figure) in accordance with the horses' understanding of what it is to drive, we are directed, brought up, educated in accordance with man's conception of what it is to be a man. Behold therefore what we lack: exaltation, and what follows in turn from this, that we only can stand so little . . .

Once it was different. Once there was a time when it pleased the Deity (if I may venture to say so) to be Himself the coachman; and He drove the horses in accordance with the coachman's understanding of what it is to drive. Oh, what was a man not capable of at that time!

Think of to-day's text! [Acts 2:1–12] There sit twelve men, all of them belonging to that class of society which we call the common people. They had seen Him whom they adored as God, their Lord and Master, crucified; as never could it be said of anyone even in the remotest, it can be said of them that they had seen everything lost. It is true, He thereupon went triumphantly to heaven—but in this way also He is lost to them: and now they sit and wait for the Spirit to be imparted to them, so that thus, execrated as they are by the little nation they belong to, they may preach a doctrine which will arouse against them the hate of the whole world— and that on the most terrible terms, against its will.

It is Christianity that had to be put through. These twelve men, they put it through. They were in a sense men like us— but they were well driven, yea, they were well driven!

Friedrich Nietzsche (1844-1900)

The Joyful Wisdom
We Fearless Ones

WHAT OUR CHEERFULNESS SIGNIFIES

The most important of more recent events—that "God is dead," that the belief in the Christian God has become unworthy of belief—already begins to cast its first shadows over Europe. To the few at least whose eye, whose *suspecting* glance, is strong enough and subtle enough for this drama, some sun seems to have set, some old, profound confidence seems to have changed into doubt: our old world must seem to them daily more darksome, distrustful, strange and "old." In the main, however, one may say that the event itself is far too great, too remote, too much beyond most people's power of apprehension, for one to suppose that so much as the report of it could have *reached* them; not to speak of many who already knew *what* had taken place, and what must all collapse now that this belief had been undermined—because so much was built upon it, so much rested on it, and had become one with it: for example, our entire European morality. This lengthy, vast and uninterrupted process of crumbling, destruction, ruin and overthrow which is now imminent: who has realised it sufficiently today to have to stand up as the teacher and herald of such a tremendous logic of terror, as the prophet of a period of gloom and eclipse, the like of which has probably never taken place on earth before? . . . Even we, the born riddle-readers, who wait as it were on the mountains posted 'twixt today and tomorrow, and engirt by their contradiction, we, the first-lings and premature children of the coming century, into whose sight especially the shadows which must forthwith envelop Europe *should* already have come—how is it that even we, without genuine sympathy for this period of gloom, contemplate its advent without any *personal* solicitude or fear? Are we still, perhaps, too much under the *immediate effects* of the event—and are these effects, especially as regards *ourselves,* perhaps the reverse of what was to be expected—not at all sad and depressing, but rather like a new and inde-scribable variety of light, happiness, relief, enlivenment, encouragement, and dawning day? . . . In fact, we philoso-phers and "free spirits" feel ourselves irradiated as by a new dawn by the report that the "old God is dead"; our hearts overflow with gratitude, astonishment, presentiment and expectation. At last the horizon seems open once more, grant-ing even that it is not bright; our ships can at last put out to sea in face of every danger; every hazard is again permitted to the discerner; the sea, *our* sea, again lies open before us; perhaps never before did such an "open sea" exist.

To what Extent even We are still Pious

It is said with good reason that convictions have no civic rights in the domain of science: it is only when a conviction voluntarily condescends to the modesty of an hypothesis, a preliminary standpoint for experiment, or a regulative fic-tion, that its access to the realm of knowledge, and a certain value therein, can be conceded—always, however, with the restriction that it must remain under police supervision, under the police of our distrust. Regarded more accurately, however, does not this imply that only when a conviction *ceases* to be a conviction can it obtain admission into sci-ence? Does not the discipline of the scientific spirit just commence when one no longer harbours any conviction? . . .

FRIEDRICH NIETZSCHE

It is probably so: only, it remains to be asked whether, *in order that this discipline may commence,* it is not necessary that there should already be a conviction, and in fact one so imperative and absolute, that it makes a sacrifice of all other convictions. One sees that science also rests on a belief: there is no science at all "without premises." The question whether truth is necessary, must not merely be affirmed beforehand, but must be affirmed to such an extent that the principle, belief, or conviction finds expression, that "there is *nothing more necessary* than truth, and in comparison with it everything else has only secondary value." This absolute will to truth: what is it? Is it the will *not to allow ourselves to be deceived?* Is it the will *not to deceive?* For the will to truth could also be interpreted in this fashion, provided one included under the generalisation, "I will not deceive," the special case, "I will not deceive myself." But why not deceive? Why not allow oneself to be deceived? Let it be noted that the reasons for the former eventuality belong to a category quite different from those for the latter: one does not want to be deceived oneself, under the supposition that it is injurious, dangerous, or fatal to be deceived—in this sense science would be a prolonged process of caution, foresight and utility; against which, however, one might reasonably make objections. What? is not-wishing-to-be-deceived really less injurious, less dangerous, less fatal? What do you know of the character of existence in all its phases to be able to decide whether the greater advantage is on the side of absolute distrust, or of absolute trustfulness? In case, however, of both being necessary, much trusting *and* much distrusting, whence then should science derive the absolute belief, the conviction on which it rests, that truth is more important than anything else, even than every other conviction? This conviction could not have arisen if truth *and* untruth had both continually proved themselves to be useful: as is the case. Thus—the belief in science, which now

330

undeniably exists, cannot have had its origin in such a utilitarian calculation, but rather *in spite of* the fact of the inutility and dangerousness of the "Will to truth," of "truth at all costs," being continually demonstrated. "At all costs": alas, we understand that sufficiently well, after having sacrificed and slaughtered one belief after another at this altar! Consequently, "Will to truth" does *not* imply, "I will not allow myself to be deceived," but—there is no other alternative—"I will not deceive, not even myself": *and thus we have reached the realm of morality.* For, let one just ask oneself fairly: "Why wilt thou not deceive?" especially if it should seem—and it does seem—as if life were laid out with a view to appearance, I mean, with a view to error, deceit, dissimulation, delusion, self-delusion; and when on the other hand it is a matter of fact that the great type of life has always manifested itself on the side of the most unscrupulous. Such an intention might perhaps, to express it mildly, be a piece of Quixotism, a little enthusiastic craziness; it might also, however, be something worse, namely, a destructive principle, hostile to life. . . . "Will to Truth"—that might be a concealed Will to Death. Thus the question, Why is there science? leads back to the moral problem: *What in general is the purpose of morality,* if life, nature, and history are "non-moral"? There is no doubt that the conscientious man in the daring and extreme sense in which he is presupposed by the belief in science, *affirms thereby a world other than* that of life, nature, and history; and in so far as he affirms this "other world," what? must he not just thereby—deny its counterpart, this world, *our* world? . . . But what I have in view will now be understood, namely, that it is always a *metaphysical belief* on which our belief in science rests—and that even we knowing ones of today, the godless and anti-metaphysical, still take *our* fire from the conflagration kindled by a belief a millennium old, the Christian belief, which was also the belief of Plato, that God is truth, that the truth is divine. . . . But what if this itself always becomes more untrustworthy, what if nothing any longer proves itself divine, except it be error, blindness, and falsehood—what if God himself turns out to be our most persistent lie?

MORALITY AS A PROBLEM

A defect in personality revenges itself everywhere: an enfeebled, lank, obliterated, self-disavowing and disowning personality is no longer fit for anything good—it is least of all fit for philosophy. "Selflessness" has no value either in heaven or on earth; the great problems all demand *great love,* and it is only the strong, well-rounded, secure spirits, those who have a solid basis, that are qualified for them. It makes the most material difference whether a thinker stands personally related to his problems, having his fate, his need, and even his highest happiness therein; or merely impersonally, that is to say, if he can only feel and grasp them with the tentacles of cold, prying thought. In the latter case I warrant that nothing comes of it: for the great problems, granting that they let themselves be grasped at all, do not let themselves *be held* by toads and weaklings: that has ever been their taste—a taste also which they share with all high-spirited women. How is it that I have not yet met with any one, not even in books, who seems to have stood to morality in this position, as one who knew morality as a problem, and this problem as *his own* personal need, affliction, pleasure and passion? It is obvious that up to the present morality has not been a problem at all; it has rather been the very ground on which people have met after all distrust, dissension and contradiction, the hallowed place of peace, where thinkers could obtain rest even from themselves, could recover breath and revive. I see no one who has ventured to *criticise* the estimates of moral worth. I miss in this connection even the attempts of scientific curiosity, and the fastidious, groping imagination of psychologists and historians, which easily anticipates a problem and catches it on the wing, without rightly knowing what it catches. With difficulty I have discovered some scanty data for the purpose of furnishing a *history of the origin* of these feelings and estimates of value (which is something different from a criticism of them, and also something different from a history of ethical systems). In an individual case I have done everything to encourage the inclination and talent for this kind of history—in vain, as it would seem to me at present. There is little to be learned from those historians of morality (especially Englishmen): they themselves are usually, quite unsuspiciously, under the influence of a definite morality, and act unwittingly as its armour-bearers and followers—perhaps still repeating sincerely the popular superstition of Christian Europe, that the characteristic of moral action consists in abnegation, self-denial, self-sacrifice, or in fellow-feeling and fellow-suffering. The usual error in their premises is their insistence on a certain *consensus* among human beings, at least among civilised human beings, with regard to certain propositions of morality, from thence they conclude that these propositions are absolutely binding even upon you and me; or reversely, they come to the conclusion that *no* morality is binding, after the truth has dawned upon them that among different peoples moral valuations are *necessarily* different: both of which conclusions are equally childish follies. The error of the more subtle amongst them is that they discover and criticise the probably foolish opinions of a people about its own morality, or the opinions of mankind about human morality generally (they treat accordingly of its origin, its religious sanctions, the superstition of free will, and such matters), and they think that just by so doing they have criticised the morality itself. But the worth of a precept, "Thou shalt," is fundamentally different from and independent of such opinions about it, and must be distinguished from the weeds of error with which it has perhaps been overgrown: just as the worth of a medicine to a sick person is altogether independent of the question whether he has a scientific opinion about medicine, or merely thinks about it as an old wife would do. A morality could even have grown *out of* an error: but with this knowledge the problem of its worth would not even be touched. Thus, no one hitherto has tested the *value* of that most celebrated of all medicines, called morality: for which purpose it is first of all necessary for one—*to call it in question.* Well, that is just our work.

Our Note of Interrogation

But you don't understand it? As a matter of fact, an effort will be necessary in order to understand us. We seek for words; we seek perhaps also for ears. Who are we after all? If we wanted simply to call ourselves in older phraseology, atheists, unbelievers, or even immoralists, we should still be far from thinking ourselves designated thereby: we are all three in too late a phase for people generally to conceive, for *you,* my inquisitive friends, to be able to conceive, what is our state of mind under the circumstances. No! we have no longer the bitterness and passion of him who has broken loose, who has to make for himself a belief, a goal, and even a martyrdom out of his unbelief! We have become saturated with the conviction (and have grown cold and hard in it) that things are not at all divinely ordered in this world, nor even according to human standards do they go on rationally, mercifully, or justly: we know the fact that the world in which we live is ungodly, immoral, and "inhuman"—we have far too long interpreted it to ourselves falsely and mendaciously, according to the wish and will of our veneration, that is to say, according to our *need*. For man is a venerating animal! But he is also a distrustful animal: and that the world is *not* worth what we believed it to be worth is about the surest thing our distrust has at last managed to grasp. So much distrust, so much philosophy! We take good care not to say that the world is of *less* value: it seems to us at present absolutely ridiculous when man claims to devise values *to surpass* the values of the actual world—it is precisely from that point that we have retraced our steps; as from an extravagant error of human conceit and irrationality, which for a long period has not been recognised as such. This error had its last expression in modern Pessimism; an older and stronger manifestation in the teaching of Buddha; but Christianity also contains it, more dubiously, to be sure, and more ambiguously, but none the less seductive on that account. The whole attitude of "man *versus* the world," man as world-denying principle, man as the standard of the value of things, as judge of the world, who in the end puts existence itself on his scales and finds it too light—the monstrous impertinence of this attitude has dawned upon us as such, and has disgusted us—we now laugh when we find, "Man *and* World" placed beside one another, separated by the sublime presumption of the little word "and"! But how is it? Have we not in our very laughing just made a further step in despising mankind? And consequently also in Pessimism, in despising the existence cognisable *by us?* Have we not just thereby awakened suspicion that there is an opposition between the world in which we have hitherto been at home with our venerations—for the sake of which we perhaps *endure* life—and another world *which we ourselves are:* an inexorable, radical, most profound suspicion concerning ourselves, which is continually getting us Europeans more annoyingly into its power, and could easily face the coming generation with the terrible alternative: Either do away with

FRIEDRICH NIETZSCHE

your venerations, or—*with yourselves!*" The latter would be
Nihilism—but would not the former also be Nihilism? This
is *our* note of interrogation.

BELIEVERS AND THEIR NEED OF BELIEF

How much *faith* a person requires in order to flourish,
how much "fixed opinion" he requires which he does not
wish to have shaken, because he *holds* himself thereby—is
a measure of his power (or more plainly speaking, of his
weakness). Most people in old Europe, as it seems to me,
still need Christianity at present, and on that account it still
finds belief. For such is man: a theological dogma might be
refuted to him a thousand times—provided, however, that
he had need of it, he would again and again accept it as
"true"—according to the famous "proof of power" of which
the Bible speaks. Some have still need of metaphysics; but
also the impatient *longing for certainty* which at present
discharges itself in scientific, positivist fashion among large
numbers of the people, the longing by all means to get at
something stable (while on account of the warmth of the
longing the establishing of the certainty is more leisurely
and negligently undertaken): even this is still the longing
for a hold, a support; in short, the *instinct of weakness,*
which, while not actually creating religions, metaphysics,
and convictions of all kinds, nevertheless, preserves them. In
fact, around all these positivist systems there fume the vapours of a certain pessimistic gloom, something of weariness,
fatalism, disillusionment, and fear of new disillusionment
—or else manifest animosity, ill-humour, anarchic exaspera-
tion, and whatever there is of symptom or masquerade
of the feeling of weakness. Even the readiness with which
our cleverest contemporaries get lost in wretched corners
and alleys, for example, in Vaterländerei (so I designate
Jingoism, called *chauvinisme* in France, and *deutsch* in

Germany), or in petty aesthetic creeds in the manner of Parisian *naturalisme* (which only brings into prominence and uncovers *that* aspect of nature which exictes simultaneously disgust and astonishment—they like at present to call this aspect *la vérité vraie*), or in Nihilism in the St. Petersburg style (that is to say, in the *belief in unbelief*, even to martyrdom for it): this shows always and above all the need of belief, support, backbone, and buttress. . . . Belief is always most desired, most pressingly needed, where there is a lack of will: for the will, as emotion of command, is the distinguishing characteristic of sovereignty and power. That is to say, the less a person knows how to command, the more urgent is his desire for that which commands, and commands sternly—a God, a prince, a caste, a physician, a confessor, a dogma, a party conscience. From whence perhaps it could be inferred that the two world-religions, Buddhism and Christianity, might well have had the cause of their rise, and especially of their rapid extension, in an extraordinary *malady of the will*. And in truth it has been so: both religions lighted upon a longing, monstrously exaggerated by malady of the will, for an imperative, a "Thou-shalt," a longing going the length of despair; both religions were teachers of fanaticism in times of slackness of will-power, and thereby offered to innumerable persons a support, a new possibility of exercising will, an enjoyment in willing. For in fact fanaticism is the sole "volitional strength" to which the weak and irresolute can be excited, as a sort of hypnotising of the entire sensory-intellectual system, in favour of the overabundant nutrition (hypertrophy) of a particular point of view and a particular sentiment, which then dominates—the Christian calls it his *faith*. When a man arrives at the fundamental conviction that he *requires* to be commanded, he becomes "a believer." Reversely, one could imagine a delight and a power of self-determining, and a *freedom* of will, whereby a spirit could bid farewell to every belief, to every wish for certainty, accustomed as it would be to support itself on slender cords and possibilities, and to dance even on the verge of abysses. Such a spirit would be the *free spirit par excellence*.

THE ORIGIN OF THE LEARNED

The learned man in Europe grows out of all the different ranks and social conditions, like a plant requiring no specific soil: on that account he belongs essentially and involuntarily to the partisans of democratic thought. But this origin betrays itself. If one has trained one's glance to some extent to recognise in a learned book or scientific treatise the intellectual *idiosyncrasy* of the learned man—all of them have such idiosyncrasy—and if we take it by surprise, we shall almost always get a glimpse behind it of the "antecedent history" of the learned man and his family, especially of the nature of their callings and occupations. Where the feeling finds expression, "That is at last proved, I am now done with it," it is commonly the ancestor in the blood and instincts of the learned man that approves of the "accomplished work" in the nook from which he sees things; the belief in the proof is only an indication of what has been looked upon for ages by a laborious family as "good work." Take an example: the sons of registrars and office-clerks of every kind, whose main task has always been to arrange a variety of material, distribute it in drawers, and systematise it generally, evince, when they become learned men, an inclination to regard a problem as almost solved when they have systematised it. There are philosophers who are at bottom nothing but systematising brains—the formal part of the paternal occupation has become its essence to them. The talent for classifications, for tables of categories, betrays something; it is not for nothing that a person is the child of his parents. The son of an advocate will also have to be an advocate as investigator: he seeks

338

as a first consideration, to carry the point in his case, as a second consideration, he perhaps seeks to be in the right. One recognizes the sons of Protestant clergymen and schoolmasters by the naïve assurance with which as learned men they already assume their case to be proved, when it has but been presented by them staunchly and warmly: they are thoroughly accustomed to people *believing* in them—it belonged to their fathers' "trade"! A Jew, contrariwise, in accordance with his business surroundings and the past of his race, is least of all accustomed to people believing him. Observe Jewish scholars with regard to this matter—they all lay great stress on logic, that is to say, on *compelling* assent by means of reasons; they know that they must conquer thereby, even when race and class antipathy is against them, even where people are unwilling to believe them. For in fact, nothing is more democratic than logic: it knows no respect of persons, and takes even the crooked nose as straight. (In passing we may remark that in respect to logical thinking, in respect to *cleaner* intellectual habits, Europe is not a little indebted to the Jews; above all the Germans, as being a lamentably *déraisonnable* race, who, even at the present day, must always have their "heads washed"* in the first place. Wherever the Jews have attained to influence, they have taught to analyse more subtly, to argue more acutely, to write more clearly and purely; it has always been their problem to bring a people "to *raison*.")

The Origin of the Learned once more

To seek self-preservation merely, is the expression of a state of distress, or of limitation of the true, fundamental instinct of life, which aims at the *extension of power*, and

---

* In German the expression *Kopf zu waschen*, besides the literal sense, also means "to give a person a sound drubbing."—T.R.

with this in view often enough calls in question self-preservation and sacrifices it. It should be taken as symptomatic when individual philosophers, as for example, the consumptive Spinoza, have seen and have been obliged to see the principal feature of life precisely in the so-called self-preservative instinct—they have just been men in states of distress. That our modern natural sciences have entangled themselves so much with Spinoza's dogma (finally and most grossly in Darwinism, with its inconceivably one-sided doctrine of the "struggle for existence"), is probably owing to the origin of most of the inquirers into nature: they belong in this respect to the people, their forefathers have been poor and humble persons, who knew too well by immediate experience the difficulty of making a living. Over the whole of English Darwinism there hovers something of the suffocating air of over-crowded England, something of the odour of humble people in need and in straits. But as an investigator of nature, a person ought to emerge from his paltry human nook: and in nature the state of distress does not *prevail,* but superfluity, even prodigality to the extent of folly. The struggle for existence is only an *exception,* a temporary restriction of the will to live; the struggle, be it great or small, turns everywhere on predominance, on increase and expansion, on power, in conformity to the will to power, which is just the will to live.

In Honour of Homines Religiosi

The struggle against the church is certainly (among other things—for it has a manifold significance) the struggle of the more ordinary, cheerful, confiding, superficial natures against the rule of the graver, profounder, more contemplative natures, that is to say, the more malign and suspicious men, who with long continued distrust in the worth of life, brood also over their own worth—the ordinary instinct of the people, its sensual gaiety, its "good heart," revolts against them. The entire Roman Church rests on a Southern suspicion of the nature of man (always misunderstood in the North), a suspicion whereby the European South has succeeded in the inheritance of the profound Orient—the mysterious, venerable Asia—and its contemplative spirit. Protestantism was a popular insurrection in favour of the simple, the respectable, the superficial (the North has always been more good-natured and more shallow than the South), but it was the French Revolution that first gave the sceptre wholly and solemnly into the hands of the "good man" (the sheep, the ass, the goose, and everything incurably shallow, bawling, and fit for the Bedlam of "modern ideas").

In Honour of Priestly Natures

I think that philosophers have always felt themselves very remote from that which the people (in all classes of society nowadays) take for wisdom: the prudent, bovine, placidity, piety, and country-parson meekness, which lies in the meadow and *gazes* at life seriously and ruminatingly—this is probably because philosophers have not had sufficiently the taste of the "people," or of the country-parson, for that kind of wisdom. Philosophers will also perhaps be the last to acknowledge that the people *should* understand something of that which lies furthest from them, something of the great *passion* of the thinker, who lives and must live continually in the storm-cloud of the highest problems and the heaviest repsonsibilities (consequently, not gazing at all, to say nothing of doing so indifferently, securely, objectively). The people venerate an entirely different type of men when on their part they form the ideal of a "sage," and they are a thousand times justified in rendering homage with the highest eulogies and honours to precisely that type of men— namely, the gentle, serious, simple, chaste, priestly natures

341

and those related to them—it is to them that the praise falls
due in the popular veneration of wisdom. And to whom
should the multitude have more reason to be grateful than
to these men who pertain to its class and rise from its ranks,
but are persons consecrated, chosen, and *sacrificed* for its
good—they themselves believe themselves sacrificed to God,
before whom every one can pour forth his heart with impu-
nity, by whom he can *get rid* of his secrets, cares, and worse
things (for the man who "communicates himself" gets rid
of himself, and he who has "confessed" forgets). Here there
exists a great need: for sewers and pure cleansing waters are
required also for spiritual filth, and rapid currents of love
are needed, and strong, lowly, pure hearts, who qualify and
sacrifice themselves for such service of the non-public health-
department—for it *is* a sacrificing, the priest is, and continues
to be, a human sacrifice. . . . The people regard such sacrificed, silent, serious men of "faith" as *"wise,"* that is to say,
as men who have become sages, as "reliable" in relation to
their own unreliability. Who would desire to deprive the
people of that expression and that veneration? But as is fair
on the other side, among philosophers the priest also is still
held to belong to the "people," and is *not* regarded as a sage,
because, above all, they themselves do not believe in "sages,"
and they already scent "the people" in this very belief and
superstition. It was *modesty* which invented in Greece the
word "philosopher," and left to the playactors of the spirit
the superb arrogance of assuming the name "wise"—the
modesty of such monsters of pride and self-glorification as
Pythagoras and Plato.

WHY WE CAN HARDLY DISPENSE WITH MORALITY

The naked man is generally an ignominious spectacle—I
speak of us European males (and by no means of European
females!). If the most joyous company at table suddenly

found themselves stripped and divested of their garments through the trick of an enchanter, I believe that not only would the joyousness be gone and the strongest appetite lost —it seems that we Europeans cannot at all dispense with the masquerade that is called clothing. But should not the disguise of "moral men," the screening under moral formulae and notions of decency, the whole kindly concealment of our conduct under conceptions of duty, virtue, public sentiment, honourableness, and disinterestedness, have just as good reasons in support of it? Not that I mean hereby that human wickedness and baseness, in short, the evil wild beast in us, should be disguised; on the contrary, my idea is that it is precisely as *tame animals* that we are an ignominious spectacle and require moral disguising—that the "inner man" in Europe is far from having enough of intrinsic evil "to let himself be seen" with it (to be *beautiful* with it). The European disguises himself *in morality* because he has become a sick, sickly, crippled animal, who has good reasons for being "tame," because he is almost an abortion, an imperfect, weak and clumsy thing. . . . It is not the fierceness of the beast of prey that finds moral disguise necessary, but the gregarious animal, with its profound mediocrity, anxiety and ennui. *Morality dresses up the European*—let us acknowledge it!—in more distinguished, more important, more conspicuous guise, in "divine" guise.

THE ORIGIN OF RELIGIONS

The real inventions of founders of religions are, on the one hand, to establish a definite mode of life and everyday custom, which operates as *disciplina voluntatis,* and at the same time does away with ennui; and on the other hand, to give to that very mode of life an *interpretation,* by virtue of which it appears illumined with the highest value; so that it henceforth becomes a good for which people struggle, and

343

under certain circumstances lay down their lives. In truth, the second of these inventions is the more essential: the first, the mode of life, has usually been there already, side by side, however, with other modes of life, and still unconscious of the value which it embodies. The import, the originality of the founder of a religion, discloses itself usually in the fact that he *sees* the mode of life, *selects* it, and *divines* for the first time the purpose for which it can be used, how it can be interpreted. Jesus (or Paul), for example, found around him the life of the common people in the Roman province, a modest, virtuous, oppressed life: he interpreted it, he put the highest significance and value into it—and thereby the courage to despise every other mode of life, the calm fanaticism of the Moravians, the secret, subterranean self-confidence which goes on increasing, and is at last ready "to overcome the world" (that is to say, Rome, and the upper classes throughout the empire). Buddha, in like manner, found the same type of man—he found it in fact dispersed among all the classes and social ranks of a people who were good and kind (and above all inoffensive), owing to indolence, and who likewise owing to indolence, lived abstemiously, almost without requirements. He understood that such a type of man, with all its *vis inertiae*, had inevitably to glide into a belief which promises *to avoid* the return of earthly ill (that is to say, labour and activity generally)—this "understanding" was his genius. The founder of a religion possesses psychological infallibility in the knowledge of a definite, average type of souls, who have not yet recognised themselves as akin. It is he who brings them together: the founding of a religion, therefore, always becomes a long ceremony of recognition.

The "Genius of the Species"

The problem of consciousness (or more correctly: of becoming conscious of oneself) meets us only when we begin

344

to perceive in what measure we could dispense with it: and it is at the beginning of this perception that we are now placed by physiology and zoology (which have thus required two centuries to overtake the hint thrown out in advance by Leibnitz). For we could in fact think, feel, will, and recollect; we could likewise "act" in every sense of the term, and nevertheless nothing of it all need necessarily "come into consciousness" (as one says metaphorically). The whole of life would be possible without its seeing itself as it were in a mirror: as in fact even at present the far greater part of our life still goes on without this mirroring—and even our thinking, feeling, volitional life as well, however painful this statement may sound to an older philosopher. *What* then is *the purpose* of consciousness generally, when it is in the main *superfluous?* Now it seems to me, if you will hear my answer and its perhaps extravagant supposition, that the subtlety and strength of consciousness are always in proportion to the *capacity for communication* of a man (or an animal), the capacity for communication in its turn being in proportion to the *necessity for communication:* the latter not to be understood as if precisely the individual himself who is master in the art of communicating and making known his necessities would at the same time have to be most dependent upon others for his necessities. It seems to me, however, to be so in relation to whole races and successions of generations: where necessity and need have long compelled men to communicate with their fellows and understand one another rapidly and subtly, a surplus of the power and art of communication is at last acquired, as if it were a fortune which had gradually accumulated, and now waited for an heir to squander it prodigally (the so-called artists are these heirs, in like manner the orators, preachers, and authors: all of them men who come at the end of a long succession, "late-born" always, in the best sense of the word, and as has been said, *squanderers* by their very nature). Granted that this observation is correct, I may proceed further to the conjecture that *consciousness generally has only been developed under the pressure of the necessity for communication*—that from the first it has been necessary and useful only between man and man (especially between those commanding and those obeying), and has only developed in proportion to its utility. Consciousness is properly only a connecting network between man and man—it is only as such that it has had to develop; the recluse and wild-beast species of men would not have needed it. The very fact that our actions, thoughts, feelings and motions come within the range of our consciousness—at least a part of them—is the result of a terrible, prolonged "must" ruling man's destiny: as the most endangered animal he *needed* help and protection; he needed his fellows, he was obliged to express his distress, he had to know how to make himself understood—and for all this he needed "consciousness" first of all: he had to "know" himself what he lacked, to "know" how he felt, and to "know" what he thought. For, to repeat it once more, man, like every living creature, thinks unceasingly, but does not know it; the thinking which is becoming *conscious of itself* is only the smallest part thereof, we may say, the most superficial part, the worst part—for this conscious thinking alone is *done in words, that is to say, in the symbols for communication,* by means of which the origin of consciousness is revealed. In short, the development of speech and the development of consciousness (not of reason, but of reason becoming self-conscious) go hand in hand. Let it be further accepted that it is not only speech that serves as a bridge between man and man, but also the looks, the pressure and the gestures; our becoming conscious of our sense impressions, our power of being able to fix them, and as it were to locate them outside of ourselves, has increased in proportion as the necessity has increased for communicating them to *others* by means of signs. The sign-inventing man is at the same time the man who is always more acutely self-

346

conscious; it is only as a social animal that man has learned to become conscious of himself—he is doing so still, and doing so more and more. As is obvious, my idea is that consciousness does not properly belong to the individual existence of man, but rather to the social and gregarious nature in him; that, as follows therefrom, it is only a relation to communal and gregarious utility that it is finely developed; and that consequently each of us, in spite of the best intention of *understanding* himself as individually as possible, and of "knowing himself," will always just call into consciousness the non-individual in him, namely, his "averageness"—that our thought itself is continuously as it were *outvoted* by the character of consciousness, by the imperious "genius of the species" therein—and is translated back into the perspective of the herd. Fundamentally our actions are in an incomparable manner altogether personal, unique and absolutely individual—there is no doubt about it; but as soon as we translate them into consciousness, they *do not appear so any longer*. . . . This is the proper phenomenalism and perspectivism as I understand it: the nature of *animal consciousness* involves the notion that the world of which we can become conscious is only a superficial and symbolic world, a generalised and vulgarised world; that everything which becomes conscious *becomes* just thereby shallow, meagre, relatively stupid—a generalisation, a symbol, a characteristic of the herd; that with the evolving of consciousness there is always combined a great, radical perversion, falsification, superficialisation, and generalisation. Finally, the growing consciousness is a danger, and whoever lives among the most conscious Europeans knows even that it is a disease. As may be conjectured, it is not the antithesis of subject and object with which I am here concerned: I leave that distinction to the epistemologists who have remained entangled in the toils of grammar (popular metaphysics). It is still less the antithesis of "thing in itself" and phenomenon, for we

347

do not "know" enough to be entitled even *to make such a distinction*. Indeed, we have not any organ at all for *knowing,* or for "truth": we "know" (or believe, or fancy) just as much as may be of use in the interest of the human herd, the species; and even what is here called "usefulness" is ultimately only a belief, a fancy, and perhaps precisely the most fatal stupidity by which we shall one day be ruined.

THE ORIGIN OF OUR CONCEPTION OF "KNOWLEDGE"

I take this explanation from the street. I heard one of the people saying that "he knew me," so I asked myself: What do the people really understand by knowledge? what do they want when they seek "knowledge"? Nothing more than that what is strange is to be traced back to something *known.* And we philosophers—have we really understood *anything more* by knowledge? The known, that is to say, what we are accustomed to so that we no longer marvel at it, the commonplace, any kind of rule to which we are habituated, all and everything in which we know ourselves to be at home: what? is our need of knowing not just this need of the known? the will to discover in everything strange, unusual, or questionable, something which no longer disquiets us? Is it not possible that it should be the *instinct of fear* which enjoins upon us to know? Is it not possible that the rejoicing of the discerner should be just his rejoicing in the regained feeling of security? . . . One philosopher imagined the world "known" when he had traced it back to the "idea": alas, was it not because the idea was so known, so familiar to him? because he had so much less fear of the "idea"—Oh, this moderation of the discerners! let us but look at their principles, and at their solutions of the riddle of the world in this connection! When they again find aught in things, among things, or behind things that is unfortunately very well known to us, for example, our multiplication table, or our logic, or our willing

348

and desiring, how happy they immediately are! For "what is known is understood": they are unanimous as to that. Even the most circumspect among them think that the known is at least *more easily understood* than the strange; that for example, it is methodically ordered to proceed outward from the "inner world," from "the fact of consciousness," because it is the world which is *better known to us!* Error of errors! The known is the accustomed, and the accustomed is the most difficult of all to "understand," that is to say, to perceive as a problem, to perceive as strange, distant, "outside of us." . . . The great certainty of the natural sciences in comparison with psychology and the criticism of the elements of consciousness—*unnatural* sciences, as one might almost be entitled to call them—rest precisely on the fact that they take *what is strange* as their object: while it is almost like something contradictory and absurd *to wish* to take generally what is not strange as an object. . . .

Jacques Maritain (1882-   )

The Range of Reason
The Meaning of Contemporary Atheism

The subject discussed in this chapter involves many deep and intricate problems. I do not pretend to dogmatize about them; the views that I shall put forward are no more than tentative views, which originate in a desire to look for the hidden spiritual significance which lies within the present agony of the world.

VARIOUS KINDS OF ATHEISM

Let us try, first, to establish in a more systematic way the distinction, indicated in the two previous chapters, between the diverse forms of atheism. This distinction can be made from either of two points of view: from the point of view of the attitude of the human being who professes himself to be an atheist; or from the point of view of the logical content of various atheistic philosophies.

From the first point of view, or with regard to the manner in which atheism is professed, I have already remarked that there are, in the first place, *practical atheists,* who believe that they believe in God but who in actual fact deny His existence by their deeds and the testimony of their behavior. Then there are *pseudo-atheists,* who believe that they do not believe in God but who in actual fact unconsciously believe in Him, because the God whose existence they deny is not God but something else. Finally there are *absolute*

350

atheists, who really do deny the existence of the very God in Whom the believers believe—God the Creator, Savior and Father, Whose name is infinitely over and above any name we can utter. Those absolute atheists stand committed to change their entire system of values and to destroy in themselves everything that could possibly suggest the name they have rejected; they have chosen to stake their all against divine Transcendence and any vestige of Transcendence whatsoever.

From the second point of view, that is, with regard to the logical content of various atheistic philosophies, I would divide atheism into negative and positive atheism.

By *negative atheism* I mean a merely negative or destructive process of casting aside the idea of God, which is replaced only by a void. Such a negative atheism can be shallow and empirical, like the atheism of the *libertins* in the XVIIth century—then it digs a hollow in the center of the universe of thought which has taken shape through the centuries around the idea of God, but it does not bother about changing that universe; it is merely concerned with making us live a comfortable life, enjoying the freedom of doing exactly as we please. On the other hand, negative atheism can be lived at a profound and metaphysical level: in which case the hollow it creates at the heart of things extends to and lays waste our whole universe of thought; the freedom it claims for the human Self is absolute independence, a kind of divine independence that this Self, like Dostoievsky's Kirilov, has no better way of affirming than by suicide and voluntary annihilation.

By *positive atheism* I mean an active struggle against everything that reminds us of God—that is to say antitheism rather than atheism—and at the same time a desperate, I would say heroic, effort to recast and reconstruct the whole human universe of thought and the whole human scale of values in accordance with that state of war against God. Such positive

351

atheism was the tragic, solitary atheism of a Nietzsche; such is today the literary, fashionable atheism of existentialism; such is the revolutionary atheism of dialectical materialism. The latter is of special interest to us, because it has succeeded in getting a considerable number of men to accept wholeheartedly this new kind of faith, and to give themselves to it with unquestionable sincerity.

Now when I speak of contemporary atheism, I have in mind atheism seen under the last aspect I have just mentioned; I consider it the most significant form of atheism, one which spells a new and unheard of historic event because it is an atheism at once *absolute* and *positive*. Human history has been confronted, for almost a century now, with the stormy bursting forth of an atheism which is both *absolute* (making man actually deny God Himself) and *positive* (anti-theism, demanding to be lived in full by man and to change the face of the earth). I have outlined in the preceding chapter the ideological process which terminated in this atheism which is both absolute and positive.

THE TWO-FOLD INCONSISTENCY OF CONTEMPORARY ATHEISM

An Act of Faith in Reverse Gear

After these preliminary signposts I should like to point out that today's absolute-positive atheism involves a dual inconsistency.

How does absolute-positive atheism come to birth in the mind of a man? At this point we are faced with a remarkable fact. A man does not become an absolute atheist as a result of some inquiry into the problem of God carried on by speculative reason. No doubt he takes into account the negative conclusions afforded in this connection by the most radical forms of rationalist or positivist philosophy; he does not neglect, either, the old platitude which will have it that the scientific explanation of the universe purely and simply got

352

clear of the existence of God. But all that is for him a
second-hand means of defense, not the prime propelling and
determining incentive. Neither those philosophical conclusions nor that nonsensical commonplace does he submit to
any critical examination. He takes them for granted. He
believes in them. And why? By virtue of an inner act of freedom, in the production of which he commits his whole personality. The starting point of absolute atheism is, in my
opinion, a basic act of moral choice, a crucial free determination. If at the moment when he takes stock of himself and
decides upon the whole direction of his life, a man confuses
the transition from youth to manhood with the refusal not
only of childhood's subordinations but of any subordina-
tion whatsoever; if he thus considers the rejection of any
transcendent law as an act of moral maturity and emancipation; and if he decides to confront good and evil in a totally
and absolutely free experience, in which any ultimate end
and any rule coming from above are cast aside forever—such
a free moral determination, dealing with the primary values
of existence, will mean that this man has entirely excluded
God from his own universe of life and thought. Here is, in
my opinion, the point at which absolute atheism begins in
the depths of a man's spiritual activity

But what is this I have just been describing if not a kind
of act of faith, an act of faith in reverse gear, whose content
is not an adherence to the transcendent God but, on the
contrary, a rejection of Him?

Thus it is that absolute atheism is positive atheism. As I
stated above, and this must be stressed once again: "It is
in no way a mere absence of belief in God. It is rather a
refusal of God, a fight against God, a challenge to God."
The absolute atheist is delivered over "to an inner dialectic
which obliges him ceaselessly to destroy any resurgence in
himself of what he has buried. . . . In proportion as the dialectic of atheism develops in his mind—each time he is con-

fronted with the natural notion of and tendency to an ultimate End, or with the natural notion of and natural interest in absolute values or unconditioned standards, or with some metaphysical anxiety—he will discover in himself vestiges of Transcendence which have not yet been abolished. He must get rid of them. God is a perpetual threat to him. His case is not a case of practical forgetting, but a case of deeper and deeper commitment to refusal and fight." He is bound to struggle against God without pause or respite, and to change, to recast everything in himself and in the world on the base of that anti-theism.

Now what does all this mean? Absolute atheism starts in an act of faith in reverse gear and is a full-blown religious commitment. Here we have the first internal inconsistency of contemporary atheism: it proclaims that all religion must necessarily vanish away, and it is itself a religious phenomenon.

An Abortive Protest and Rupture

The second inconsistency is very like the first one. Absolute atheism starts as a claim of man to become the sole master of his own destiny, totally freed from any "alienation" and heteronomy, made totally and decisively independent of any ultimate end as well as of any eternal law imposed upon him by any transcendent God. According to atheistic theorists, does not the idea of God originate in an alienation of human nature separated from its true subject, and transmuted into an ideal and sublimated image whose very transcendence and sovereign attributes ensure man's submission to an enslaved state of existence? Is it not by getting rid of that sublimated image and of any transcendence, that human nature will achieve the fullness of its own stature and freedom and bring about the final reconciliation between essence and existence?"

354

The Range of Reason

But what is the actual end-all of the philosophy of absolute Immanence which is all one with absolute atheism?
Everything which was formerly considered superior to time
and participating in some transcendent quality—either ideal
value or spiritual reality—is now absorbed in the movement
of temporal existence and the all-engulfing ocean of Becoming and of History. Truth and justice, good and evil, faith-
fulness, all the standards of conscience, henceforth perfectly
relativized, become radically contingent: they are but changing shapes of the process of History: just as for Descartes
they were but contingent creations of divine Freedom. The
truth, at any given moment, is that which conforms with
the requirements of History's begettings. As a result truth
changes as time goes on. An act of mine which was meritori-
ous today will be criminal tomorrow. And that is the way my
conscience must pass judgment on it. The human intellect
and moral conscience have to become heroically tractable.
And what of the Self, the person, the problem of human
destiny? A total rejection of Transcendence logically entails
a total adherence to Immanence. There is nothing eternal
in man; he will die in the totality of his being; there is
nothing to be saved in him. But he can give himself, and
give himself entirely, to the Whole of which he is a part,
to the boundless flux which alone is real and which bears the
fate of mankind. By virtue of his decisive moral experience itself, and of that primary moral choice—against any
ultimate End—which I have tried to describe, and which
commits the human personality far more profoundly than
individualistic egoism or epicureanism can do, the absolute
or positive atheist hands himself over, body and soul, to the
ever-changing and all-engulfing Whole—be it the social or
the cosmic totality. It is not only that he is satisfied to die
in it, as a blade of grass in the loam, and to make it more
fertile by dissolving in it. He is also willing to make of his

own total being, with all its values and standards and beliefs, an offering given, as I said above, to that great Minotaur that is History. Duty and virtue mean nothing else to him than a total submission and immolation of himself to the sacred voracity of Becoming.

Here we are confronted with a new variety of mystical "pure love"—giving up every hope for personal redemption —a real unselfishness, self-denial and self-sacrifice, a total and absolute disinterestedness—but a monstrous one, paid for at the price of the very Self, and the existence and dignity of the human Person: at the price of that which, in each one of us, is an end in itself and the image of God. Christ had said: "He who loses his own soul for Me, shall find it,"* because losing one's own soul for God is delivering it over to absolute Truth and Goodness and Love, to the eternal Law itelf which transcends all the contingency and mutability of Becoming. The positive atheist delivers over his own soul—and not in order to save it—to a worldly demiurge crazy for human minds to bend and bow and yield at the event's sweet will.

I am not belittling the spiritual significance of the moral attitude of the absolute atheist. On the contrary, I am emphasizing the kind of mystical disinterestedness, and the elements of greatness and generosity which are implied in it. But I say that this moral attitude also involves a basic inconsistency, and that the whole process is in the end a failure. That rupture with God began as a claim to total independence and emancipation, as a proud revolutionary break with everything that submits man to alienation and heteronomy. It ends up in obeisance and prostrate submission to the all-powerful movement of History, in a kind of sacred surrender of the human soul to the blind god of History.

* Matth. 10, 39.

THE ATHEIST AND THE SAINT

The Initial Act of Rupture Brought About by the Saint

The failure I have just mentioned reveals to us a fact which has, to my mind, a deep significance: I mean the fact that absolute atheism has a revolutionary power which materially speaking is exceedingly strong, but spiritually speaking is very weak indeed, minute, and deceptive; I mean the fact that its radicalism is an inevitably self-deluded radicalism, for a genuinely revolutionary spirit does not kneel before History, it presumes to make history; I mean the fact that absolute atheism falls short of that uncompromising protest, of that absolute non-compliance the semblance—and the expectation—of which make it seductive for many people.

Thus, we arrive at the point I should like especially to discuss. Which of these two, the Atheist or the Saint, is the more uncompromising and thorough-going, the harder, the more intractable; which has his axe more deeply embedded in the root of the tree? Which brings about the more complete and far-reaching, the cleaner and more radical break?

Let us try to imagine what takes place in the soul of a saint at the crucial moment when he makes his first irrevocable decision. Let us consider St. Francis of Assisi when he threw away his raiment and appeared naked before his bishop, out of love for poverty; or St. Benedict Labre when he decided to become a verminous beggar wandering along the roads. At the root of such an act there was something so deep in the soul that it hardly can be expressed, I would say a simple refusal—not a movement of revolt which is temporary, or of despair, which is passive—rather a simple refusal, a total, stable, supremely active refusal to accept things as they are: here it is not a question of knowing whether things and nature and the face of this world are good in their essence—to be sure they are good; being is good insofar as it is being; grace perfects nature and does

357

not destroy it—but these truths have nothing to do with the inner act of rupture, of break, that we are now contemplating. This act is concerned with a fact, an existential fact: Things as they are are not tolerable, positively, definitely not tolerable. In actual existence the world is infected with lies and injustice and wickedness and distress and misery; the creation has been so marred by sin that in the nethermost depths of his soul the saint refuses to accept it as it is. Evil —I mean the power of sin, and the universal suffering it entails, the rot of nothingness that gnaws everywhere—evil is such, that the only thing at hand which can remedy it, and which inebriates the saint with freedom and exultation and love, is to give up everything, the sweetness of the world, and what is good, and what is better, and what is pleasurable and permissible, in order to be free to be with God; it is to be totally stripped and to give himself totally in order to lay hold of the power of the Cross; it is to die for those he loves. That is a flash of intuition and of will over and above the whole order of human morality. Once a human soul has been touched by such a burning wing, it becomes a stranger everywhere. It may fall in love with things, it will never rest in them. To redeem creation the saint wages war on the entire fabric of creation, with the bare weapons of truth and love. This war begins in the most hidden recesses of his own soul and the most secret stirrings of his desire: it will come to an end with the advent of a new earth and new heaven, when all that is powerful in this world will have been humiliated and all that is despised will have been exalted. The saint is alone in treading the winepress, and of the peoples there is no man with him.*

And I would say that in that way of which I have just spoken his God has given him the example. For, in calling the intellectual creatures to share in His own uncreated life,

* Isaiah, 63, 3.

God uproots them from the very life of which they are possessed as rooted in nature. And Jews know that God is a hidden God, Who conceals His name and manifests Himself to mankind in prodigies and in the stormy visions of the prophets, in order to renew the face of the earth, and Who has separated for Himself His people from all the nations of the world. And Christians know that God is both so dissatisfied with that lost world which He had made good and which evil has ruined—and at the same time so carried away by love—that He has given His Son and delivered Him over to men, in order to suffer and to die, and in this way redeem the world.

The Great God of Idolaters

To this true God the saint is entirely given. But there are false gods; even, as I shall shortly say, there is a spurious and distorted image of God that can be called the King or Jove of all false gods, the great god of the idolaters. With regard to *this* god, the saint is a thorough atheist, the most atheistic of men—just because he adores *only* God.

Let us dwell a moment on this point. And let us consider the merely rational, merely philosophical concept of God. This concept is twofold: there is the true God of the philosophers, and there is the false god of the philosophers. The true God of the philosophers is but the true God Himself, the God of the saints, the God of Abraham, Isaac and Jacob— imperfectly and inchoatively known, known in those attributes only which can be reached by our natural forces: Such a merely rational notion of God is in actual fact open to the supernatural.

But now suppose for yourselves a merely rational notion of God which would know the existence of the Supreme Being, but would disregard at the same time what St. Paul called His glory, deny the abyss of freedom which is meant by His transcendence, and chain Him to the very world He has made. Suppose for yourselves a merely rational—and warped—notion of God which is closed against the supernatural, and makes impossible the mysteries that are hidden in God's love and freedom and incommunicable life. Here we would have the false god of the philosophers, the Jove of all false gods. Imagine a god bound to the order of nature who is no more than a supreme warrant and justification of that order, a god who is responsible for this world without the power of redeeming it, a god whose inflexible will, that no prayer can reach, is pleased with and hallows all the evil as well as all the good of the universe, all the trickery, wickedness and cruelty together with all the generosity which are at play in nature, a god who blesses iniquity and slavery and misery, and who sacrifices man to the cosmos, and makes the tears of the children and the agony of the innocents a stark ingredient of, and a tribute offered without any compensation to the sacred necessities of eternal cycles or of evolution. Such a god would be the unique supreme Being but made into an idol, the naturalistic god of nature, the Jupiter of the world, the great god of the idolaters and of the powerful on their thrones and of the rich in their earthly glory, the god of success which knows no law, and of mere fact set up as law.

I am afraid that such was the God of our modern rationalistic philosophy, the God perhaps of Leibniz and Spinoza, surely the God of Hegel.

Such was also, in quite another mood, not rationalistic, but magical, the God of pagan antiquity, or rather one of the countenances of that double-faced God. For the pagan God was ambiguous; on the one hand he was the true God of nature and reason, the unknown God of Whom St. Paul spoke to the Athenians; and on the other hand he was the false god of naturalism, the self-contradictory god I have just described, and who does get on very well with the Prince of this world.

The Range of Reason

It could be added that among Christian sects, some wild Gnostics, especially the followers of Marcion, who regarded the God of the Old Covenant as an evil world-maker in conflict with the Redeemer, mistook for the Creator the same false god I have been discussing, the same absurd Emperor of the world.

And this brings me to the point I want to drive home. The saint, when he brings about the great act of rupture which I stressed earlier, rejects by the same stroke, breaks and annihilates, with an irresistible violence, this spurious Emperor of the world, this false god of naturalism, this great god of the idolaters, the powerful and the rich, who is an absurd counterfeit of God, but who is also the imaginary focus whence the adoration of the cosmos radiates, and to whom we pay tribute each time we bow down before the world. With regard to this god the saint is a perfect atheist. Well, were not the Jews and the first Christians often called atheists by the pagans at the time of the Roman Empire? There was a hidden meaning in this slander.*

The Case of the Absolute Atheist

But let us turn at present to our modern atheists, our true and actual atheists—what can we say about them? I would suggest that, in the sense I have just emphasized, the absolute atheist is *not atheist enough*. He, too, is indignant against the Jupiter of this world, against the god of the idolaters, the powerful and the rich; he too decides to get rid of him. But instead of hurling against that false god the strength of the true God, and of giving himself to the work of the true God, as the saint does, the atheist, because he rejects the true God, can only struggle against the Jupiter of this world by calling on the strength of the immanent god

---

* St. Justin said: "We are called atheists. And yes we confess it, we are atheists of those so-called gods." 1st *Apology*, VI, n. I.

361

of History, and by dedicating himself to the work of that immanent god.

It is indeed because he believes in the revolutionary disruptive power of the impetus of History, and because he expects from it the final emancipation of man, that the atheist delivers over his own soul to the blind god of History. Yet he is caught in a trap. Wait a while, and the blind god of History will appear just as he is—yes, the very same Jupiter of this world, the great god of the idolaters and the powerful on their thrones and the rich in their earthly glory, and of success which knows no law, and of mere fact set up as law. He will reveal himself as this same false god in a new disguise and crowned by new idolaters, and meting out a new brand of power and success. And it is too late for the atheist. As we saw at the beginning, he is possessed by this god. He is on his knees before History. With respect to a god who is not God, he is the most tractable and obedient of the devotees.

And so his break with this world of injustice and oppression was but a shallow and temporary break. More than ever he is subservient to the world. In comparison with the saint, who consummates in his own flesh his initial rupture with the world, and every day dies unto himself, and is blessed with the beatitudes of the poor and the persecuted and all the other friends of God, and who enjoys the perfect freedom of those who are led by the Spirit, the atheist is, it seems to me, a very poor replica of the liberated mind and the heroic insurgent. Nevertheless, as I have tried to point out, it is by an ill-directed longing for inner freedom and for non-acceptance of things as they are that he has been led astray. A somewhat paradoxical, yet, in my opinion, true statement about absolute atheism would be to say that it deprives God and mankind of some potential saints, in bringing to bankruptcy their attempt at heroic freedom, and turning their effort to break with the world into a total and servile subservience to the world. With all his sincerity and

362

devotion, the authentic, absolute atheist is after all only an abortive saint, and, at the same time, a mistaken revolutionist.

THE SAINT AND TEMPORAL HISTORY

A Lost Opportunity

There is now another paradox, this time in an opposite direction. If we look at the saint, it seems that the inner act through which he achieves his total break with the world and total liberation from the world, making him free from everything but God, will inevitably overflow from the realm of spiritual life onto the realm of temporal life. Thus, if he is not dedicated solely to a contemplative state of existence, he will be led to act as a ferment of renewal in the structures of the world, as a stimulating and transforming energy in social matters and in the field of the activities of civilization.

And this is true, of course. As a matter of fact, it is what has been taking place for centuries. The Fathers of the Church were great revolutionaries. Thomas Aquinas in the order of culture, St. Vincent de Paul in the social field, were eminent examples of genuine radicals, whose initiative brought about decisive changes in the history of civilization. For centuries temporal progress in the world has been furthered by the saints.

Yet, here is the paradox that I just mentioned—the day when, in the course of modern history, a particularly inhuman structure of society, caused by the Industrial Revolution, made the problem of social justice manifestly crucial; when, at the same time, the human mind became aware of the *social* as a specific object of knowledge and activity, and when the first attempts to create workers' organizations provided the beginnings of a historical force capable of acting upon social structures—then was it not the moment for the saints to take the lead in the protest of the poor and in the movement of labor toward its historical coming of age? In actual fact, except for a few men of faith, like Ozanam in France and Toniolo in Italy (they are not yet canonized, but some day they might be), the task, as we know, was not conducted by saints. It even happened that atheists, instead of saints, took the lead in social matters, much to the misfortune of all.

Why such a tragic vacancy? It seems difficult not to see in it a kind of punishment of the Christian world, which for a long period has more or less failed Christianity in its practical behavior, and despised the lessons of the saints, and abandoned to their fate, here below, that great flock which also belongs to Christ, that immense herd of men whom destitution and unlivable conditions of existence kept chained to hell on earth. Let us not be mistaken. During the time of which I am speaking, the saints were not lacking on the earth; there was a considerable flowering of saints in the last century. But they did not pass beyond the field of spiritual, apostolic or charitable activities: they did not cross the threshold of temporal, social, secular activity. And thus the gap was not filled, because in the historical age which is ours, the indirect repercussion of the inner renewal of conscience upon the external structures of society is definitely not enough, although it answers a basic need and has made progressively more possible such social changes as the abolition of slavery. A specifically social activity, an activity which directly aims at improving and recasting the structures of temporal life, is also needed.

Why has this kind of activity been neglected by a great many Christians in the past? Is it on account of their supposed contempt for the world, as people say? Nonsense! The saints break with the world, but they have no contempt for creation; that they leave to apprentices. As for the general run of Christians, one need but look at them—at ourselves—(as François Mauriac reminded us rather bluntly in the sec-

ond *Semaine des Intellectuels Catholiques*)* to be assured
that we do not despise the world in the least and that we are
"of the earth," as it is said in the new devotional jargon. No;
the reason for which activities directly aiming at the struc-
tural changes required by social justice have been lacking
for so many centuries, is quite simple: the means of exercising such activities were non-existent. In the seventeenth century Saint Vincent de Paul could found hospitals but he
could not found trade unions. It was only after the Industrial Revolution and the way in which it developed that the
possibility of directly social activity could enter people's
imaginations, and that such a directly social, and not only
spiritual or charitable, activity has become a crying need.

Perhaps a concrete example will help to make clear the
difference between the two kinds of activity I have mentioned. A poor priest named Cottolengo, who was a saint
(though his name is not to be found in the *Encyclopaedia
Britannica*) founded in Turin, in the first half of the past
century, a hospital that rapidly grew into a sort of huge city
of all kinds of infirmity and human misery; hundreds of the
poor were fed and cared for every day. But Cottolengo had
established the rule that none of the money contributed
for the support of his Institute should ever be saved and
invested. Money each day received from the Providence of
God should be spent each day, for "sufficient unto the day
is the evil thereof."* There is even a story that one evening,
as he saw that his assistants had set aside a certain amount
of money for the morrow, Cottolengo threw that money out
of the window—which in our modern world is the height
of insanity, and perhaps of sacrilege. This course of action
was in itself perfectly revolutionary, and all the more revo-

* See *Foi en Jesus-Christ et Monde d'aujourd'hui*. Editions de Flore,
Paris, 1949.
* Matth. 6, 34.

lutionary in that it succeeded (Cottolengo's work has thrived in an astounding manner; it is now one of the most important institutions in Turin). Yet such a course of action, for all its spiritual significance, remained of no social consequence. It transcended the social problem. The social problem must be managed and solved in its own order. For half a century men of good will have realized better and better that the temporal mission of those who believe in God is to take over the job. Still, we must not forget that, even in the simple perspective of the temporal community, Christian social action is not enough; political action is even less so, however necessary both of them may be. What is required of those who believe in God is a witness of God; and what the world demands and expects of the Christian is first, and foremost to see the love of truth and brotherly love made genuinely present in and through man's personal life—to see a gleam of the Gospel shining in the one place where the crucial test and crucial proof are to be found, namely the obscure context of relations from person to person.

The Christian World is Neither Christianity Nor the Church

I have just spoken of the historical deficiencies of the Christian world. Parenthetically, in order to avoid any misunderstanding, I should like to point out that by these words, "the Christian world," I am designating a sociological category, which is involved in the order and history of temporal civilizations, and is a thing of this world. The Christian world is neither Christianity nor the Church. The failures of the Christian world have no power to tarnish the Church or Christianity.

There has been, moreover, a good deal of confusion on this score. Neither Christianity nor the Church have a mission to make men happy, their business is to tell them the truth—not to bring about justice and freedom in the political society, but to give mankind salvation and eternal life.

No doubt this lays upon them the additional task of quickening the energies of justice and love in the depths of temporal existence and thus making that existence more worthy of man. Yet the successful accomplishment of such a task depends on the way in which the divine message is received. It is at this point that we are confronted with the responsibilities of the Christian world, that is, of the social groups of Christian denomination at work in secular history.

It is nonsense to reproach the Christians, as we often see it done today, with not having baptized "the Revolution," and with not having devoted their whole energies to "the Revolution." The messianic myth of "the Revolution" is a secularized perversion of the idea of the advent of God's Kingdom; it is apt to warp the course of human history, and to turn into failures the particular, genuine and genuinely progressive revolutions—the revolutions without a capital R—that are bound to follow one another as long as human history endures. But it is not nonsense to reproach Christians in the world with having failed to bring about at certain given times such needed particular revolutions. It is not nonsense to reproach them, more generally, with being sinners—they know very well that they are—who more or less always betray Christianity. Most important of all, it is certainly not nonsense to reproach the many people in modern times who are paying lip-service to the God in Whom they think they believe, with being in fact practical atheists.

Men Today Need Signs

According to one of our previous remarks, if a new age of civilization is to come rather than a new age of barbarism, the deepest requirement of such an age will be the sanctification of secular life, a fecundation of social, temporal existence by spiritual experience, contemplative energies and brotherly love.

I dare say that we have not yet reached that stage. For the

moment we are at the lowest point; human history today is
in love with fear and absurdity, human reason with despair.
The powers of illusion are spreading all over the world,
throwing all compasses off direction. The faculty of language
has been so dishonored, the meaning of words so thoroughly
falsified; so many truths, met with at every corner in press
or radio reports, are at each moment so perfectly mixed with
so many errors similarly advertized, and trumpeted to the
skies, that men are simply losing the sense of truth. They
have been lied to so often that they have become addicted,
and need their daily dose of lies as a daily tonic. They look
as if they believed in all this; but they are beginning to lead
a kind of clandestine mental life in which they will believe
nothing they are told, but will rely only upon savage experience and elementary instincts. They are surrounded on all
sides by spurious marvels and false miracles, which dazzle
and blind their minds.

Things being as they are, it seems clear that the wisest
reasonings and the most eloquent demonstrations and the
best managed organizations are definitely not enough for the
men of this time. Men today need *signs*. They need deeds.
Above all they need tangible signs to reveal to them the
reality of things divine. Yet there is everywhere a considerable shortage of thaumaturges, though they probably are the
kind of a commodity we need the most.

At this point I should like to bring back to our minds a
saying of Pascal. "We always behave," Pascal has said, "as
if we were called upon to make the truth triumph, whereas
we are called upon only to struggle for it."

It does not rest with us to give men miracles. It is up to
us to practice what we believe.

Here it seems well to stress one of the deepest meanings
of absolute atheism. In so doing we shall but be brought
back to the conclusion of the preceding chapter. As I put it,
absolute atheism is "a translation into crude and inescapable

terms, a ruthless counterpart, an avenging mirror, of the practical atheism of too many believers who do not actually believe." It is both the fruit and the condemnation of practical atheism, its image reflected in the mirror of divine wrath. If this diagnosis is true, then we must go on to say that it is impossible to get rid of absolute atheism without first getting rid of practical atheism. Furthermore this has become clear to everyone that from now onwards a decorative Christianity is not enough, even for our existence in this world. The faith must be an actual faith, practical and living. To believe in God must mean to live in such a manner that life could not possibly be lived if God did not exist. Then the earthly hope in the Gospel can become the quickening force of temporal history.

SUGGESTIONS FOR FURTHER READING

St. Thomas Aquinas, *Summa Contra Gentiles,* Book II, "Creation."

Henri Bergson, *The Two Sources of Morality and Religion.*

G. K. Chesterton, *Orthodoxy.*

S. L. Frank, *A Solovyov Anthology.*

Etienne Gilson, *The Elements of Christian Philosophy.*

Søren Kierkegaard, *Works of Love; Concluding Unscientific Postscript.*

C. S. Lewis, *Mere Christianity.*

Jacques Maritain, *On the Uses of Philosophy.*

Hugo Meynell, *Sense, Nonsense and Christianity.*

Friedrich Nietzsche, *Thus Spake Zarathustra.*

Index

Index